Island Refuge

*Britain and Refugees from
the Third Reich*
1933–1939

Island Refuge

*Britain and Refugees from
the Third Reich*
1933-1939

A. J. SHERMAN

UNIVERSITY OF CALIFORNIA PRESS
Berkeley and Los Angeles

University of California Press
Berkeley and Los Angeles

ISBN 0–520–2595–4

Library of Congress Catalog Card Number:
73–86850

Printed in Great Britain by
Clarke, Doble & Brendon Limited
Plymouth

To my parents

Contents

ERRATUM.

Line 12 on page 135 should read:

"Government bitterly criticised the IGC for 'refusing to deal with"

Preface

THIS is a book which describes Great Britain's response to the exodus of refugees from the Third Reich in the years 1933 to 1939. It is concerned primarily with the evolution of British Government policy toward refugees, and relies mainly on unpublished Foreign Office and Home Office papers which have only recently been released for public scrutiny. A consideration of the sociology and psychology of the refugees themselves, of their adjustment to Britain and of their contributions to British life, lies outside the scope of this work, which investigates political decision-making in a situation that posed many highly emotional and contentious issues in both domestic and foreign policy.

I have been fortunate in the generous assistance of many individuals throughout the preparation of this work. It is a pleasure to acknowledge my gratitude to the Warden and Fellows of St Antony's College, Oxford, for affording me the opportunity to pursue my research in their most congenial company. This study was made under a fellowship granted by the Foreign Area Fellowship Program of the American Council of Learned Societies and the Social Science Research Council, whose support is acknowledged with thanks.

My research was carried out for the most part in London, where I was helpfully received by the librarians and staff of the Public Record Office, the Foreign and Commonwealth Office Library, the Royal Institute of International Affairs, and the Wiener Library. I am particularly grateful to the Departmental Record Officer of the Home Office for granting me access to certain materials; and to the Board of Deputies of British Jews for permission to examine their archives at Woburn House. I am also indebted to the custodians of private papers at Cambridge and Liverpool Universities; and to the United Nations Library, Geneva; the American Jewish Archives, Cincinnati; the Zionist Archives, Jerusalem; and the Weizmann Archives in Rehovoth. The Librarian of St Antony's College, Miss Anne Abley, was throughout a source of valuable assistance, which I acknowledge with thanks.

A number of people generously accorded me personal interviews : I am grateful in particular to Dr Eduard Rosenbaum, Lord Sherfield, Mr M. Stephany, Miss J. Stiebel, Sir Siegmund G. Warburg and Dr Robert Weltsch. The late Judge Neville Laski, Q.C. and the late Professor Norman Bentwich also kindly assisted me with insights and recollections.

I should like also to thank those colleagues and friends who have read my manuscript and given me most helpful advice and criticism : Mr Chimen Abramsky, Dr Yehuda Bauer, Professor James Joll, Dr and Mrs T. W. Mason, Miss Elizabeth Monroe, Professor S. K. Orgel, Dr P. G. J. Pulzer, Professor Hans Rogger, Mr C. I. Seton-Watson, and Professor Peter Stansky. Professors Henry F. Graff, Christoph M. Kimmich, James P. Shenton, and Robert K. Webb generously encouraged me at earlier stages in this enterprise, and to them too I should like to express my thanks.

Finally, a word of deepest gratitude to Dr Gerhard Adler and to Dr Edward F. Edinger, without whose inspiration and devoted encouragement this work and all it represents would not have been accomplished.

A.J.S.
Oxford
March, 1973

List of Abbreviations

*See Bibliography for full details of manuscript and
published sources*

CAB, C.P.	Cabinet Papers
CO	Colonial Office
DBFP	*Documents on British Foreign Policy,* 3rd Series
DGFP	*Documents on German Foreign Policy,* Series D
FO	Foreign Office
FRUS	*Foreign Relations of the United States*
H.C. Deb.	Hansard, House of Commons Debates, 5th Series
H.L. Deb.	Hansard, House of Lords Debates
HO	Home Office
RGBl	*Reichsgesetzblatt*
WA	Weizmann Archives
WH	Woburn House, Board of Deputies of British Jews
ZA	The Central Zionist Archives

1

Introduction

One refugee is a novelty, ten refugees are boring, and a hundred
refugees are a menace.[1]

VERY shortly after the rise of Adolf Hitler to power in Germany in
January 1933, the British Government was confronted with a
domestic and international problem for which it was uniquely
unprepared : a wave of refugees fleeing from political, racial and
religious persecution. Earlier post-World War I mass movements
of refugees—notably of Russians, Armenians and Greeks—with
which other European governments were wearily familiar, had
largely by-passed Great Britain, and there were few useful recent
precedents for dealing with large numbers of would-be immigrants
to the United Kingdom and the Empire, some merely politically
embarrassing but virtually all unwanted potential competitors in the
drastically shrunken labour markets of the Depression years.

Soon after their appearance on the international scene refugees
from the Third Reich[2] represented very little of a novelty, still less
of a bore, but indeed something of a menace : they embodied a
stubbornly intractable problem which subjected both Ministers and
civil servants to a cross-fire of intensely uncomfortable political
pressures. There were on the one hand eloquent representations
both public and private from Parliament, Jewish groups, the
Quakers and other sources to do something for the refugees on
humanitarian grounds. Other groups and individuals, slower off
the mark and at least initially less vocal, were nonetheless insistent

[1] Quoted by Donald P. Kent, *The Refugee Intellectual* (New York, 1953),
p. 172.
[2] See Appendix I for a discussion of refugee statistics.

in urging that the number of refugees admitted to Great Britain and the Empire be limited as much as possible. Intense lobbying on the part of many groups, sometimes in competition with one another, produced a policy perhaps inevitably seldom entirely consistent in either conception or execution. A survey of that policy does however refute the widely-held view, based largely on the dramatic clash over Palestine, that the British Government was both ungenerous and indifferent to the fate of refugees from the Nazi regime.

The relentlessly rising numbers of those fleeing from the Reich confronted the Government in London with the necessity to formulate and then often revise policies in several areas. The earliest and most urgent issue concerned the admission of refugees to the United Kingdom itself, whose uniquely favourable geographical position to control immigration was buttressed by legislation conferring wide discretionary powers upon the Home Secretary in deciding on the admission, expulsion or naturalisation of aliens.[3] Later the question of admission to the overseas territories, including Palestine, also assumed great importance. Among these territories, the self-governing Dominions—Canada, Australia, New Zealand, South Africa and Eire—each had its own independent aliens policy, agreeing only in a general preference for immigration from the British Isles; London bore no responsibility for making immigration policy in the Dominions, and was wary of even giving the appearance of a wish to intervene in this sphere of jealously-guarded national prerogative.

The British Government did however retain authority to promulgate immigration policy in certain overseas dependencies, the principal one of which in relation to the refugee problem was Palestine, where the League of Nations mandate under which Great Britain administered the country specifically enjoined the Government to 'facilitate Jewish immigration under suitable conditions'. These conditions were until 1937 defined in purely economic terms, as the economic capacity of Palestine to absorb new arrivals.[4]

Policy decisions had in addition to be made on such international

[3] See Appendix II, Immigration Regulations.
[4] Ibid.

aspects of the problem as the extent to which Great Britain should cooperate in League of Nations and other efforts to assist refugee migration. The League had created in 1921 a High Commission to deal with the international problem represented by more than a million Russian refugees; during the years that followed, the High Commissioner for Refugees, Dr Fridtjof Nansen, was required also to aid in the relief and settlement of Greek, Armenian, Assyrian and other refugee groups. By 1930 some progress had been made in defining the legal status of these largely stateless persons—most had been provided with identity papers which became known as 'Nansen passports'—and in their settlement in Europe and else-where. After Dr Nansen's death in 1930 the legal and political protection of refugees was transferred to the Nansen International Office for Refugees, a body directly responsible to the League Assembly, which also provided for the Office's administrative expenses in the confident expectation that the Office and its task could be wound up by the end of 1938. The British Government consistently regarded the problem of 'Nansen' refugees as one not substantially affecting British interests, since very few of these individuals had been admitted to British territories, and remained correspondingly aloof from League refugee work on their behalf.

There was also the effect of the refugee question on relations with Germany, the United States, and several Eastern European countries to be considered. These questions were in turn bound up with the larger issue of which British interests were specifically affected by the refugee movement, and whether Great Britain had in diplomatic usage any *locus standi* to intervene in one or another aspect of the refugee problem, which from Berlin's point of view remained a largely internal question brooking no interference from the League of Nations or any outside power.

In considering its attitude to the refugee question, each Government department was burdened by its own particular anxiety: for the Home Office it was, overwhelmingly, the large numbers of British unemployed and the possible importation through inadvertence of an undesirable 'racial problem'; for the Foreign Office, fraying relations with Berlin and the desire to avoid criticism from Washington and later from new allies such as Poland and Rumania;

for the Treasury, the spectre of unlimited financial liability for the settlement and possible relief of needy migrants; and for the Colonial Office, Palestine and the entire constellation of issues in the Arab-Jewish conflict. Behind all these concerns was the nightmare, based on repeated urgent representations from the Polish Government and broad hints from other Eastern European regimes, that an over-generous response to the plight of refugees from the Reich might create a precedent which could inspire the expulsion of millions, not thousands, of totally destitute Jews from Eastern Europe, and thus confront the British and indeed other governments with a burden of unbearable dimensions. The many millions in Eastern Europe who might yet become stateless cast a shadow which lengthened in direct proportion to the worsening in the situation of refugees from the Reich.

That situation itself underwent an evolution between 1933 and 1939 in which a number of periods may be distinguished. The first extended from January 1933 when Hitler took office as Chancellor to the promulgation of the so-called Nuremberg Laws in September 1935. The first refugee exodus, relatively small in numbers, was also rather tentative in character, as many of the refugees fled to France and other neighbouring European countries in the expectation that the Nazi regime would somehow be replaced, or at least become sufficiently moderate so as to permit them to resume residence in Germany. Moreover, these first refugees benefited from regulations which still permitted them to rescue a substantial fraction of their property, as well as from a sympathetic attitude on the part of many governments outside Germany. The Nuremberg Laws, however, with their sudden inclusion in the pariah class of many 'non-Aryans' as well as those heretofore regarded as Jews, ushered in a period of increasing repression under whose impact many thousands of new refugees sought permanent settlement outside Germany. Emigration in the second period, from October 1935 to March 1938, proceeded steadily, even though the process was complicated by increasingly confiscatory measures by the German Government and less receptive policies in countries to which the refugees turned for asylum. The incorporation of Austria into the Reich in March 1938 inaugurated the third phase, which lasted until November of that year. This period saw a massive flight characterised by widespread panic, the virtual expulsion of refugees stripped of almost all their property, and the hasty tightening of immigration regulations by countries all over the world anxious to deflect the tide of migrants to some other and preferably far distant shore.

The slender hope that the German Government might permit its unwanted nationals to leave with that minimum of property rendering them acceptable to other countries as immigrants was shattered, along with any lingering illusions that life in the Reich itself might remain barely tolerable for Jews and 'non-Aryans', by the organised pogrom of November 9–10, 1938, which came to be known as *Kristallnacht*. The ensuing wave—the fourth period—of flight, during which most privately-organised efforts for orderly migration broke down in chaos, was complicated also by the exodus from those parts of Czechoslovakia which had been transferred to the Reich under the provisions of the Munich Agreement. Faced with vast numbers of penniless and demoralised refugees, most countries closed their doors to both permanent settlers and transmigrants; private relief organisations and international refugee agencies struggled desperately but unsuccessfully to deal with the new developments. With the absorption of rump Czechoslovakia into the Reich in March 1939, the fifth and final pre-war phase of the refugee movement began. It saw the widest possible territorial spread of the problem, with refugees streaming to every continent, frequently on ships which wandered for weeks in search of some port where they could dump their unwanted passengers. Shanghai, the one port in the world which required no landing papers, became the uncertain refuge for many thousands. Other thousands from the Reich and from the impoverished and desperate Jewries of Poland and Rumania attempted the hazards and hardships of the clandestine routes to Palestine. With the Gestapo simply pushing refugees over the Reich frontiers, several European governments, in sheer self-preservation, established temporary camps to harbour refugees pending their further migration. Territorial settlement schemes in ever more exotic corners of the globe were explored and debated.

B

But time, that most critical factor in the migratory equation, had almost run out. With the outbreak of war in September 1939 and successive German occupation of countries on the Continent which had sheltered refugees, the entire problem assumed dimensions and posed policy issues radically differing from those of the pre-war period with which this work is concerned.

2

First Wave

January 1933 — September 1935

Indeed, at the beginning of the persecution . . . there was something like an awakening of conscience and an outburst of pity. France and other European countries opened their borders to the refugees. . . . But this attitude was short-lived.[1]

ON January 30, 1933, Adolf Hitler took office as Chancellor of Germany in a National Socialist–Nationalist coalition government which at the outset was unable to claim a majority in the Reichstag. Within six months, however, the National Socialists had subjugated all their political opponents and were implacably launched on a policy of 'coordinating' almost every sphere of German life. German nationals who were unable to adjust to this *Gleichschaltung* of German politics and society, or who were for whatever reasons unwelcome to the National Socialist regime—their number included Jews, pacifists, liberals, 'Marxists' of every hue, members of certain Churches, dissenting Conservatives or indeed schismatic National Socialists—were subjected to an intensive campaign of persecution, which was expressed in legislation, administrative regulations, court decisions and the informal and avowedly extra-legal methods of local and national Party leaders and organisations. The result and declared purpose of all these measures, official and unofficial, was to make life in the new Reich intolerable for unwanted categories of German citizens. Dismissed *en masse* from public and, in many cases, private employment, subjected not infrequently to physical abuse, internment or other indignities, those affected sought refuge either in flight or in the hope, soon to be destroyed by further develop-

[1] Eugene M. Kulischer, *Europe on the Move* (New York, 1948), p. 190.

ments, that the policy of discrimination would be abandoned, or at least its intensity diminished.

The initial wave of terrorism following Hitler's coming to power, during which many prominent Jews, pacifist or left-wing politicians and journalists were forced to seek refuge outside Germany, was not based on specific legislative or administrative authority. Following the dissolution of the Reichstag, however, the Government proceeded to enact in legislation a persecutory regime foreshadowed in the Nazi party programme. The statutory foundation for the entire body of subsequent discriminatory legislation was the Law of April 7, 1933 for the Reconstruction of the Civil Service,[2] which provided sweepingly that civil servants of 'non-Aryan descent' were to be summarily retired. A 'non-Aryan' was defined in a regulation of April 11, 1933[3] as a person one of whose grandparents or parents was 'Jewish', which in its turn was defined as adhering to the Jewish religion. Those officials who were serving members of the Civil Service before August 1, 1914, or who fought at the front during World War I, or who had lost a father or a son in that conflict were however exempted initially from the scope of the new legislation. The definition of 'Aryan' and the 'Veterans' clause' were henceforth to serve as guides for the application of administrative measures to Jews throughout Germany.

A series of ordinances and decrees clarifying and extending the provisions of the basic law led to the dismissal of thousands of university and school teachers, employees of national and municipal enterprises, judicial officers of all kinds, scientists, public health and welfare officers and others. Those branches of the German legal profession outside the ranks of the Civil Service were 'coordinated' under a Law on Admission to the Bar of April 7, 1933;[4] here too, lawyers who were in practice before August 1914, or who could comply with the requirements of the 'Veterans' clause', were in theory re-admitted to the Bar, but often enough excluded in practice.

Those Jewish doctors who were employed in municipal and State

---

[2] *Gesetz zur Wiederherstellung des Berufsbeamtentums, RGBl*, 1933, I, 175.
[3] Ibid., p. 195.
[4] Ibid., p. 188.

services were dismissed along with other civil servants. The numbers of Jewish panel doctors in National Health Insurance practice, which was widespread in Germany, were restricted by a special decree of April 22, 1933. These restrictions were gradually extended to doctors and dentists in other group practices by decisions of the Medical Association. 'Coordination' in education kept pace with that in other fields : on April 25, 1933 schools, other than primary schools, were ordered by law to limit the number of their 'non-Aryan' students to 5 per cent of the student body, and no new 'non-Aryan' students in excess of 1·5 per cent of the student body were to be admitted.

Germany's cultural life too was forced into conformity with the new order, through the establishment of guild associations, *Reichskammern*, for the press, cinema, theatre, music, radio, painting, literature and architecture. Admission to each of these individual associations, grouped in the *Reichskulturkammer* under the direct authority of the Minister for Enlightenment and Propaganda, could be refused if the prospective applicant did not 'inspire the confidence or possess the ability necessary for the carrying on of his activity'. It was made clear that political opponents of the regime and 'non-Aryans' would be unable to qualify for admission; exclusion from the appropriate association was however an absolute bar to the exercise of the particular cultural pursuit in question.[5]

Also among the early measures inviting emigration from the Reich was a Law of July 14, 1933 providing for denationalisation by individual decree of those naturalised in Germany between November 9, 1918 and January 30, 1933, whose naturalisation was now regarded as 'undesirable'. The same law also provided for the denationalisation of those German nationals already residing outside Germany who 'prejudiced German interests by an attitude contrary to the duty of loyalty' toward the Reich.[6] Determinations of status under the terms of this legislation were to be made according to 'national racial' principles; the mere fact of absence from Germany was in many cases deemed sufficient to deprive individuals

---

[5] See Oscar I. Janowsky and M. M. Fagen, *International Aspects of German Racial Policies* (New York, 1937), pp. 158–161.

[6] Ibid., pp. 217–223.

of their German nationality. As a practical matter, even those refugees whose nationality had not formally been withdrawn often found it impossible to claim the protection of German consular authorities abroad—and many of them had in any case been forced to leave Germany without going through the formalities necessary to acquire papers proving their nationality.

The first systematic attempt to make good the election undertaking of the National Socialists to destroy the economic influence of the Jews in Germany was the national boycott of Jewish establishments decreed on April 1, 1933. Although there had been unofficial sporadic closings and acts of terrorism against Jewish-owned businesses as early as February 1933, the decision to institute a nationwide boycott of Jewish businesses was taken by Hitler and Goebbels in late March and was justified in Party propaganda as a defensive response to the 'international Jewish agitation' against Germany, which had itself been expressed in a spasmodic boycott of German exports, especially in the United States.[7] The day of the boycott, with its accompaniment of S.A. demonstrations, strident posters threatening reprisals against those patronising Jewish shops and other businesses, and scattered violence, saw a virtually complete closure of Jewish establishments. The subsequent international condemnation of the boycott was sufficiently severe to impress Government and Party officials—particularly those responsible for the German economy—with the necessity for future caution in orchestrating potentially disruptive nationwide measures of this kind. Subordinate local government and Party functionaries, however, unconcerned with Germany's foreign exchange position or her international markets, and inspired by the continuing propaganda of Goebbels and Streicher, instigated a series of quasi-legal measures—individual boycotts, 'spontaneous' attacks on individuals or their businesses, police denunciations, press attacks—which had the result, even before the promulgation of the Nuremberg Laws in September 1935 and the subsequent forced 'Aryanisation' of many businesses, of compelling the emigration of many Jews, initially from smaller towns and cities to Berlin and other centres, and then abroad.

[7] See Helmut Genschel, *Die Verdrängung der Juden aus der Wirtschaft im Dritten Reich* (Göttingen, 1966), pp. 44–47.

As the pressures on opponents, real or imaginary, of the new regime mounted throughout 1933, so did the numbers of emigrants. The greatest number of these fled between March and July 1933, initially to France, the Netherlands and other countries bordering on Germany. By the end of 1933, it was estimated that about 60,000 refugees had left Germany, of whom some 80 per cent were Jews.[8]

The emigrants from Germany, whatever their material circumstances or their political affiliations, faced many obstacles in attempting the move to other countries. Not least of these was the necessity to possess valid travel documents. In the early years of emigration, refugees in possession of German passports usually had no difficulty in renewing them at German Consulates abroad; by 1938, such renewal was most often refused, thus rendering the refugee *de facto* stateless. Those refugees who had been denationalised by decree— they were for the most part Jews of Eastern European origin—were of course stateless *de jure* from the start. Moreover, many of the political refugees either crossed the frontier illegally, or were simply expelled from Germany without any papers. As the exodus from Germany increased, however, practically every European country tightened its immigration regulations and its frontier security; a refugee without valid papers was illegally present in any country and thus liable to arrest and deportation, frequently into a neighbouring country from which he would also be subject to expulsion, and for the same reason.

Even for refugees with valid papers, permission to enter various countries was often impossible to obtain, because such permission was closely linked with the question of how much capital the intending immigrant could bring with him. Most countries had very limited immigration quotas in any case, or at least stringent regulations concerning permission for immigrants to take up employment. Certain types of skilled labourers, technicians and agricultural workers were the only categories of labour which were in any demand; unfortunately, the overwhelming proportion of emigrants from Germany, particularly the Jews, belonged to the professional

[8] See Norman Bentwich, *The Refugees from Germany, 1933–1935* (London, 1936), p. 33.

or business classes.[9] Those emigrants willing and able to learn new skills nevertheless faced grave financial difficulties; in the world-wide economic depression, no country was willing to risk the importation of potential or actual paupers, and practically every European and non-European country demanded of the would-be migrant some convincing demonstration of means sufficient to ensure his not becoming a public charge.

The intending emigrant from Germany had of course initially to dispose of his business or other property, real estate, furnishings, and personal assets of all kinds, frequently at a small fraction of their true value: the good-will of a going business concern was for example very seldom recoverable by its owner. A series of regulations of increasing severity was to culminate, by 1938, in setting conditions for the sale of all property which made it virtually impossible to retrieve more than a minute fraction of its value. Out of the meagre proceeds of such sales the costs of travel, shipping, visa and other fees had to be paid, and in the case of most non-European countries, these were particularly high. The so-called *Reichsfluchtssteuer*, or 'flight tax', which had been introduced in 1931 to conserve Germany's foreign exchange reserves, was retained by the Nazi regime, and from 1934 was levied on any emigrant who possessed a capital of more than RM50,000 or who since 1931 had an income of more than RM20,000 in any one year; the emigrant was required to pay to the Reich 25 per cent of the last assessed value of all his property.[10] The remainder of the emigrant's capital was retained in Germany and paid into a special blocked mark account which could only be realised abroad, at a rate which fluctuated but which tended steadily downward as the uses to which blocked marks could be applied were progressively limited. The losses on transfer of blocked marks varied from 20–50 per cent in

---

[9] In June 1933, 61·26 per cent of all Jews employed in Germany were engaged in commercial or service occupations; 12·46 per cent were civil servants or members of the professions. See Esra Bennathan, 'Die demographische und wirtschaftliche Struktur der Juden', p. 106, in W. E. Mosse (ed.), *Entscheidungsjahr 1932* (Tübingen, 1965).

[10] See Genschel, *Verdrängung*, pp. 256–264. The income of the Reich Government from *Reichsfluchtssteuer* was RM 1 million in 1932–33; RM 45 million in 1935–36; RM 70 million in 1936–37; RM 81 million in 1937–38; and RM 342 million in 1938–39.

the case of transfers to Palestine to 20–95 per cent for other countries.

Emigrants not only encountered extreme difficulty in transferring funds: they were also forbidden in many cases, particularly after 1938, to export merchandise, furniture, the tools of a trade, furs or jewellery. There were other exactions, legal and otherwise, to be paid by intending emigrants, and the number of these mounted annually; all emigrants had in addition to reckon with the costs of establishing themselves in a new country with whatever resources they might have succeeded in retaining. The material losses thus incurred throughout the process of emigration have been estimated at an average of 30–50 per cent of the emigrants' entire capital for the years 1933 to 1937; for the years from 1937 to the outbreak of the war, such losses amounted to 60–100 per cent of emigrants' capital.[11]

The appearance in the early months of 1933 of large numbers of despoiled and panicky German refugees in European countries excited widespread indignation and sympathy, and inspired the formation of numerous private committees and associations for the relief and resettlement of the victims. Great Britain was no exception to this general rule, and there as elsewhere the lead was taken by the Jewish community, which created in early 1933 a fund-raising body, the Central British Fund for German Jewry, later to become known as the Council for German Jewry. The fund represented all sections of the Anglo-Jewish community, and was in close touch with the central body of the German Jewish community, which organised and administered a comprehensive network of relief, retraining and emigration programmes in Germany. Sums raised by the Central British Fund and other specialised fund-raising organisations were allocated to an entire range of subsidiary bodies which dealt with relief, emigration, training and other aspects of refugee work.

The immediate needs of the first refugees arriving in England were met by the Jews' Temporary Shelter in London, whose President since World War I had been Mr Otto M. Schiff, himself born in Germany, and a partner in the City merchant banking firm of

[11] Genschel, op. cit., p. 261.

Bourke, Schiff & Co. Schiff's efforts on behalf of Jewish migrants had begun with Belgian relief work in the First World War; his activities had for many years brought him into close contact with the Home Office and other Government departments, where his reputation for reliability was such that often administrative decisions in aliens' cases were taken on little more than his personal recommendation.[12] In the early months of 1933 Schiff organised a Jewish Refugees Committee (later the German Jewish Aid Committee) to arrange for the admission of refugees to Britain, their maintenance, training, employment or re-migration. Schiff's personal relationships with Home Office officials, and the unquestioned authority of his Committee's guarantee, meant in practice that individuals were admitted to Britain, or their stay prolonged, on the simple undertaking of the Committee to place them in suitable employment or training, or to maintain them pending their move to other countries.[13]

The Society of Friends shared with the Jewish organisations the main burden of work for German refugees in Great Britain. Its German Emergency Committee, with offices in Paris, Prague and in Germany, was also established early in 1933, and both raised funds and disbursed them on behalf of the refugees. In addition, the Society of Friends frequently joined the Jewish bodies in negotiations with the Home Office and other Government departments on questions affecting refugees in Britain.

The special needs of the academic refugees were early recognised and met by the formation in April 1933 of the Academic Assistance Council, later the Society for the Protection of Science and Learning, on the initiative of Lord Beveridge, then Director of the London School of Economics. The Council, whose members were prominent academics, scientists and men in public life, devoted its efforts toward the placement of academic exiles in universities, industry and research institutions. Student refugees who could demonstrate outstanding ability were in many cases enabled to con-

[12] Schiff was awarded the OBE for his World War I refugee efforts, and CBE for his work with refugees from Germany. See obituary, *The Times*, November 17, 1952.

[13] See Norman Bentwich, *They Found Refuge* (London, 1956), pp. 14–29, 50–56.

tinue their training by a previously established body, the International Student Service, which provided study grants and training facilities. The International Solidarity Fund of the Labour Party and Trades Union Council was also active in the early stages of the refugee movement, engaging in relief work on behalf of those trade unionists, members of cooperative societies, Social Democrats or other refugees who had been forced for political reasons to flee Germany.

As it became generally recognised that the German refugee problem was not exclusively a Jewish concern, church groups came into existence to aid 'non-Aryan' refugees, many of whom were professing Christians. Such groups included committees of the Church of England, the Church of Scotland, and the Catholic Church; and the International Hebrew Christian Alliance. These bodies and several others subsequently pooled their efforts in the Christian Council for Refugees from Germany and Central Europe, which raised funds and was also in contact with the Home Office on questions affecting refugees.

Those private organisations and individuals who interested themselves shortly after Hitler's accession to power in the fate of German refugees recognised that the problem with which they were concerned raised issues of Government policy which went far beyond the immediate emergency and its concomitant relief effort. It was conceded by refugee groups that the economic situation in Great Britain, and the overwhelmingly middle-class character of the German emigration, made a large-scale absorption of refugees in Great Britain impracticable. Nevertheless, the partisans of more liberal immigration policies urged from the outset greater generosity on the part of the British Government, both at home and in the overseas territories for which Britain was responsible.

The tone for much subsequent Parliamentary debate was set by an early exchange, on February 21, 1933, when Colonel Josiah Wedgwood, Labour MP for Newcastle-under-Lyme and a consistently staunch champion of the refugee cause, asked the Home Secretary, Sir John Gilmour, if he would 'take into consideration some relaxation of the Aliens Act to afford refuge to the Marxists from Germany',[14] and was given the reply that

[14] 274 H.C. Deb., 1597.

the general principle on which the Aliens Order is administered is that aliens are only allowed to come in for residence if their settlement here is consonant with the interests of this country . . . the interests of this country must predominate over all other considerations.

The opposite pole in what was to be a continuing debate on refugees was stated nearly as early, on March 9, when the Home Secretary was asked by Mr E. Doran, the Unionist Member for Tottenham North, if 'he will take steps to prevent any alien Jews entering this country from Germany?' In reply, Sir John Gilmour said that it was

not within the contemplation of the law that there should be discrimination against aliens on grounds of religious belief or racial origin, but there are adequate powers under the Aliens Order to protect this country from any undesirable influx of aliens. . . .

In a further exchange of some bitterness, Mr Doran asserted that 'hundreds of thousands of Jews are now leaving Germany and scurrying from there to this country', and, after asking rhetorically 'are we prepared in this country to allow aliens to come in here from every country while we have 3,000,000 unemployed?' he added 'If you are asking for a von Hitler [sic!] in this country, we will soon get one.'[15]

Awareness in Parliament of a growing refugee problem was matched in Whitehall, which was furnished with accurate information through diplomatic sources on the extent of the growing repression in Germany. In addition, Ministers and civil servants were the object of representations by private groups and individuals concerned over the developments in Germany. On March 2, the Foreign Minister, Sir John Simon, informed the British Ambassador in Berlin that 'representative English Jews have been expressing to the Prime Minister and myself their profound alarm at the risks to which their co-religionists may be exposed in Germany in view of Nazi "incitement" ', and authorised the Ambassador to inform the German Foreign Minister 'privately and confidentially' of these representations.[16] Shortly thereafter, Viscount Robert Cecil wrote

[15] 275 H.C. Deb., 1351–1352.
[16] Simon to Rumbold, March 2, 1933, FO 371/16718, C 2013/319/18.

privately to Sir Robert Vansittart, Permanent Under Secretary at the Foreign Office, urging that

there is a case, especially in view of our position in Palestine, at any rate to make enquiries on the subject [of persecutions] in Germany. Anti-Semitism on a large scale there is bound to complicate our own problems of Government.[17]

And from Berlin itself, the British Passport Control Officer reported : 'This office is overwhelmed with applications from Jews to proceed to Palestine, to England, to anywhere in the British Empire.'[18]

By the end of March, the Home Office, which had also begun to receive an increasing number of applications for entry and extensions of stay from 'aliens of Jewish origin', requested the Foreign Office officially to supply it with information

regarding the situation in Germany in so far as it relates to the Jewish community and the extent to which numbers of the community may be driven to seek a refuge abroad through acts of violence, destitution, or any other like cause.[19]

Anticipating what was later to become a highly controversial issue, the Home Office also sought the aid of the Foreign Office in ascertaining the numbers and type of Jewish refugees from Germany in various countries, the conditions governing their stay, and other arrangements for dealing with them.[20]

The boycott of April 1, 1933 and actions preceding and accompanying it led to a sharp increase in the rate of emigration from Germany, and to the appearance at ports in Great Britain of significantly large numbers of visitors from Germany, many of whom were in fact refugees. The problem had already become too large to be ignored.

Recognising the sensitive nature of the dilemma with which Immigration Officers were now confronted, the Home Secretary

[17] Cecil to Vansittart, March 24, 1933, FO 371/16720, C 2745/319/18.
[18] Foley to Central Department, March 29, 1933, FO 371/16721, C 3405/319/18.
[19] Holderness to Under-Secretary of State, March 31, 1933, FO 371/16740, C 2979/1621/18.
[20] See telegrams of inquiry sent to British representatives at Paris, Brussels, The Hague, Copenhagen, Berne, Vienna, Prague, Warsaw, Riga, Stockholm, Oslo, April 5, 1933, FO 371/16720, C 3159/319/18.

sought the guidance of his Cabinet colleagues, informing them officially on April 5 that there had recently been a large influx of Germans 'mainly of the professional classes and probably Jews',[21] and that although these persons had satisfied the Immigration Officers as to the means at their disposal, many of them had admitted that they were refugees. After reviewing the relevant provisions of the Aliens Order, 1920, the Home Secretary reported that all the Germans allowed to land as visitors had had time conditions attached to their stay, and that this practice would be continued. The Secretary acknowledged that

in theory, the Home Office will have power to regulate the stay of such people by refusing to grant further extensions, but in practice it may prove very difficult to insist on their return to Germany while present conditions continue in that country.

The Cabinet was further informed that representatives of the Jewish community had visited the Home Office and had proposed

(a) that all German Jewish refugees from Germany should be admitted without distinction; (b) that German Jews already admitted for the purpose of visits or who may be admitted in the future should be allowed during the present emergency to prolong their stay indefinitely.

The representatives of the Jewish community formally undertook that 'all expense, whether in respect of temporary or permanent accommodation or maintenance will be borne by the Jewish community without ultimate charge to the State', adding that

it is appreciated that these arrangements can at the best be only temporary and negotiations are in progress with a view to the ultimate transmigration of the refugees to countries other than England.

The Jewish community had estimated that the numbers of refugees coming to Great Britain 'might be as many as 3,000 to 4,000'.[22]

---

[21] Cabinet Committee on Aliens Restrictions, memorandum by the Home Secretary, The Present Position in Regard to the Admission of Jewish Refugees from Germany to this Country, April 7, 1933, C.P. 96/33.

[22] See Proposals of the Jewish Community as Regards Jewish Refugees from Germany, Appendix I to memorandum by the Home Secretary, April 7, 1933, C.P. 96/33. The undertaking was signed by Neville Laski, President of the London Committee of Deputies of British Jews (the Board of Deputies), Lionel L. Cohen, Chairman of the Law and Parliamentary Committee of the Board of Deputies, L. G. Montefiore, President of the Anglo-Jewish Association, and Otto M. Schiff, Chairman of the Jewish Refugees Committee.

The undertaking that no Jewish refugee would become a public charge was explicitly relied on by Government officials on many occasions; it was to be upheld until the outbreak of war in September 1939.

After a short discussion, the Cabinet agreed that a committee of its members should be appointed to examine the proposals of the Jewish community and report to the full Cabinet.[23] When the Committee reported two days later, it acknowledged that it was not possible to say how many of Germany's 500,000 Jews might try to leave, but that the number might be 'substantial'. Taking note of the Jewish community's offer to guarantee 'temporary maintenance for the refugees, and to facilitate their ultimate transportation to countries other than the United Kingdom', the Committee considered and rejected the alternatives of either making restrictions on entry more severe, or relaxing them so as to extend to German Jews without means, or to those requiring employment, the same privileges of entry enjoyed by German Jews with financial resources who were in most cases seeking to visit friends or relatives. The Committee affirmed that

so far as Palestine is concerned, the number of Jewish refugees who could be allowed to enter the country is strictly conditioned by what the country can absorb. The matter is strictly one for the High Commissioner, but there is no reason to suppose that room could be found in Palestine in the near future for any appreciable number of German Jewish refugees. The number of refugees who might be transmigrated to the Colonies generally, must be treated as negligible.[24]

Cautiously, the Committee concluded that it would be best to maintain for the time being the existing arrangements for admission and exclusion of German Jewish refugees, but that these arrangements should be strengthened by adding the condition that the refugee should register with the police upon reaching his destination in the

[23] See Cabinet 23 (33), Conclusion 5, April 5, 1933. The Cabinet Committee was composed of the Home Secretary as Chairman; the Foreign Secretary; the Colonial Secretary; the President of the Board of Trade; the Minister of Labour; and the First Commissioner of Works.
[24] Cabinet Committee on Aliens Restrictions, Report, April 7, 1933, C.P. 96 (33). Throughout its Report, the Committee apparently considered the German refugee problem to be an exclusively Jewish one; non-Jewish political or other refugees are not mentioned.

United Kingdom. The British Jewish community were to be apprised of this decision and to be further informed that in cases where refugees desired to extend permission for their temporary stays,

the Government would be prepared to consider a further extension provided that the Jewish community were prepared to guarantee, so far as it might be necessary, adequate means of maintenance for the refugees concerned.

The Committee also ventured the opinion that it might be desirable if the refugee situation deteriorated to 'arrange for the problem to be considered by the International Office for Refugees of the League of Nations'.

Meeting on April 12, the Cabinet once again considered the refugee question; in the course of discussion it was pointed out that it would be in the public interest to

try and secure for this country prominent Jews who were being expelled from Germany and who had achieved distinction whether in pure science, applied science, such as medicine or technical industry, music or art. This would not only obtain for this country the advantage of their knowledge and experience, but would also create a very favourable impression in the world, particularly if our hospitality were offered with some warmth.[25]

Ministers displayed sensitivity to possible foreign criticism as well as the exigencies of the domestic situation : the minutes record that

while fully realising the importance of not allowing this country to be flooded with foreign refugees who would before long either become a burden to the community or replace other workers who would become a burden, the Cabinet were anxious to avoid the other danger of creating an atmosphere in Europe critical to this country.

The Cabinet thereupon agreed to approve the proposals of its Committee on Aliens Restrictions, and to invite that Committee to consider the suggestion of possible offers of hospitality to refugees from Germany who were 'eminent in science, technology, art, music, etc.'. The Cabinet Committee on Aliens Restrictions appears however

[25] See Cabinet 27 (33), Conclusion 8, April 12, 1933.

not to have held any further meetings to discuss this or other aspects of the refugee question.[26]

The Home Secretary had also informed his fellow-Ministers that he faced a Parliamentary question as to whether 'the Government will be prepared to consider the granting of asylum to German Jews in this country on a self-supporting financial basis', and submitted a draft reply for their consideration. The Cabinet approved the reply, whose sonorous formula was to be repeated on many subsequent occasions :

the interests of this country must predominate over all other considerations, but subject to this guiding principle each case will be carefully considered on its individual merits . . . in accordance with the time-honoured tradition of this country no unnecessary obstacles are placed in the way of foreigners seeking admission.[27]

Concern in Parliament and in the country over the refugee issue was growing, however, and was reflected in the frequency and tone of Parliamentary questions. Miss Eleanor F. Rathbone, Member for English Universities, asked the Home Secretary on April 13 whether he was aware that 'Jewish and Socialist refugees from Germany are being freely admitted into France, Switzerland and other Continental countries', and asked further if the immigration laws of Great Britain were being modified on their behalf. On the same day, Mr E. Doran asked for the 'total number of alien Jews who have arrived in the United Kingdom within the past month' and was informed that no such statistics were available.[28]

Later on April 13, the refugee question was discussed at some length in a Commons debate on the adjournment.[29] Colonel Wedgwood led off with a strong plea that the House and the country should 'realise the value of brains and the duty of hospitality to the oppressed' and open the doors to refugees from Germany. Mr Clement Attlee of the Labour Party also urged action on the Government, and suggested that Great Britain, as the holder of the Palestine mandate, had a particular responsibility vis-à-vis refugees from

---

[26] See FO 372/2949, T 4351/509/378. A Cabinet Committee on Refugees was established in January 1939. See Chapter 7.
[27] See 276 H.C. Deb., 2557–2558.
[28] 276 H.C. Deb., 2719, 2734.
[29] Ibid., 2744–2812.

c

Germany, and that Palestine could absorb a very much larger population. Sir Herbert Samuel, a former High Commissioner of Palestine, more cautiously ventured that

something may be done possibly in Palestine, and perhaps something
may be done by a little relaxation of the very severe conditions of
admission into this country. . . . But the main solution must come out
of Germany itself.

The Foreign Secretary, Sir John Simon, replying on behalf of the
Government, expressed the opinion that the debate had been useful
in giving voice to the 'deep, general and, I might say, universal
feeling that is entertained in this country on the recent treatment
of Jews and other minorities in Germany'. Acknowledging that the
events in Germany had presented the Government with quite particular problems, and that considerable numbers of people were
applying to enter England, the Foreign Secretary proclaimed himself as

belonging to that school which holds, on the whole, and with the long
view, that the admission to this country of people of good character
who bring their trade and experience with them, is a gain and not a
loss to this country.

He added his conviction that 'the sentiment of our own people will
not wish us to be unfeeling or niggardly' in administering the immigration laws. Turning to the Palestine situation, Simon announced,
to the approval of the House, several concessions recently authorised
by the High Commissioner for Palestine for Jewish immigrants from
Germany.[30] He ended the debate by affirming that it would not be
in the interests of the German Jews themselves for the British
Government to intervene with the authorities in Berlin on their
behalf—but he hoped that the debate had served to echo British
opinion, and that 'friendly but firm remonstrance' might have its

---

[30] These concessions were: an advance of 1,000 certificates on account of the
Labour Schedule for the half-year beginning April 1; the allocation to the
British Passport Control Officer, Berlin, of blocks of 200 immigration certificates
for grant without reference to Jerusalem to immigrants possessing a minimum
capital of £1,000; a 'liberal review' of applications for immigration certificates
by members of certain skilled trades and crafts, with a minimum capital of
£500; finally, the High Commissioner had given orders that there should be
considerate treatment for applications by German Jews already within Palestine
for the admission of parents or other relatives.

effect in Germany. The Foreign Secretary's hope was to be a vain one: the only immediate effect of the Commons debate was a sharp protest by the German Ambassador in London.

As the German exodus showed no signs of abating throughout the spring and summer months of 1933, the attention of the Foreign Office and other Government departments turned to the possibility, foreshadowed in the Cabinet Committee's report, of referring the refugee question to the League of Nations. Private organisations and individuals concerned with refugees were also pressing for a British Government initiative in bringing the German refugee problem to the attention of the League. The Society of Friends, leaders of the Labour Party, notably George Lansbury and Arthur Henderson, and the League of Nations Union all addressed the Foreign Secretary in this sense. These petitions were answered with a certain weary patience by Foreign Office officials who pointed out the incontrovertible fact that the refugees from Germany still possessed German passports, were not technically stateless, and therefore could not claim the protection of the Nansen Office.[31] Following an internal review of the entire question, the Foreign Office addressed an official letter to the Home Office advising that the question of Jewish refugees from Germany lay outside the technical scope of the Nansen Office, and that

a suggestion by His Majesty's Government that the League should consider measures of assistance for German nationals leaving Germany would be regarded in that country as an act of unwarranted interference, if not of hostility, and Sir John Simon could not advise that it should be made.[32]

International action on behalf of those being persecuted in at least one part of the Reich, Upper Silesia, was however initiated by a refugee from that region who sent a petition to the League on May 19, 1933, protesting against the Nazi regime of discrimination there, and relying on the minorities protection clauses of the Geneva Convention of 1922 pursuant to which the territory was administered by Germany. The Council of the League, including the repre-

[31] See Simon to Henderson, May 26, 1933, FO 371/16724, C 4550/319/18.
[32] Foreign Office to Home Office, May 20, 1933, FO 371/16274, C 4549/319/18.

sentative of Great Britain, concurred in a report condemning Germany for its violation of the 1922 Convention, and an undertaking was extracted from the German Government to restore and henceforth respect the rights of the Jewish minority in Upper Silesia.[33]

By June, the French, Dutch and Belgian representatives to the International Labour Conference at Geneva all raised the issue of the influx of German refugees and its disruptive effect on their respective labour markets. With the concurrence of the British delegate to the Conference, the International Labour Office was thereupon requested to study the matter without interfering in Germany's internal affairs, and to advise what measures might be taken to place German refugees in various countries. It was emphasised that such measures were to be devised so as to avoid any harm to the economic welfare of countries in which the refugees might find asylum. Consideration in Whitehall of the proposed International Labour Office enquiry revealed, however, considerable misgivings on the part of both the Home Office and the Colonial Office. A Home Office spokesman at an interdepartmental meeting felt that 'information as to the present position as regards this country might serve to encourage an influx of refugees from Germany, which we wished to avoid.' The Colonial Office for its part 'deprecated any enquiry by the International Labour Office which might involve an attempt by the International Labour Office to determine whether or not more room could be found for Germans in Palestine, since this matter was entirely within the High Commissioner's discretion.' It was nevertheless agreed, at the urging of the Foreign Office, that it would not be possible for the British delegate to oppose the enquiry, since to do so 'might be construed as indicating a lack of sympathy with the position of the refugees'.[34]

Responding to the move at Geneva, Mr Neville J. Laski, the Chairman of the Joint Foreign Committee of the Jewish Board of Deputies and the Anglo-Jewish Association, and official spokesman of the British Jewish community in foreign affairs, wrote to Sir Robert Vansittart in July to express doubt that the International

---

[33] This undertaking was largely ignored, and ceased to have any value when Germany withdrew from the League. See Janowsky and Fagen, *German Racial Policies*, pp. 110–115.

[34] Home Office note, June 19, 1933.

Labour Office was equipped for the task which had just been given it, and to request that the British Government place the entire matter of German refugees on the agenda of the September meeting of the League Assembly.[35] The Laski-Vansittart exchange of views, which included a call at the Foreign Office, instituted a review of policy within the Department, which was now also seized of the ominous information that a German law had been passed on July 14 providing for revocation of grants of naturalisation and for the withdrawal of German citizenship in certain cases.[36]

Discussions within the Foreign Office revealed that the chief objection to taking any initiative with the League was the conviction that the British Government by so doing would inevitably assume the onerous responsibility for suggesting an overall solution to the problem. While the delicate state of Anglo-German relations preoccupied the Foreign Office, the Colonial Office was concerned lest a British Government lead at Geneva imply a willingness to take some special action on the refugees' behalf, such as their admission in considerable numbers to Palestine.[37]

In its official reply to the Joint Foreign Committee, the Foreign Office justified its refusal to raise the German refugee problem with the League by referring to the 'very much smaller number of such refugees in this country than in most other countries concerned.[38] An internal memorandum on the situation was more specific:

The number of such refugees in the United Kingdom is still comparatively small . . . (according to the Home Office, round about 1,000), but the competent authorities have no desire to see it increased . . . the Home Office, Colonial Office, Dominions Office and Ministry of Labour are especially anxious to avoid being placed in the position of having either to turn down, or to act upon any immigration or settlement recommendations coming from such a source [the League]; and they therefore do not want the matter referred to the League *at all* if that can be avoided . . . they are *a fortiori* averse from any suggestion that HM Government should . . . take the initiative. . . . It

[35] See Laski to Vansittart, July 28, 1933, FO 371/16727, C 6821/319/18.

[36] See Newton to Simon, July 19, 1933, FO 371/16726, C 6540/319/18.

[37] See minute August 4, 1933, FO 371/16756, C 7078/6839/18 and minutes August 3–5, 1933 on FO 371/16727, C 6821/319/18.

[38] See Perowne to Montefiore, August 25, 1933, FO 371/16756, C 6966/6839/18.

may be noted *en passant* that placing the matter on the agenda involves (1) giving notice three weeks in advance; (2) giving reasons before the Assembly for placing the matter on the agenda; and (3) proposing a definite course of action. Both (2) and (3) would be highly embarrassing to HMG.[39]

The issue was not however permitted to rest there. The Jewish organisations returned to the charge, this time proposing the appointment of a League Commission, or at least a Commissioner, to assist in settling the refugees from Germany, and urging again that the British Government sponsor such a proposal before the Assembly.[40] The Joint Foreign Committee's consistent aim, shared by other groups concerned with the fate of the refugees, was to have the refugee problem officially recognised as 'a concern of the League', thus paving the way for a potential claim on the intervention of the Nansen Office, and establishing a lever to exert more effective diplomatic pressure on Germany to stop creating refugees. The Foreign Office was prepared by September to concede that the League would probably 'in the long run' have to deal with the German refugee question, but again it was predicted that a League Commission 'could scarcely fail to make recommendations which it would be inconvenient for His Majesty's Government to implement and embarrassing for them to reject.[41] The Foreign Secretary, to whom the question was referred for an opinion, agreed that the British Government should not take the lead, but suggested that if 'other Governments *propose* such action, I should be prepared to support it.[42] Another member of the Department added:

if we are assured that the Jewish Organisations will not favour any scheme which would be a charge on public funds, we should feel much freer to give them moral support.

The official reply to the Joint Foreign Committee repeated that the British Government was unable to take the lead at Geneva, but might support initiatives of other Governments 'more directly con-

[39] Perowne, memorandum, FO 371/16756, C 7075/6839/18.
[40] See Montefiore to Vansittart, September 1, 1933, FO 371/16757, C 7877/6839/18.
[41] See Perowne, minute, September 6, 1933, FO 371/16757, C 7877/6839/18.
[42] Simon, minute, September 13, 1933, ibid. Both the French and the Netherlands Governments had already requested talks with the British Government on the subject of German refugees.

cerned'. The Joint Foreign Committee was also requested to send the Foreign Office its views as to how the expenses of any League-sponsored refugee schemes should be borne.[43]

Throughout the summer months, as the Foreign Office and the refugee organisations sparred warily on the subject of League of Nations intervention, there was a series of Parliamentary questions, along by then traditional lines, on one or another aspect of the refugee question, and in particular immigration into Palestine. The even predictability of these expressions of Parliamentary concern was varied by an altogether novel intervention by Commander Oliver Locker-Lampson, MP, who introduced a Bill on July 26 'to promote and extend opportunities of citizenship for Jews resident outside the British Empire'.[44] In introducing his Bill, which would 'promote and extend citizenship in Palestine for Jews deprived of citizenship elsewhere', Commander Locker-Lampson reminded the House that 'it is un-English, it is caddish to bully a minority' and suggested that the British Empire should 'stand by Jewry in its trouble'. He added that Great Britain had been granted the mandate of Palestine 'to help fulfil the Messianic miracle there', and his Bill therefore proposed to extend Palestinian citizenship to all persecuted Jews. The *Nationality of Jews Bill* was presented accordingly, and read a first time; it was not however printed, and never came up for a second reading.[45]

The question of the worsening refugee situation—flight had continued unabated in June, July and August—was finally raised at the League Assembly by the Netherlands Government, which sponsored a Resolution on September 29 inviting the League Council to formulate plans for an international solution to the German refugee problem.[46]

[43] Wigram to Montefiore, September 19, 1933, FO 371/16757, C 7877/6839/18.

[44] See 280 H.C. Deb., 2604–2606.

[45] A Foreign Office minute on an extract from the debate states that the 'House was greatly moved by Commander Locker-Lampson's oration'. July 31, 1933, FO 371/16726, C 6709/319/18. Locker-Lampson, Conservative MP for the Handsworth Division of Birmingham, had extended hospitality to Albert Einstein when Einstein was en route to refuge in the United States.

[46] See League of Nations Document A.33. 1933, Geneva, September 29, 1933, *Assistance to Refugees*, Draft Resolution submitted by the Netherlands Delegation. The Netherlands Government was persuaded to put forward its Resolu-

In its telegram of instructions for the British delegate at Geneva, the Foreign Office conceded that while

we could scarcely refuse our general support for proposal that the Council should consider this question . . . the British Delegation should refrain from too explicitly associating itself with it and from taking the lead in any way. It should also be made clear . . . that His Majesty's Government . . . cannot bear any part of the expenses arising from the application of any recommendation. . . .

Further points to be borne in mind by the British delegate were the following : criticisms of Germany, or acrimony in the debate were to be avoided; the British Government would not agree to any exceptions to the principle that immigration into Palestine must be limited by the economic absorptive capacity of the country; and, finally, the state of the British labour market would be the 'paramount consideration' for the Government in considering any concrete proposals ultimately made.[47]

As a sop to German susceptibilities the Netherlands resolution was referred by the Assembly to its Second Committee for examination; that Committee dealt solely with technical matters such as health and communications. Discussion was carefully confined to economic and technical aspects of the problem, and on October 12, the Council—the German representative abstaining—appointed a High Commissioner for Refugees (Jewish and other) coming from Germany, to coordinate international efforts on behalf of the German refugees. The High Commissioner nominated by the Council was an American, James G. McDonald, President of the Foreign Policy Association. The British Jewish organisations and the Jewish Agency for Palestine had hoped it might be possible to persuade Viscount Cecil of Chelwood to accept the High Commissionership; they considered Mr McDonald lacked sufficient international experience and stature to be effective in this post. The appointment of a United States citizen was however deemed of overriding importance in view of the need to attract substantial funds from America. The

tion by the Jewish relief committee for German refugees in the Netherlands; its approach to the Netherlands Government was apparently made at the suggestion of the British Jewish organisations. See L. De Jong, *Het Koninkrijk der Nederlanden in de tweede wereldoorlog* (The Hague, 1969), Vol. I, 497.

[47] Simon to Ormsby-Gore, October 3, 1933, FO 371/16757, C 8669/6839/18.

Foreign Office for its part considered it undesirable to have a British subject as High Commissioner, since he 'might think himself bound to ask us to relax our restrictions in the UK and in Palestine, and such a request coming from a British High Commissioner might be difficult to refuse'.[48]

The new High Commissioner's authority was very carefully circumscribed : he was to be responsible not to the League itself, but to a Governing Body consisting of representatives of twelve governments interested in the German refugee problem; he and the Governing Body were to constitute an entirely autonomous organisation, whose administrative and other expenses would be met from funds contributed by private organisations and individuals rather than governments.[49] To emphasise the High Commission's separation from the League, it made its headquarters in Lausanne rather than in Geneva.

With the support of the Archbishop of Canterbury, the British Jewish organisations put forward the name of Viscount Cecil of Chelwood as British representative on the Governing Body, and the Foreign Office prepared to appoint him formally, although considerable apprehension was expressed that Lord Cecil's strong point was 'not the slavish carrying out of instructions'.[50] The Colonial Office, which had from the outset shown distinct nervousness over the implications for Palestine of the formation of a refugee High Commission, proposed its own candidate, Lord Rennell, for the Governing Body representative, but it objections to Lord Cecil were rather brusquely set aside by the Foreign Office, which speculated that the Colonial Office had withdrawn its objections to Cecil because 'Dr Weizmann has come to some arrangement with Mr McDonald [the High Commissioner for Refugees] by which the latter will not interest himself in Palestine, but leave it to Dr Weiz-

[48] See Cadogan, minute, October 30, 1933, FO 371/16758, C 9378/6839/18, and M. Shertok, Notes of Interviews with the Society of Friends and with the Bishop of Chichester with Regard to the Office of the High Commissioner for Refugees from Germany, October 18, 1933, ZA, L 13/154a.

[49] In contrast, the administrative expenses of the Nansen Office were met from the League budget. An initial loan of 25,000 Swiss francs was, however, advanced to the High Commissioner for Refugees from Germany for setting up his office; this sum was repaid in January 1934.

[50] See minutes, October 30, 1933, FO 371/16758, C 9378/6839/18.

mann's Zionist Committee'.[51] Lord Cecil was duly appointed British representative on the Governing Body, although more than one Government department remained apprehensive concerning both him and the new High Commission. J. V. Perowne of the Foreign Office wrote :

I have spoken to Sir E. Holderness H.O. and he thinks that either the Home Secretary or Sir G. Hacking shd. see Ld. Cecil & try to impress upon him how important it is that our present favourable position as regards the present numbers of refugees here shd. not be prejudiced by any recommendations made to the Governing Body.[52]

The views of the Home Office were further referred to in a letter Perowne addressed to a member of the British Embassy in Paris, who had enquired as to possible openings for German Jewish refugees in Great Britain or the Dominions :

For your private information the Home Office are not at all dissatisfied with the present position as regards the numbers and quality of refugees from Germany over here (which compares very favourably with that of some other countries including France). But we most certainly don't want present numbers increased and it is our policy therefore to do *nothing* to *encourage* further immigration . . . you should be careful to make it clear . . . that you have no sort of reason to suppose that there could possibly be any opening for anyone here in the United Kingdom.[53]

In advance of the new High Commission's first meeting Lord Cecil was issued with detailed instructions which embodied the views of all Government departments concerned with the refugee question.[54] He was generally to use his influence to avoid discussion or recommendations in the Governing Body 'likely to provoke resentment in Germany'. As to finance, the British Government could not consider

making any financial contribution at all towards expenditure connected either with the High Commissioner's office or with the application of any schemes which may be elaborated with a view to assisting the refugees.

[51] See Wigram, minute, November 13, 1933, FO 371/16758, C 9897/6839/18.
[52] Perowne, minute, November 21, 1933, FO 371/16758, C 10172/6839/18.
[53] Perowne to Peake, November 20, 1933, FO 371/16740, C 10229/1621/18.
[54] See Simon to Cecil, December 1, 1933, FO 371/16758, C 10564/6839/18.

All such expenses were to be defrayed by private organisations and individuals concerned with refugees. Lord Cecil was instructed further to bear in mind the settled policy of the Government that control of immigration into Palestine, and the determination of that country's economic capacity to absorb immigrants, must remain exclusively the responsibility of the High Commissioner for Palestine. As for other dependent territories within the Empire, the Colonial Office would be prepared to 'consider sympathetically any concrete proposals' which might be put forward, although generally there would be 'very little scope for the immigration of persons of a white race' into the majority of the Colonies. Within the United Kingdom itself, 'owing to the acute unemployment . . . there are no prospects for Germans seeking employment in commerce or industry'. A saturation point had also been reached in the medical profession, and no guarantees could be given that foreign doctors, even after obtaining a British degree, would be permitted to establish themselves in practice. Finally, further numbers of students and research workers could not be absorbed in Great Britain, and there would therefore be 'little or no possibility of finding useful openings in this country for more refugees of the professional classes'.

Armed with these instructions, Cecil proceeded to Lausanne where the first session of the Governing Body was held from December 5 to 8, 1933.[55] The Governing Body unanimously elected Cecil its Chairman, despite his reluctance to assume the position. A small Permanent Committee of the Governing Body was constituted to act as an executive organ in the intervals between the three sessions a year of the Governing Body. In addition, an Advisory Council, representing certain private Jewish and non-Jewish organisations concerned with refugee work was nominated to assist the Governing Body in its deliberations.[56] On substantive questions, the Govern-

[55] Cecil, report, December 8, 1933, FO 371/17698, C 39/23/18.
[56] These were, of the Jewish organisations: American Joint Distribution Committee, Jewish Colonisation Association; Jewish Agency for Palestine, representatives of the major American, English, French, Dutch and Polish Jewish organisations and the Comité des délégations juives, representing Jewish communities of central and eastern Europe, Greece and Italy. The non-Jewish organisations were: Society of Friends, Caritas Catholica, L'Office central d'entr'aide des Eglises and the Conseil oecuménique du Christianisme pratique, the Comité de placement des intellectuels réfugiés, Fédération internationale

ing Body agreed readily that 'Europe was full, and that there was little hope of absorbing the refugees permanently. Their future, therefore, depended upon the possibility of their settlement in other countries.' The major problem in such settlement was how to facilitate movement of refugees from one country to another, and in this connection the question of passports or other identity papers was an urgent one : many refugees were without any passports, or possessed lapsed or invalid papers of various kinds. These *de facto* stateless persons, unable to claim the protection of even the Nansen Office, were forced into a clandestine existence, and were frequently expelled from one country to another in an endless series of perforce illegal entries and re-entries. No solution of this problem was reached at the Lausanne meeting, largely because none of the Government representatives had instructions to deal with it.[57]

Upon receipt of Lord Cecil's official report,[58] the Foreign and Home Offices proceeded to consider the entire complex question of travel documents, a question which was to preoccupy them for several months, with the Home Office consistently reserving the right to refuse admission to any alien whose travel documents, whatever their nature, did not bear a return visa to another country.[59]

des Syndicats professionels, and a joint representation of The Emergency Committee in Aid of Displaced German Scholars, The Academic Assistance Council and the International Student Service. Other members were L'Union internationale de secours aux enfants and the Comité national français de secours aux réfugiés, a French Government-sponsored body.

[57] An international conference, in which fifteen States took part, had been held at Geneva in October 1933 in order to draft a convention for the international legal protection of refugees. Great Britain declined to attend the conference, on the grounds that the refugees whose status was to be discussed— so-called 'Nansen' refugees—were not in Great Britain in sufficient numbers so warrant such attendance. The Convention resulting from this conference was opened to accession early in 1934, but the British Government continued until 1936 to withhold its accession because, according to a Foreign Office memorandum, 'it was felt that it might be difficult, under the growing pressure from societies interested in the German refugee problem, to resist a demand for the extension of the terms of the Convention to all refugees and stateless persons, and the Home Office were particularly anxious to avoid any such commitment, which would appear to perpetuate the problem of German and other refugees'. Memorandum, August 9, 1935, FO 371/19677, W 5796/346/98. The Convention was ultimately ratified by Great Britain on October 14, 1936, but with a series of material reservations.

[58] December 8, 1933, FO 371/17698, C 39/23/18.

[59] See Home Office memorandum, Travel Documents for Refugees from Germany who do not Possess National Papers, January 26, 1934, FO 371/17698, C 621/23/18.

The Permanent Committee of the Governing Body of the High Commission met in London on January 30, 1934, and called on its member governments to grant facilities for vocational retraining of refugees, and on the High Commissioner himself to negotiate with governments concerning settlement and emigration schemes, the issue of work permits and of travel documents to *de jure* and *de facto* stateless refugees from Germany.[60] These recommendations were in the main acceptable to the Home Office, but in its formal comments the Office was careful to reserve the complete right to refuse a visa or leave to land in any case it saw fit. Subject to this stipulation, it would be

prepared to deal as liberally as may be possible, within the limits necessarily imposed by the economic situation of this country, with the question of the permanent settlement of individual refugees.[61]

While the Home Office and the Foreign Office were able relatively easily to answer the several queries and recommendations which were addressed to them by the High Commissioner for Refugees, the problem of how the refugees were to withdraw their assets from Germany—without which they were unwelcome in any country—proved far more intractable, and British Government intervention of but dubious value. Mr James McDonald, the High Commissioner, had himself approached the German authorities in an attempt to obtain some measure of uniformity in practice as to how much capital an emigrant proceeding elsewhere than to Palestine[62] could take with him, as well as on such questions as the pay-

[60] See Report on the Meeting of the Permanent Committee of the Governing Body of the High Commission for Refugees (Jewish and Other) coming from Germany, January 30, 1934, FO 371/17699, C 1060/23/18.

[61] Home Office to Foreign Office, April 28, 1934, FO 371/17699, C 2680/23/18.

[62] Emigrants to Palestine were able to take advantage of a special transfer arrangement, known as Haavara, or 'transfer' in Hebrew. This arrangement, which was negotiated in August 1933 by the Jewish Agency for Palestine with the German Government, enabled emigrants to transfer funds to Palestine by paying exporters in Germany in marks for the export of merchandise to Palestine, and then to obtain the equivalent amount in Palestine currency from the importer in Palestine. Under this system would-be emigrants were often able to transfer not merely the £1,000 required to qualify for entry into Palestine as 'persons of independent means' but also substantial additional sums whose investment led to a continuing expansion of the local economy. Until the end of 1934, Jewish immigrants in Palestine received some 94 per

ment of pensions and social insurance contributions to dismissed
civil servants and others, and the imposition of *Reichsfluchtssteuer* on refugees. The High Commissioner was met with
studied indifference however and was ultimately fobbed off
on a relatively junior member of the legal staff at the Wilhelmstrasse, who was not able to hold out any hope of progress. The
High Commissioner was finally informed, through the German
Ambassador in London, that the German Foreign Office would be
prepared to discuss these questions, but only if 'questions of political
principle and matters affecting internal legislation were not introduced'.[63]

Rebuffed in Berlin, the High Commissioner thereupon
approached the Foreign Office, through his deputy Mr Norman
Bentwich, to request that the British Ambassador in Berlin be instructed to urge the German Government to give sympathetic consideration to the High Commissioner's proposals. Although several
members of the Department reacted coolly to Mr Bentwich's suggestion—one minuted : 'this is really no business of ours. . . . Once
we give way on any of these suggested informal approaches to the
German Govt. in the interests of the refugees there will be no end
to the requests for intervention we shall get from the Jews'[64]
—it was ultimately decided that the British Ambassador, Sir Eric
Phipps, be authorised at his discretion to make a 'strictly unofficial
representation' about the matter if the United States Ambassador
in Berlin would take similar action on behalf of his Government.[65]
Before any joint démarche could be made however the purge of
June 30, 1934 had intervened, and it was felt by both the American
and the British Ambassadors that the disturbed atmosphere was not
propitious for urging greater generosity to enable refugees to transfer

cent of sums they had deposited in Germany for transfer; as pressures to leave
the Reich mounted, this percentage rapidly declined, and in November 1938
all further Haavara transfers were forbidden by the German authorities. See
Werner Feilchenfeld et al., *Haavara-Transfer nach Palästina und Einwanderung
deutscher Juden 1933–1939* (Tübingen, 1972).
   [63] See Cecil, Report on Second Session of the Governing Body of the High
Commission for Refugees coming from Germany, May 4, 1934, FO 371/17700,
C 4239/23/18.
   [64] Perowne, minute, June 6, 1934, FO 371/17699, C 3521/23/18.
   [65] Perowne to Phipps, June 8, 1934, FO 371/17699, C 3521/23/18.

their capital abroad. There matters rested until the early autumn, when a German regulation restricting remittances of income from Germany was promulgated, thus threatening to cut off the sole source of a limited income for many thousands of refugees outside Germany. The High Commissioner again visited Berlin, in the middle of November, and was received on this occasion by a staff member of the Reichsbank, who informed him that although the German authorities appreciated the claims of the refugees, no present solution of the transfer question could be found, given Germany's chronic and serious shortage of foreign exchange.[66] The transfer of refugees' assets from Germany was a question on which the High Commissioner, his staff, and all organisations dealing with refugees were to return repeatedly to the charge, in efforts to enlist the support of the Foreign Office for representations in Berlin. The efficacy of such representations was with equal consistency seriously questioned in Whitehall, and in the event, such informal approaches to the German authorities as were made—most usually jointly with the Americans—proved barren of any result.

While the Foreign Office was considering aspects of the refugee question affecting Anglo-German relations, and the possible extension of British Government involvement in international efforts to solve the problem, the Home Office was dealing with the day-to-day, case by case decisions affecting those refugees who were allowed to enter the United Kingdom. In this activity, the Home Office continued to work in close liaison with the Jewish Refugees Committee, under the chairmanship of Mr Otto M. Schiff: the admission of selected refugees was authorised after consultation with the Committee, in reliance on the guarantee that no individual for whom the Jewish community assumed responsibility would be permitted to become a public charge. Refugees arrived at the British ports in 1934 in comparatively small numbers, however; about 100 per month, compared with between 300 and 400 per month in 1933.[67] By January 1935, Mr Schiff could report that there had been a distinct falling off in the number of refugees dealt with by

[66] Newton to Perowne, December 11, 1934, FO 371/17702, C 8543/23/18.
[67] Figures quoted in Annex II to Report on Second Session of the Governing Body of the High Commission for Refugees coming from Germany, May 4, 1934, FO 371/17700, C 4239/23/18.

his Committee, chiefly 'owing to the realisation by them that permission to settle in this country permanently was difficult to obtain'.[68]

Although comparatively few refugees had entered Britain between 1933 and 1935—their number fluctuated between some 1,500 and 2,500—and those admitted were not permitted to take any but approved employment, the spectre of thousands of aliens flooding the job market was consistently invoked by the Beaverbrook and other segments of the popular press, and aroused alarm in certain quarters, notably among the medical profession. Representatives of British medicine were insistent in urging the Home Office not to relax restrictions on aliens, and to make it clear to foreign medical students that they could not be guaranteed admission to practice even after qualifying in British medical schools. When Lord Dawson of Penn, President of the Royal College of Physicians, called on the Home Secretary in November 1933, he conceded that there might be room in Britain for a few refugee doctors of special distinction, but 'the number that could usefully be absorbed or teach us anything could be counted on the fingers of one hand'.[69] At the time, 160 aliens were studying at British medical schools, not by any means all of them refugees.

For its part, the Home Office undertook to consult the medical organisations if the number of refugees studying medicine threatened to become too large. The British medical fraternity was able through its own licensing procedures to limit to its satisfaction the number of refugee doctors admitted to practice, but widespread misapprehension as to the numbers actually involved was to persist throughout the period 1933–1939.

Well aware of the impact of German legislative and other measures on the number of would-be immigrants, the Home Office followed developments in Germany with careful attention, enlisting the assistance of the Foreign Office to obtain information on discriminatory developments. [70] It was not of course solely the volume

[68] Aliens Committee of the Board of Deputies of British Jews, minutes, January 10, 1935, WH.

[69] See Hoare, minute, November 23, 1933, HO 45/15882, 666,764/69.

[70] E.g., Cooper to Perowne, March 31, 1934, concerning measures against 'non-Aryan' traders, and requesting further information, FO 371/17699, C 2155/23/18.

of potential emigration from Germany that concerned the Home Office, but also its character. And as the year 1934 proceeded it was in the light of this concern that the issue of political refugees came to the fore.

The settled policy of the Home Office in considering requests for the admission of political refugees had been stated in a case which arose in 1933 of a political exile from Yugoslavia :

we do not, of course, admit that there is a 'right of asylum', but when we have to decide whether a particular political refugee is to be given admission to this country, we have to base our decision not on the question whether he is recognised by his Government but on whether it is in the public interest that he should not be admitted.[71]

In the wake of the assassination of King Alexander of Yugoslavia at Marseilles in October 1934, and the subsequent appeal of the Yugoslav Government to the League of Nations, an urgent review of British Government policy on foreign political refugees was initiated in an effort to define a policy in connection with the possible conclusion of an international convention on political refugees. The Home Office prepared a full-scale memorandum on the subject for the Foreign Office, in which it was finally conceded that it would be 'impossible to make any general statement as to when asylum would be extended to a political refugee, since a decision can only be reached in the light of the circumstances of any particular case'.[72] At a joint meeting of Home Office and Foreign Office representatives held on November 29 in an effort to define policy and 'in particular, to ascertain to what extent the views of Victorian Liberalism might have been modified by later developments', the discussion demonstrated that 'no very clear policy could be said to exist', and it was ultimately decided that each particular case would have to be considered on its individual merits, and that in arriving at its decisions the Government 'would be guided by considerations of expediency, of the possible reactions upon their

[71] Holderness to Perowne, Foreign Office, March 11, 1933, FO 371/16828, C 2312/24/92.

[72] Home Office, Memorandum respecting Foreign Political Refugees in the United Kingdom, November 30, 1934, FO 371/18553, R 6774/5524/92.

D

foreign relations, and of public opinion in this country.[73] As the sense of shock at the assassination of King Alexander waned, so also did the interest at Geneva in the possibility of legislating some international control over political refugees. But the view that refugees constituted *ipso facto* an irritant to international relations and a potential menace to the domestic order in several European countries persisted and found expression in efforts to fashion effective international machinery to deal with the problem and to associate the League of Nations more closely with the work of the High Commission for Refugees from Germany.

In September 1934, the High Commissioner for Refugees from Germany called on Mr Anthony Eden, the British representative at the League of Nations, and made two requests: that the British Government take an appropriate opportunity at the League to draw attention to the work of his High Commission; and that the British Government make some contribution, however small, to the costs of administering the Commission. Eden indicated that it might be possible to accede to the first request, but it was emphasised that the whole of the High Commission's expenses, whether for relief or for administration, should continue to be borne in future, as in the past, by private organisations and individuals.[74] Later in September, the British Delegate to the Second Committee of the League of Nations Assembly paid tribute to the work of the High Commission and expressed the hope that further private financial support for the Commission's work would be forthcoming. Hewing closely to the line established for him in London, he 'avoided all reference to the part which had been, or could be, played by Governments in dealing with this problem'.[75] Apparently undaunted by his earlier rebuff, however, the High Commissioner formally requested the British Government in October to make a contribution toward the budget of the High Commission for 1935: a figure of £2,000 was suggested. Mr McDonald was informed that his proposal had been carefully considered, but that it had been found impossible to

---

[73] See Roberts, memorandum, December 5, 1934, FO 371/18462, R 6930/5524/92.

[74] See exchange of telegrams, September 19–21, 1934, FO 371/17700, C 6327/23/18.

[75] Eden to Simon, September 27, 1934, FO 371/17701, C 6546/23/18.

accede to his request; the proposal for direct Government assistance raised a 'fundamental question of principle on which . . . we cannot compromise'.[76] It had been settled, from the inception of the refugee problem, that all costs of the refugee work must be met solely from private sources.

The suggestion that the High Commission for Refugees from Germany be made an integral part of the League of Nations was first officially proposed by the Advisory Council to the High Commission in November 1934, in a cautiously-worded recommendation which the Governing Body of the High Commission then conveyed without comment to the respective Governments.[77] It was recognised immediately at the Foreign Office that this recommendation, even though not specifically endorsed by the Governing Body, raised both a political issue—the High Commission had been dissociated from the League expressly to avoid irritating Germany— and the possibility of British Government financial support being solicited.[78] In a private letter to the Foreign Secretary, Viscount Cecil strongly endorsed the notion that the High Commission and its Governing Body be reorganised as a constituent organ of the League, even if financial support from governments was not to be forthcoming. He argued that the German attitude to the Commission should no longer preclude the inclusion of the Commission in the League, and added that the Governing Body in its present form was 'of very little value' and 'almost useless except to give a kind of official air to the authority of the High Commissioner in his negotiations with various Governments'.[79] Replying, Sir John Simon

[76] Sargent to McDonald, October 29, 1934, FO 371/17701, C 7043/23/18.

[77] See High Commission for Refugees coming from Germany, Recommendations adopted at Third Session of the Governing Body, November 1–2, 1934, FO 371/17701, C 8326/23/18.

[78] See minutes on FO 371/17701, C 8326/23/18, where it was noted that although Germany had ceased to participate in the work of the League, she nevertheless formally remained a member until her withdrawal was to become effective in October, 1935.

[79] Cecil to Simon, December 27, 1934, FO 371/17702, C 8945/23/18. Lord Cecil's opinion that the members of the Governing Body were 'not persons of much importance' was echoed by Norman Bentwich, then Assistant to the High Commissioner, who recalled that 'the Governing Body was composed mainly of nondescript diplomatists who knew little, cared little, and wanted to do as little as possible about the [refugee] cause'. Norman Bentwich, *Wanderer Between Two Worlds* (London, 1941), p. 236.

relied chiefly on the argument that it was of crucial importance to do nothing which might prevent the return of Germany to the League; the inclusion of the High Commission in the League 'might just be the sort of last straw that might frighten Germany away from Geneva for good'. Furthermore, if the High Commission were to be an integral part of the League, Governments could hardly avoid incurring some financial responsibility, and the British Government had already 'more than played our part in the settlement of the refugees—17,000 out of 27,000 in Palestine alone and a greater number of refugee intellectuals . . . in the U.K. than in any other country'.[80] Lord Cecil, in a tart rejoinder, refused to accept the contention that German susceptibilities should still be catered to : 'they are a stupid people, generally speaking, and very backward in intellectual and spiritual civilisation. . . . Sweet reasonableness, I am certain, is quite thrown away upon them.'[81] Cecil further urged that the condition of the refugees was becoming particularly acute, and that he personally felt it 'repugnant to be taking exertions which are quite useless' in his capacity as President of the Governing Body.

The debate on the future of the High Commission was carried into the House of Lords by Lord Marley of the Labour Party, Chief Opposition Whip, who asked the Government on February 6 whether refugees from the Saar[82] were considered to be the responsibility of the High Commissioner for Refugees from Germany, and more generally, what action the Government was taking to aid the

[80] Simon to Cecil, January 28, 1935, FO 371/18861, C 645/232/18.
[81] Cecil to Simon, January 29, 1935, FO 371/18861, C 935/232/18.
[82] In January 1935, pursuant to the provisions of the Versailles Treaty, a plebiscite was held in the Saar Territory, which had been internationally administered under the aegis of the League of Nations. The plebiscite resulted in a vote favouring reunion with Germany, and some 7,000 refugees thereupon fled into France. The French Government maintained that the special position of the Saar made refugees from that territory an international responsibility. At the request of France, the League Council approved the extension of the Nansen passport system to Saar refugees, and entrusted their protection to the Nansen Office. Moreover, the League Assembly voted a special grant to the Nansen Office to defray administrative expenses incurred in settling Saar refugees in France and Paraguay. The prompt and effective action taken on behalf of Saar refugees contrasted painfully with the relative impotence of the High Commissioner for German refugees in dealing with the far larger problem posed by the continuing flight of his clients.

High Commissioner in his task.[83] In its brief for the Government spokesman, Lord Strathcona, the Foreign Office warned that although Lord Marley's motion did not mention the suggestion that the High Commission for Refugees from Germany should become an integral part of the League, this issue might well be raised in the course of debate.[84] Lord Strathcona was instructed that

it is, of course, important to say nothing to indicate that His Majesty's Government would be ready in any way to abandon this somewhat passive attitude [toward the High Commission for Refugees from Germany] or that they can agree to any alteration in the existing status of the High Commission. . . .

Moreover, the Government must continue to insist on the purely voluntary and private character of financial support for refugee settlement and relief. In the course of the debate itself, Lord Cecil intervened to make the broad suggestion that all the refugee organisations now be amalgamated and brought directly under the League. Strathcona, in his cautious reply for the Government, stated merely that any alteration in the status of the High Commission for Refugees would have to be considered by the Assembly of the League.

An energetic drive on the part of several organisations interested in refugee work now began: the Foreign Office was bombarded with letters and memoranda advocating Lord Cecil's proposal from the League of Nations Union, the Save the Children Fund, the Society of Friends' German Emergency Committee, the Women's International League for Peace and Freedom, and, not least, the High Commission for Refugees from Germany itself.[85] On March 19, a deputation from the Society of Friends called at the Foreign Office to urge British Government initiative in proposing that governments lend their authority and financial support to refugee settlement efforts.[86] After a preliminary ranging barrage in the form of a letter and memorandum from Professor Gilbert

---

[83] See 95 H.L. Deb., 826–833, February 6, 1935.

[84] Minutes on FO 371/18861, C 1044/232/18.

[85] See Makins, memorandum, March 6, 1935, FO 371/19676, W 2232/356/98, referring to letters from these organisations and cautioning his colleagues that 'these interests are unwearying and persistent in pursuit of their objects, and well versed in the art of concerted pressure'.

[86] See Foreign Office minute, March 19, 1935, FO 371/19676, W 2472/356/98.

Murray to the Foreign Secretary,[87] the League of Nations Union organised a large deputation which called on the Foreign Secretary on May 16 to elaborate on its proposals for a centralised refugee organisation under the League.[88] Professor Gilbert Murray and Lord Cecil maintained on this occasion that the proposals for a new League refugee body would involve only a very minor increase in cost to the Treasury; Lord Noel-Buxton, however, representing the Save the Children Fund, raised an alarming spectre by suggesting that the Government should also consider providing funds for settlement as well as administrative expenses. A representative of the Society of Friends added that funds from private sources were virtually exhausted, and it had therefore become necessary to 'knock at every door and to pull every string' in order to obtain Government assistance. The deputation was told by Sir John Simon that if the proposal for a centralised refugee organisation were to come forward at the next Assembly in Geneva, the British Government would certainly do nothing to obstruct it, but it was premature to discuss what the Government's attitude would in fact be.

The Foreign Office then proceeded to canvass other Departments for their views on this issue, and was told that the Home Office would not oppose League action on refugees, 'however inconvenient we may find it'.[89] The Treasury, however, was doubtful that the proposed amalgamation of refugee organisations under the League would result in greater efficiency or economy, and reiterated the view that it was important to uphold the League Assembly's decision to wind up the Nansen Office by 1938.[90]

---

[87] Murray to Simon, April 11, 1935, FO 371/19676, W 3336/356/98.

[88] The deputation, introduced by Lord Cecil and Professor Murray, consisted of representatives of the League of Nations Union, the Save the Children Fund, the Armenian (Lord Mayor's) Fund, the Society of Friends, and the Academic Assistance Council. In addition, representatives of the Archbishop of Canterbury, the Archbishop of Westminster and the Chief Rabbi were present. See Foreign Office memorandum, May 16, 1935, FO 371/19676, W 4285/356/98.

[89] Hoare to Makins, May 15, 1935, FO 371/19676, W 4255/356/98. The same letter expresses particular anxiety lest anything be said to the League of Nations Union deputation to indicate that the Home Office opposed its proposals, since this 'might seriously prejudice not only the Home Secretary's position in dealing with the problem in this country but also our friendly personal relations with the various organisations concerned here with refugees'.

[90] Hopkins to Under Secretary of State, May 22, 1935, FO 371/19676, W 4446/356/98.

Pursuing the hint that the British Government would not necessarily oppose another Government's initiative on the refugee question, the refugee organisations turned to the Norwegian Government, which sent a memorandum to the Secretary-General of the League, based on documents supplied by the League of Nations Union and the High Commission for Refugees from Germany, advocating the formation of a central refugee organisation at Geneva to whose administrative expenses the League Governments would contribute. The Norwegian Government was not at this stage proposing a definite plan; rather it hoped to secure a thorough discussion of the question at the next League Assembly.[91]

On July 26, the Foreign Secretary again received a League of Nations Union deputation headed by Lord Cecil, and once more reserved the British Government's attitude on a centralised refugee organisation. More formally, Lord Cecil took the opportunity of his official report on the Fourth Session of the Governing Body of the High Commission for Refugees from Germany to reiterate in very strong terms his conviction that the High Commission in its present form could accomplish little further of any help to refugees. Describing the Governing Body as 'a futile institution', Lord Cecil repeated that the High Commission as a whole had done 'little or nothing' and again urged that the activities of the High Commission, as of the Nansen Office, be transferred to the League.[92] Later in the summer, the Society of Friends, and Mrs Charles Roden Buxton in a more personal vein, wrote to the Foreign Secretary to urge favourable consideration of the Norwegian Government's proposals.[93] Viscount Cranborne of the Foreign Office learned in a private meeting with Lord Cecil that Cecil's objections to the High Commission for Refugees coming from Germany related partly to the personality of the High Commissioner—as an American, he was uniquely unsuited to urge on Latin American governments the settlement of refugees on their territories—but mostly to its con-

[91] See Foreign Office, Memorandum respecting the Refugee Question, August 9, 1935, FO 371/19677, W 5796/356/98, and minutes on Norwegian Minister's call at the Foreign Office, July 2, 1935, FO 371/19677, W 5810/356/98.

[92] Cecil, report, August 12, 1935, FO 371/18862, C 5968/232/18.

[93] Robson to Secretary of State, August 19, 1935, FO 371/19678, W 7327/356/98; Buxton to Hoare, August 26, 1935, FO 371/19678, W 7625/356/98.

stitution as a private body, whose members could speak with little or no authority. Cranborne confided on this occasion the view that the British Government was now prepared in principle to drop its opposition to the League's assumption of responsibility for all refugees, so long as a practical scheme were put forward which would not involve increased expenditure; Cranborne's fear was that in taking responsibility for all refugees the League might be 'signing a blank cheque'.[94]

Early in September, Government policy for the forthcoming League Assembly meeting was discussed at an interdepartmental meeting including representatives of the Foreign Office, Treasury and Home Office; it was decided that the British delegation at Geneva could agree to the proposal that a central League organisation dealing with all refugees should be established, provided that League funds were to be used solely for administrative expenses and not for relief or settlement, and that the new organisation limited its functions to providing legal and political protection for refugees and coordinating settlement efforts. Another condition for British Government acquiescence in the proposal was that no new categories of refugees should be included within the scope of the new organisation without the express authority of the League Council or Assembly.[95]

While the Government prepared to confront the refugee problem at Geneva, there were unmistakable signs in Germany itself that the numbers of refugees, which in the second half of 1934 and in early 1935 had appeared to be constant, were going shortly to be substantially augmented. The anti-Jewish campaign, relatively moderate until the Saar plebiscite was held, increased thereafter in tempo and ferocity. Official measures excluded Jewish candidates from the medical and dental professions, and from publishing; unofficial but highly effective pressures were exercised against Jewish-owned shops and other businesses, and the employment of Jewish doctors, lawyers and other professionals. Jews were hounded out of villages and smaller towns, and excluded in increasing measure

[94] See Cranborne, memorandum, September 2, 1935, FO 371/19678, W 7717/356/98.
[95] See Foreign Office memorandum, The League of Nations and Refugees, September 2, 1935, FO 371/19678, W 7744/356/98.

from restaurants, holiday resorts, and places of entertainment all over Germany. More ominously, on April 27, the Minister of the Interior stated in a press interview that Jews would eventually be excluded from German citizenship, as well as the holding of any public office. By early May, the British Ambassador was reporting to the Foreign Office that 'the outlook for the German Jew today is blacker than ever before. Emigration is his only hope, and even that . . . is rendered extremely difficult'. In a memorandum attached to the Ambassador's despatch, the British Passport Control Officer in Berlin, Captain F. E. Foley, added that 'the position of the Jew in Germany, even if he possesses capital, is therefore a desperate one : he is being ruined economically and at the same time he is unable to emigrate as he cannot obtain the release of even a moderate proportion of his capital sufficient to enable him to do so'.[96]

On July 16, Berlin, hitherto immune from the grosser aspects of the anti-Jewish agitation, was the scene of scattered attacks on Jewish premises and individuals. In late August the notorious Julius Streicher displayed his inimitable propaganda talents for the first time in Berlin, delivering himself of a well-seasoned blend of slander, obscene invective and dubious history in which Queen Victoria was pilloried for having ennobled the Jew Disraeli under the title of Lord Gladstone.[97] By the end of that month, it was decided in the higher echelons of the Nazi Party that undisciplined violence and isolated, uncoordinated anti-Jewish actions were henceforth to be discouraged : the campaign against Germany's Jews was to be put on a strictly legal basis and enforced uniformly throughout the Reich. The stage was thus set for the promulgation of the Nuremberg Laws, which at one blow defined and effectively isolated all 'non-Aryans' in Germany—thus vastly increasing the dimensions and severity of the refugee problem.

[96] Phipps to Simon, May 10, 1935, FO 371/18861, C 3853/232/18.
[97] See Newton, memorandum on the Jewish Question in Germany, August 26, 1936, FO 371/19919, E 5444/94/31.

3

The Tightening Vice
September 1935 — February 1938

Was er glaubt ist einerlei,
in der Rasse liegt die Schweinerei.

THE vague menace of renewed anti-Jewish agitation became legislative reality on the occasion of the Nazi Party rally in Nuremberg.
There, on September 13, 1935 Chancellor Hitler gave orders that
laws be enacted 'for the protection of German blood and honour'
and for a new definition of Reich citizenship. In two days of feverish
work the drafting experts of the Interior Ministry completed the
statutes, which were then duly passed by the Reichstag meeting in
extraordinary session.

The Law for the Protection of German Blood and Honour[1] forbade marriages and intercourse outside marriage between Jews and
persons of 'German or related blood', as well as the employment
by Jews of female citizens of 'German or related blood' under forty-
five years of age as domestic servants. Jews were likewise forbidden
to display the Reich flag. The terms 'Jew' and 'German or related
blood' were left undefined, but this omission was corrected in
November, when a regulation was issued defining 'Jews' and those
of 'mixed Jewish blood', known as *Mischlinge*.[2] The maze of legis-

[1] *Gesetz zum Schutz des deutschen Blutes und der deutschen Ehre, RGBl,*
1935, I, 1146. See Raoul Hilberg, *The Destruction of the European Jews*
(Chicago, 1961), pp. 46–53, for a description of the drafting of the Nuremberg
legislation.
[2] See First Regulation to the Reich Citizenship Law, *RGBl,* 1935, I, 1333,
which divided the German nation into the following categories:
    1. Aryans
    2. Non-Aryans: *Jews*—Persons with three or four Jewish grandparents, or
                with two Jewish grandparents, if they belonged to the

lation, administrative regulation and court decisions which sprang from the original Nuremberg laws had the practical effect of dividing 'non-Aryans' into the two classes of Jews and *Mischlinge*. Jews, as defined, were disfranchised, barred from all State employment, and excluded from the *Reichskulturkammern* which regulated admission to the cultural professions, as well as from active military service and national labour service. *Mischlinge*, for their part, retained the franchise, and continued to be liable for military call-up and labour service; as 'non-Aryans', however, they were excluded from State service, the *Reichskulturkammern*, and any position of command in the armed services. The *Mischlinge*, although labouring under these and subtler disabilities, were not henceforth subjected to measures which were taken against 'Jews' as defined; most *Mischlinge* were thus to escape the ultimate stages of the Final Solution.

The second law passed at Nuremberg in September 1935, the Reich Citizenship law,[3] made a distinction between *Reichsbürger*, who had to be persons of 'German or related blood', and who therefore enjoyed the full political rights of citizens, and *Staatsbürger*, who were not of 'German or related blood' and who therefore declined to an inferior status akin to that of guests or wards of the Reich.

The Nuremberg legislation was to alter decisively the dimensions of the refugee problem : trapped within the new set of definitions most Jews and 'non-Aryans' now realised that their hopes of remaining in Germany and being permitted a reasonable existence there were illusory; the comparatively selective restrictions and disabilities previously promulgated could now be added to at will. Refugees outside Germany thereupon sought with increased urgency for places of permanent settlement, and would-be emigrants increased their pressure to leave Germany. Emigration between Sep-

Jewish religion, or were married to a Jew on September 15, 1935.
Mischlinge of the first degree—Persons with two Jewish grandparents who did not belong to the Jewish religion and were not married to a Jew on September 15, 1935.
Mischlinge of the second degree—Persons with one Jewish grandparent.

[3] *Reichsbürgergesetz, RGBl*, 1935, I, 1146.

tember 1935 and the end of 1937 did not accelerate more than moderately, largely because of the continuing extreme difficulty of removing capital abroad, but it became steady, with a view to permanent expatriation : Jewish emigration from Germany, estimated at 20,000 in 1935, increased to 24,000 in 1936 and levelled off in 1937 to some 23,000.

The Nuremberg Laws themselves contained no provisions for accelerating the departure of Jews and 'non-Aryans' from German economic life, and initially their influence on the more enthusiastic among the Party faithful seemed a calming one : the wave of violent anti-Jewish excesses that had taken place throughout the spring and summer ebbed perceptibly.[4] The propaganda campaign against Jewish participation in the economy continued, however, if at a more carefully regulated pace.

With the example of dismissals of Jews and 'non-Aryans' from the Civil Service and cultural enterprises to guide them, directors of a wide variety of businesses proceeded to sack their Jewish employees, frequently by strained interpretations of employment contracts, or by pressures leading to 'voluntary' transfers abroad or resignations. Lump-sum payments, pensions, or other severance provisions grew progressively worse as the number of dismissals increased. These dismissals were of course a strong incentive to the emigration of the individuals involved.

The independent Jewish-owned enterprises, ranging in size from the thousands of small shops and other businesses to several major industrial or financial concerns, were from the autumn of 1935 'aryanised' in increasing numbers, despite the fears of Government economic experts as to the possible negative effects this might have on certain branches of the economy. The 'aryanisation' process, which was at least in form voluntary until November 1938, represented in fact the transfer of assets, under pressure, to buyers who were frequently competitors in the same field. The forms this pressure took were as varied as the enterprises themselves. Party-inspired boycotts, for example, tended to make it worthwhile for suppliers to refuse sales to Jewish enterprises; industry-wide cartels allocating raw materials would cut out their Jewish members;

[4] See Genschel, *Verdrängung*, pp. 115–119.

Government authorities used their licensing and raw-materials allocation powers selectively. For the smaller establishment, particularly in a provincial town or village, simple blackmail, sustained boycott, or physical intimidation would often be enough to 'induce' a sale. German enterprises throughout the Reich were now beginning to be able to purchase Jewish firms on highly favourable terms, with the assistance of the banks, which on their own initiative had developed a highly lucrative business in 'aryanisations', collecting handsome commissions for bringing buyers and sellers together, charging high interest rates on loans to finance purchases, and frequently also assuring themselves by contractual arrangements of obtaining subsequent banking business from the 'aryanised' firm. In addition to their brisk activity as agents, the banks were not slow to seize opportunities to deal as principals, and to acquire for their own portfolios shares in the more attractive Jewish banks or other enterprises which might come on to the market.[5]

The Nuremberg legislation and its consequences were anxiously noted by the High Commission for Refugees from Germany, whose Governing Body officially called the attention of governments to the new persecution and consequent fresh exodus of refugees, and referred to the growing burden on the private organisations.[6] The High Commissioner called at the Foreign Office on October 17 to request once more that the British Ambassador in Berlin be authorised, jointly with his American colleague, to approach the German Government and urge that arrangements be made for the orderly transfer of refugees' property, so that a flight of impoverished people might be avoided. The Foreign Office was however reluctant to accept Mr McDonald's suggestion, fearing that any such initiative on behalf of the refugees would almost certainly be rebuffed by the Germans. One member of the Department summarised its anxieties :

. . . might it not be even worse if the German Government agreed to discuss this matter with Sir Eric Phipps? If the German Govern-

[5] See figures on 'aryanisations' in Genschel, *Verdrängung*, p. 135.

[6] Permanent Committee, Governing Body of the High Commission for Refugees from Germany, Recommendation Concerning the Situation of Jews in Germany, October 16, 1935, FO 371/18862, C 7298/232/18.

ment were to enter into private negotiations with us regarding the
emigration of Jews, they would certainly not be moved by considerations arising out of the sufferings of the Jews, or the inconvenience
occasioned to foreign governments by the emigration of destitute
foreigners. Their object would probably be to persuade us to take a
number of German Jews, whose presence in Germany was, in their
opinion, undesirable. And I think that we should take care to avoid
being drawn into any discussion turning on the disposal of more
German Jews in the United Kingdom. Moreover, if we are to start
any negotiations with the German Government, it would be better
if the matter were one affecting British interests :—the interests of
British subjects; it seems undesirable that we should waste much of
our scanty powder and shot over German Jews who wish to leave
Germany, no matter how much we may sympathise with the plight
of these unfortunate people. On the other hand . . . we cannot refuse
Mr McDonald's request out of hand. We may be certain that if we
did so, our action would be much criticised here. Lord Cecil and the
Jewish Associations in this country would enquire why we were not
now prepared to take action similar to that which we had, in fact,
taken last year.[7]

The Ambassador in Berlin predicted shortly after McDonald's
visit that the position of German Jews under the new legislation

will be so bad that no further aggravation will be possible . . . the net
is being drawn round the Jewish community more systematically and
effectively than in the days of the so-called 'isolated action'.[8]

In a further despatch, enclosing a report from the Munich Consul
General on persecution of Jews, Sir Eric Phipps stated that similar
reports were reaching him from other quarters, and that they confirmed the view that 'a systematic and official drive is being made,
which will have the effect of rendering the position of Jews here
almost intolerable'.[9] Further corroboration of the Ambassador's grim
prediction was received very shortly thereafter, in a confidential
memorandum prepared for his superiors by the Palestine Government's Commissioner for Migration and Statistics, Mr E. Mills,
who had just completed a visit to Germany to consult with the
Passport Control Officer in Berlin. Mills reported starkly that 'the
Jew is to be eliminated, and the State has no regard for the manner

[7] Baxter, minute, October 18, 1935, FO 371/18862, C 7298/232/18.
[8] Phipps to Hoare, October 24, 1935, FO 371/18862, C 7242/232/18.
[9] Phipps to Hoare, November 5, 1935, FO 371/18863, C 7504/232/18.

of the elimination'.[10] Planned emigration was therefore the only possible solution, although there was undoubtedly a risk of inflaming anti-Semitism in countries of immigration if large numbers of Jews were introduced into them. Mills added that international action—which must be preceded by the informing of opinion among 'responsible people' in each country—was required, but it remained to be seen whether a centralised refugee organisation under the League could be effective where the High Commissioner for Refugees had not been.

In early December, Sir Eric Phipps commented further on McDonald's suggestion for British representations to the German Government. Agreeing that

the position of the Jews is becoming so desperate as to make it more apparent every day that . . . the present Nazi policy threatens the Jewish population in the Reich with extermination,

Phipps nevertheless rejected the notion that a catastrophic exodus of Jews was to be feared, on the purely practical grounds that no country except Palestine—and even Palestine only to a limited extent—was willing to accept Jewish immigrants without sufficient capital. The dwindling number of German Jews who still possessed some capital were, however, prevented from taking it with them. It followed that unless funds from outside Germany were forthcoming to finance their emigration, the vast majority of German Jews would have to remain where they were. The Ambassador felt that any joint appeal by the British and United States Governments requesting the German Government to soften its anti-Jewish policy was foredoomed to failure; the German Government would not bow to world opinion on this point, and any representations would be deeply resented. The stark dilemma, Sir Eric pointed out in conclusion, was that if financial help were to be forthcoming from outside Germany on a scale generous enough to enable the Jewish community to leave, the German Government would have even less inducement to make life tolerable for those Jews left in Germany. Since some Jews had inevitably to remain in Germany, it seemed wisest to wait and see what Dr Hjalmar Schacht of the

[10] E. Mills, report, November 12, 1935, FO 371/19919, C 541/16/18.

Reichsbank might be able to do to 'secure the issue of reasonable regulations regarding the position of Jews in business before any steps are taken to consider the possibility of assistance from outside for Jewish emigrants'.[11]

The generally-recognised worsening of the German refugee situation was reflected at the League of Nations, where the Sixth Committee of the League Assembly had discussed at its September 1935 meeting the entire question of international assistance to refugees, recommending that an expert committee should be appointed to report on arrangements for reorganising and coordinating the work of the Nansen Office and the High Commission for Refugees from Germany. In adopting this recommendation the Assembly acknowledged for the first time that refugees from Germany were properly a concern of the League; Germany's withdrawal from the League had removed the political obstacle to this conclusion, and the British Government was therefore able to agree to the Assembly's action.[12] The expert committee was duly appointed by the League Council and met at Geneva in November in efforts to prepare a report for consideration by the League Assembly in January, 1936.

Meanwhile, James G. McDonald, whose resignation as High Commissioner for Refugees from Germany had for some months been expected, sent a lengthy letter of resignation to the Secretary-General of the League. In his widely-publicised letter, dated December 27, 1935, McDonald described in detail the measures of persecution employed against Germany's Jewish and 'non-Aryan' population, and predicted a steadily increasing flight from that country. He argued that only an organisation directly under the authority of the League could now cope with the German refugee problem, and called for 'friendly and firm intervention with the German Government' on the part of the League, its members and all other members of 'the community of nations' to 'remove or mitigate the causes which create German refugees'. He based the demand for such intervention on the legal notion that the German Jews con-

[11] See Phipps to Eden, December 10, 1935, FO 371/18863, C 8183/232/18.
[12] See Foreign Office, Memorandum concerning the Refugee Question, September 1, 1936, FO 371/20482, W 10548/172/98.

stituted a minority whose protection—like that of all racial, religious, or linguistic minorities—had been 'hardening into an obligation of the public law of Europe'.

The McDonald letter, with its appended analysis of German legislative and other measures and their effects in creating refugees, was at first studiously ignored, then violently attacked in Germany. The letter did however arouse widespread public interest outside Germany, particularly in Great Britain and the United States, in both of which it was extensively commented on in the press. To the Foreign Office, McDonald's letter was nevertheless 'an unwise document, which did a disservice to the real interests of the Jews in Germany', and in which 'the guiding hand of Zionism was apparent'.[13]

Mr McDonald's resignation served also to focus interest on a far-ranging scheme, elaborated at the instance of leading British Jewish organisations, for the systematic and gradual emigration over a period of four years of the largest possible number of German Jews. The scheme, launched by Sir Herbert Samuel, Lord Bearsted, and Mr Simon Marks, envisaged the assisted emigration each year of some 16,000 young men and women, and 7,000 children, at least half of whom it was hoped to settle in Palestine. In addition, nearly an equal number of older persons were to be emigrated annually, financing their emigration from their own resources. In order to implement the scheme, the Council for German Jewry was established, and Sir Herbert Samuel, Lord Bearsted and Mr Marks departed for the United States in mid-January 1936 in order to coordinate with American Jewish organisations the raising of a world fund of £3,000,000 over four years to carry out the emigration. The plan also assumed for its success—an assumption fraught with grave doubts—that the German Government could be induced to enable emigrants to transfer their capital out of Germany.

The Foreign Office favoured the Bearsted proposal as a limited,

[13] See Foreign Office memorandum, September 1, 1936, FO 371/20482, W 10548/172/98. McDonald's letter was in fact drafted in close consultation with, if not actually by, the principal Jewish refugee organisations represented on the High Commission's Advisory Council. Private communication to the author by the late Judge Neville J. Laski, Q.C.

reasonable and potentially practicable solution of the problem. 'It seems quite plain', wrote a member of the Department

that if we go to the Germans with a practical scheme of this sort [the Bearsted plan] we are far more likely to achieve some sort of alleviation of the Jewish lot than if we address to them windy appeals in the name of 'humanity and decency'.[14]

In the event, both 'windy appeals' and 'practical schemes' proved unable to budge the obdurate refusal of the German authorities to permit emigrants to take with them any reasonable proportion of even the comparatively small sums left after the liquidation of their assets in Germany.

Early in January 1936 the League Committee of Experts submitted its Report to the Council,[15] making separate proposals regarding both 'Nansen' refugees—Russians, Armenians and 'assimilated' groups—and refugees from Germany. The principal interim proposal on German refugees was for the appointment of a new High Commissioner who would be empowered to convene an international conference to establish a uniform type of legal protection for German refugees analogous to that existing for 'Nansen' refugees. The High Commissioner was in addition to consult with governments on the possibility of receiving and placing refugees; the Report was however deliberately ambiguous as to whether he was intended to negotiate directly with the German Government or merely with governments in countries of refuge.

The Committee's permanent proposals for German refugees envisaged the establishment of a service for their protection separate from the Nansen Office, but so administered that upon the winding up of the Nansen Office the service could be transformed into an autonomous international organisation under the auspices of the League. These permanent proposals were deliberately drafted in the vaguest terms; the Committee had wished to establish uniformity between the treatment of German and 'Nansen' refugees, but was apprehensive that if it recommended assimilating German refugees to those cared for by the Nansen Office, the Soviet Govern-

---

[14] Perowne, minute, January 3, 1936, FO 371/19918, C 47/16/18.

[15] See Committee on International Assistance to Refugees, report, January 3, 1936, League of Nations Publication XII.B. International Bureaux. 1936. XII. B.1.; text in FO 371/20479, W 282/172/98.

ment—which was adamant in insisting on a strict timetable for liquidation of the Nansen Office—would consider that a 'backdoor' continuation of the Office was proposed, and thus attempt to block constructive proposals on behalf of all classes of refugees.

The publication of the Committee's report confronted the British Government with the need to define its policy on German refugees in advance of the League Council meeting and an interdepartmental meeting was accordingly held on January 15,[16] at which it was agreed that there should be no objection to the appointment of a High Commissioner to carry on after Mr McDonald's departure. The representative of the Home Office expressed considerable apprehension, however, over the convening of an international conference to consider the legal status of refugees; it was settled after some discussion that a conference would in principle be acceptable, but that the British delegate to the League Council should use his best efforts to narrow its scope. The proposed consultation of the High Commissioner with governments concerning possibilities for receiving and placing refugees also aroused the alarm of the Home Office, whose representative declared that the British Government and others would be 'bound to return a discouraging reply' to any formal questionnaire of the High Commissioner's. Any suggestion of outside scrutiny of its procedures, or of pressure from an international body to admit more refugees, was to be consistently opposed by the Home Office, whose position on this sensitive issue was almost invariably supported by the Foreign Office. The Colonial Office spokesman registered the concern of his Department over any further efforts to increase Jewish immigration into Palestine, citing as the reason for this anxiety the 'uncertainty of the economic future of the territory', and recommending that it be made quite clear to the High Commissioner for Refugees that he was authorised only to ask governments about the possibilities of accepting immigrants : 'it would be quite inadmissible that the High Commissioner should himself conduct an examination of the capacity of any particular territory to absorb emigrants'. The proposal that the High Commissioner should negotiate with the German Government on

---

[16] See Record of Interdepartmental Meeting on International Assistance to Refugees, January 15, 1936, FO 371/20480, W 557/172/98.

the emigration of Jews still in Germany caused the Foreign Office representative to raise a point of principle: the proposal appeared to contemplate a wide extension of the League's powers to interfere in the internal affairs of other countries; it was very doubtful that the British Government would accept the notion that the League should negotiate for the transfer of a section of one country's population to other countries: 'i.e. the creation of refugees'. The Home Office representative, on the other hand, pointed out that the High Commissioner could hardly fail as a practical matter to concern himself with the 'German end of the problem'; the question of transferring capital, for example, directly affected refugees already outside Germany, who depended on such transfers for their support. He added that what the refugee organisations were hoping for was a High Commissioner of sufficient stature to 'rattle a sabre' at Hitler. The meeting agreed to defer a final decision on the High Commissioner's powers until the views of other delegations at Geneva could be obtained.

The refugee organisations, for their part, and certain individuals interested in refugee matters were preoccupied as the time for the League Council's meeting approached by the question of who the new High Commissioner should be, and how wide his authority. Among those who approached the Foreign Office to propose candidates for the post of High Commissioner were Sir Henry Strakosch, Sir Arthur Salter, Professor Norman Bentwich, and even a Miss Ginsberg, Assistant Librarian at the League of Nations in Geneva, who was described in a faintly irritated minute by R. M. Makins as 'an intriguing Jewess; it is by no means clear on whose behalf she has been acting'.[17] The choice ultimately fell on Major-General Sir Neill Malcolm, a much-decorated retired Army officer whose most recent post had been General Officer Commanding in Malaya. Malcolm agreed to accept the post despite his initial misgivings concerning its demands on a man of his age and indifferent health; he had been seriously wounded on war service and was very lame.[18]

The scope of the new High Commissioner's authority proved an altogether more contentious issue than his appointment. At the

[17] Minutes, January 8, 1936, FO 371/19919, C 300/16/18.
[18] See Namier to Weizmann, January 27, 1936, WA.

January meeting of the League Council, the refugee organisations and such Jewish bodies as the World Jewish Congress and the Jewish Agency for Palestine lobbied energetically for two major proposals : first, that Jews in Germany should be recognised by the Council as having 'minority rights', and that the Council should publicly comment on the points raised in Mr McDonald's letter of resignation; second, that the new High Commissioner should be authorised to deal with Jews inside Germany, and that he should be specifically empowered to negotiate with the German Government on the transfer of refugees' capital. The organisations also advocated that the League should make some financial contribution to the administrative expenses of the High Commission. The British representative successfully opposed the proposal that the High Commissioner should negotiate with the German Government, and 'the principle was laid down that the High Commissioner was not concerned with Jews until they had left Germany'. It was also established that the High Commissioner was not to concern himself with settlement and relief : these were the responsibility of the private organisations, with which the High Commissioner was to maintain liaison. The Council ultimately defined the duties of the new High Commissioner as preparing for an intergovernmental conference which would define the legal status of refugees coming from Germany, consulting with governments on admission and employment possibilities, and arranging liaison with the private organisations dealing with settlement and relief.[19]

The refugee organisations, disturbed by the Council's narrow definition of the High Commissioner's competence, continued to urged on the Foreign Office their view that the transfer of emigrants' funds from Germany was essential to the success of any orderly emigration programme, and that only a High Commissioner empowered by the League could deal successfully with the German authorities on the transfer question. The Jewish refugee committees argued further that Jewish refugees were not in the same position as other refugees, who only became refugees upon leaving their countries; the German Government's often expressed intention to get rid of all the Jews in Germany made German Jews *de facto*

[19] See Makins, minute, January 25, 1936, FO 371/20480, W 811/172/98.

refugees before they had crossed the frontier, and therefore suitable subjects for League intervention. This view, with its potential unsettling of established international law doctrines, was vigorously opposed by the Foreign Office, which rejected any notion that a person was a 'refugee' until he had actually been forced to leave his country. Hewing consistently to the line that it was improper to give a mandate to any League official empowering him to intervene in the internal affairs of any one country, the Foreign Office doubted in any case that the German Government, with its well-known antipathy to the League of Nations as an institution, would prove amenable to approaches by a League official, particularly on behalf of German Jews. The persistent lobbying of Jewish representatives such as Professor Lewis B. Namier on this contentious issue provoked a spasm of irritation at the Foreign Office, where Lord Cranborne wrote :

I am glad no encouragement was given to Professor Namier. He is a most tiresome person, & we already know he is not to be trusted. We cannot say often enough to Jews of this type that people do not become refugees until they leave their country of origin. While they are still there, their treatment is a question of internal policy, & however much the League may disapprove, there are no legitimate grounds on which it can interfere in the internal affairs of a sovereign state. When they leave, it will do anything it can to assist their resettlement.[20]

Sir Neill Malcolm duly convened an intergovernmental conference which met at Geneva from July 2 to 4, 1936 to consider a Provisional Arrangement[21] for according a uniform legal status to refugees from Germany. The Arrangement provided for the issue of a certificate of identity, analogous to the 'Nansen passport', for refugees from Germany who might be without passports or other

[20] Cranborne minute on Makins note reporting a conversation with Professor Namier, April 22, 1936, FO 371/20480, W 2959/172/98.

[21] The several international 'Arrangements' concluded between the World Wars to establish a legal regime for refugees and stateless persons—the earliest was adopted in July 1922, and provided for the issue of 'Nansen passports' to stateless Russians—were highly anomalous instruments : although in treaty form, they did not contain concrete undertakings but merely 'recommended' that a given course of action be taken by signatories. They were in any event frequently signed by governments only with material reservations. See R. Yewdall Jennings, 'Some International Law Aspects of the Refugee Question', *British Year Book of International Law*, 1939, p. 99.

valid papers and also aimed to protect refugees against arbitrary expulsion and being sent back to Germany. The Arrangement also contained provisions defining the personal status of refugees in their country of asylum, thus enabling them legally to contract marriage or divorce, acquire property, and avail themselves of certain civil rights.[22]

The fact that a special Arrangement had now been concluded for refugees from Germany enabled the Home Office to withdraw its long-standing objections to British accession to the Convention relating to the International Status of Refugees of October 28, 1933;[23] the Home Office had hitherto resisted such accession because it felt that once the Convention affording legal protection to 'Nansen' refugees had been accepted, there would be pressures to extend its benefits to German and perhaps unknown future classes of refugees. The Refugee Convention of 1933, and the appropriate reservations to be made on accession, were therefore the first items on the agenda as the Foreign Office, in consultation with the Home Office and the Treasury, established British policy for the September 1936 League Assembly.

As in the summer of 1935, the Foreign Office was approached by organisations concerned with refugees and urged to take certain specific action at the League Assembly. The Joint Foreign Committee, the representative body of the British Jewish community for foreign questions, presented a memorandum to the Foreign Office on June 9, 1936, requesting the British Government *inter alia* to make diplomatic representations to the German Government for the cessation of persecution in Germany and to support proposals to enlarge the powers of the High Commissioner so as to permit him to negotiate directly with the German Government.[24] On July 16

[22] See Cooper, Report on Conference, July 16, 1936, FO 371/20481, W 6478/172/98. The text of the Provisional Arrangement concerning the Status of Refugees coming from Germany is reproduced in FO 371/20482, W 13150/172/98. The Arrangement was signed on September 25, 1936 by Mr E. N. Cooper, of the Home Office, who accompanied his signature with certain minor reservations.

[23] The British Government signed an Instrument of Accession to the Convention of October 28, 1933 on October 14, 1936. The accession was made subject to a number of reservations. See FO 371/20482, W 11937/172/98.

[24] See Brotman to Vansittart, June 9, 1936, FO 371/20481, W 5370/172/98.

a delegation from the Joint Foreign Committee called at the Foreign Office and was given a sympathetic hearing, although their requests met with temporising or discouraging replies: the Foreign Office view remained that any representations to the German Government on questions which Berlin regarded as purely internal were bound only to envenom the situation and could not in any event help those suffering from persecution.[25] On another but related front, the League of Nations Union also presented a memorandum to the Foreign Office, pressing the case for the unification of all the League's refugee activities under a single authority;[26] it was not felt necessary at the Foreign Office to reply to this memorandum in any detail in advance of the Assembly meeting.

An interdepartmental meeting attended by Treasury, Home Office and Foreign Office representatives met on September 10 and agreed that it would be desirable to avoid as far as possible any discussion of the German refugee question at the League Assembly. This position was based on advice from the British Embassy in Berlin, which deplored the effect a succession of anti-Nazi speeches at Geneva might have on both the position of the Jews in Germany and the forthcoming negotiations among the Locarno Powers: it was feared that an irritated German Government might be even less prepared to 'cooperate in seeking a new international understanding, and to resume membership of the League of Nations'.[27]

The Home Office representative reported that the British Jewish refugee organisations felt for their part that settlement and emigration efforts would be seriously prejudiced if the High Commissioner were to be authorised to intervene with governments in countries of refuge; it was explained that quiet representations to governments by private organisations frequently enabled concessions on immigration to be granted without public discussion, amendment

[25] See Mounsey, minute, July 16, 1936, FO 371/20481, W 6434/172/98. Mounsey surmised that the delegation had approached the Foreign Office as 'mouthpieces and perhaps safety valves for other associated bodies who are desirous of organising more vigorous counter movements'.

[26] See League of Nations Union memorandum, July 25, 1936, FO 371/20482, W 9832/172/98.

[27] See Newton to Mounsey, August 27, 1936, FO 371/19919, C 6217/16/18, and record of interdepartmental meeting, September 10, 1936, FO 371/20482, W 1131/172/98.

of existing laws, and possible criticism of government immigration policies. The High Commissioner in his perforce official approaches could not hope to achieve comparable results. In its brief, the Home Office amplified this point, citing the example of British experience since 1933 :

If it had then been proposed to open the doors of this country to six or seven thousand refugees of all classes from Germany there would have been so much criticism that the hands of the Home Office would have been very severely tied. In point of fact there has been little hostility to the policy of the rigid but sympathetic control exercised by the Home Office, with the result that several thousand desirable, industrious, intelligent and acceptable persons have been added to the population. They have brought with them considerable capital, and established industries which have already given employment to more British subjects than the total number of refugees from Germany who are now living in the United Kingdom.[28]

The meeting decided that the High Commissioner should not be granted authority to negotiate with the German Government on the question of transfer of property. It was felt by all present that here too the private organisations would be able to deal with the German Government on an unofficial basis, and therefore with greater prospects of success, than the High Commissioner. It was also agreed that it would be inopportune to press for amalgamation of the Nansen Office and the High Commission for Refugees from Germany; both organisations were scheduled in any case to be wound up at the end of 1938 and if it were decided to prolong their existences a merger could then be considered.

At the League Assembly itself the question of international assistance to refugees was again referred to the Sixth Committee, which after considerable discussion and an unedifying wrangle over a proposal to grant funds for the settlement of 200 families of Saar refugees in Paraguay accepted a report and resolutions which were subsequently adopted by the Assembly. These called for the continuation as separate entities until the end of 1938 of the Nansen Office and the High Commission for Refugees from Germany. Sir Neill Malcolm was officially appointed High Commissioner until

[28] Home Office, memorandum, September 8, 1936, FO 371/20482, W 11192/172/98.

December 31, 1938, with the object of 'liquidating, so far as possible, the problem of refugees coming from Germany'. His duties were to include approaching governments to secure their accession to the Provisional Arrangement of July 4, 1936, and to prepare a conference to conclude an international convention on the status of refugees from Germany. On questions of emigration and final settlement he was to 'encourage initiative on the part of private organisations' and to support that initiative in suitable cases by negotiations with the governments of countries of refuge. Finally, he was to submit an interim report to the 1937 Assembly and a further report to the 1938 Assembly, which would embody his 'definite proposals in regard to the future'. A modest appropriation out of League funds to defray the High Commissioner's administrative expenses was also voted.[29]

Every delegation at Geneva was uneasily aware that other, still shadowy masses of potential refugees were waiting in the wings. The Spanish Civil War had not yet ended, but thousands of Spaniards had already been displaced, and many thousands more seemed likely to become refugees no matter which side triumphed. Even more disturbing, at the meeting of the Second (Economic) Committee of the Assembly, the Polish Foreign Minister had officially raised the question of the emigration of his country's 'surplus' Jewish population. Acknowledging that Poland's economic position did not permit her to finance this proposed emigration, nor indeed to allow emigrants to take any of their assets out of Poland with them, he demanded that facilities be somehow found for an annual emigration of 80,000 to 100,000 persons. He explained that such numbers could not of course be accommodated in any of the likely countries of emigration, and a scheme was therefore to be launched to explore the possibilities of settlement in Madagascar. Palestine, under British administration, was the only country, the Polish representative emphasised, which offered even a limited solution of his country's 'Jewish problem'.[30]

Discussion of the refugee problem at Geneva had also taken

[29] MacDonald to Secretary of State, report, October 10, 1936, FO 371/20482, W 14376/172/98.

[30] See James W. Parkes, *The Emergence of the Jewish Problem, 1878–1939* (London, 1946), p. 140.

place against a sombre background of increasing turmoil in the one country to which the largest number of German Jewish refugees had turned : again, Palestine.[31] The numbers of Jewish immigrants to Palestine had risen dramatically from the very first year of the Nazi regime in Germany : authorised Jewish immigration leapt upward from 9,553 in 1932 to 30,327 in 1933, 42,359 in 1934 and an all-time high of 61,854 in 1935.[32] By April 1936, the Arab population in Palestine, thoroughly aroused by the swelling influx, rebelled and mounted a general strike which gradually hardened into guerilla warfare in which public and private property was damaged or destroyed and attacks made on British troops and officials, their supporters among the Arabs, and randomly selected targets among the Jews. The stated aim of the general strike was to bring about the prohibition of further Jewish immigration and the transfer of Arab lands to Jews; and to force the British Government to establish a Palestine National Government responsible to a representative elected council in which the Arabs would be a majority. On May 18, the Colonial Secretary announced that after order had been restored in Palestine a Royal Commission would be appointed to investigate the causes of the disturbances. The personnel of the Commission and its terms of reference were announced at the end of July, but the situation in Palestine continued to worsen until the end of September. By that time, British troop reinforcements had arrived in sufficient numbers to quell armed resistance, and on October 12 the general strike ended, on the orders of the Arab Higher Committee.

Under the terms of the Mandate, it was the duty of the Palestine Government to 'facilitate Jewish immigration under suitable conditions'; this injunction had been interpreted by applying the principle of economic absorptive capacity to regulate Jewish immigration. The absorptive capacity of Palestine, it had been established

---

[31] From January, 1933 to the end of May, 1937, some 40,000 German Jews had entered Palestine, about 22 per cent of total Jewish immigration, according to a report by the Central Bureau for the Settlement of German Jews, a bureau of the Jewish Agency for Palestine. See Simpson, *Refugee Problem*, p. 431, and Palestine Royal Commission (Peel Commission), *Report*, Cmd. 5479 (London, 1937), p. 213.

[32] See Peel Commission, *Report*, Chapter X.

since 1931, was to be determined by reference to purely economic considerations.[33] But it became increasingly clear, in the years from 1933, that immigration itself actually led to an increase in 'economic absorptive capacity' : as immigrants came in, they created more work for local industries, and the expansion of these industries led in turn to a demand for labour, and thus an increase in the Labour Schedule component of authorised immigration. Rising immigration had in fact led to an unprecedented economic boom in Palestine, and it became obvious to the Arabs, the Government and the Jewish Agency as well that in the absence of a more restrictive immigration policy, or some pronounced deterioration of the economic situation, 'there seemed no reason why the rate of immigration should not go on climbing up and up'.[34]

Throughout the summer of 1936, while the Palestine authorities attempted to put down the disorders, a frequently bitter argument raged between the Colonial Office, the Jewish Agency and the Arabs as to whether there should be a temporary suspension of immigration into Palestine pending the report of the Royal Commission, which was waiting in London, unable to proceed with its investigation until order had been restored. Despite the widespread insecurity in Palestine, Jewish immigration had continued in 1936, although at a slower rate than in the peak year 1935.[35] The possibility of suspending immigration was first raised on July 14 by an Arab deputation which called on the Colonial Secretary. Any suggestion however that immigration might be suspended, or even curtailed, was greeted by Zionists, Zionist sympathisers and even non-Zionist Jews concerned over the refugee problem, with undis-

---

[33] See Prime Minister's letter to Dr Chaim Weizmann, February 13, 1931, quoted in Peel Commission, *Report*, p. 220.

[34] Peel Commission, *Report*, p. 62. An added stimulus to the Palestine economy was the capital brought in by immigrants qualifying for admission in category A(i), by reason of their possessing capital of £1,000 or more. 17,653 persons in this class—of whom about one-third were refugees from Germany—entered Palestine in the three years 1933 to 1936. Many of these immigrants were able to bring into Palestine far more than the £1,000 qualifying capital.

[35] Total Jewish immigration for the months January–September 1936 was 24,965; for the comparable period in 1935, the figure was 43,895. See Secretary of State for the Colonies, memorandum, Palestine Situation: Question of Temporary Suspension of Immigration, October 20, 1936, C.P. 269(36), CAB 24/264.

guised alarm; and the Colonial Secretary nervously anticipated a storm of protest from the Labour Opposition in Parliament, the Mandates Commission at Geneva, the United States press and Government, and Jewish opinion throughout the world. The High Commissioner for Palestine, Sir Arthur Wauchope, had meanwhile advised the Colonial Office that in his view a suspension of immigration could not be justified on economic grounds, and that it could not be defended, at least not in public, on political grounds.

The question was discussed by the Cabinet at several of its meetings, and it was ultimately decided at the meeting of October 28, 1936 to accept the view of the Colonial Secretary that there should be no change in policy and therefore no total suspension of immigration. This decision was taken although certain Cabinet members pointed out the dangers to Britain posed by Italy's energetic wooing of the Arabs, who were bound to be alienated by further Jewish immigration.[36] The Colonial Secretary, who had previously come to the conclusion that 'the High Commissioner [for Palestine] should in any case take a definitely conservative view in estimating the economic absorptive capacity of Palestine for the purpose of fixing the Labour Schedule for the period October 1936 to March 1937',[37] was requested by the Cabinet to ascertain the views of the High Commissioner as to the possibility of reducing the immigration of category A(i) immigrants, i.e., those with capital of £1,000 or over. The High Commissioner was also to be asked to consider whether 'if he were completely free from any commitment in this matter he would recommend a restriction on merits'. Replying to these queries, Sir Arthur Wauchope stated that 'from an economic point of view' he did not consider a restriction of capitalist immigration to be either desirable or practicable.[38]

The High Commissioner had nevertheless taken a restrictive view of 'absorptive capacity', approving a Labour Schedule for the period October 1936 to March 1937 of only 1,800, and requesting the Colonial Secretary to attempt enlisting the cooperation of Dr Chaim Weizmann in 'keeping the immigration figures as low as

---

[36] See Cabinet Conclusions 60(36)5, October 28, 1936.

[37] Colonial Secretary, memorandum cited *supra*, p. 76, note 35.

[38] Wauchope to Secretary of State for the Colonies, October 31, 1936. Quoted in C.P. 292(36).

possible'.[39] The Colonial Secretary was able to report to his colleagues at the Cabinet meeting of November 4, 1936, that he had written and spoken to Dr Weizmann, who had 'promised to make every effort to keep the numbers down'.[40] The comparatively small Labour Schedules authorised in 1936, the disturbances themselves, and the growing difficulties of German Jews in transferring their capital—even under the comparatively favourable terms of the Haavara scheme—led to a sharp drop in authorised Jewish immigration, which amounted to 29,727 for the year 1936.

The Peel Commission, which had proceeded to Palestine in November, completed its work in January and presented its Report in June, 1937. Summarising its conclusions in almost elegiac language, the Commission stated that only partition of Palestine could offer a way out of the conflict inherent in the incompatible obligations assumed by Great Britain to both Jews and Arabs. The Commission recognised that immigration was a key factor in the problem, and recommended that immigration should henceforth cease to be determined exclusively by reference to 'economic absorptive capacity'. Acknowledging that its recommendation could not be more than a mere palliative which would not appease Arab grievances, the Commission concluded that a 'political high level' of Jewish immigration should nonetheless be established for all categories of immigrants. This political maximum should be established for five years at 12,000 persons per year, within which limit the High Commissioner could admit immigrants at his discretion, subject to the economic capacity of Palestine to absorb them.

The dispute over immigration to Palestine was destined to become even more bitter as the pressures on Jews in Germany, Poland, Rumania and elsewhere increased throughout 1937 and 1938. Palestine remained the goal of impoverished and persecuted Jews from Eastern and Central Europe, and their determination to enter the country, legally or—in explosively growing numbers—illegally, brought them into repeated conflict with the British authorities.

[39] Wauchope to Secretary of State for the Colonies, October 31, 1936. Quoted in C.P. 292(36).
[40] See Cabinet Conclusions 62(36)8, November 4, 1936.

Although the problem of Jewish refugees was uppermost in the minds of Government officials throughout 1936, they were forced also to recognise that there were increasing numbers of non-Jewish refugees from Germany—'non-Aryans' and others—whose welfare was of considerable concern to Church groups. In the early months of 1936, Bishop Bell of Chichester launched an appeal for £25,000 for the assistance of the Christian refugees, but met with a very meagre response : only some £8,250 had been collected by the British Churches by November. Convinced that only with substantial outside assistance could the sum of £25,000 be raised, the Bishop wrote to the Foreign Office, proposing that the British Government make a grant of £5,000 toward the settlement of non-Jewish refugees, and that the Government also sponsor a special issue of postage stamps bearing a surcharge which would make further sums available for the refugee cause.[41] The Bishop followed his letter by a personal call on Lord Cranborne and a further letter suggesting that if the Government were unable to accede to his original request, at least it might make a limited grant to assist the ultimate settlement overseas of non-Jewish refugees temporarily resident in England and toward the education of German refugee children in English schools.[42] After consultation with the Treasury, the Foreign Office informed Bishop Bell that the Government could not accede to his requests; it would be impossible to surrender the principle that funds for settlement of refugees should come solely from private sources.

In Germany itself, the situation of Jews and 'non-Aryans' became increasingly precarious throughout the autumn of 1936 and through 1937. The tempo of 'aryanisations' of Jewish-owned enterprises perceptibly quickened after the resignation of Dr Hjalmar Schacht as Minister of Economics in November 1937. With his departure, the Ministry of Economics proceeded to define more precisely what constituted a 'Jewish' firm, and at the same time sharply reduced

[41] See Chichester to Cranborne, November 23, 1936, FO 371/20483, W 16611/172/98. The issue of surcharged stamps to raise funds for refugees had been successfully employed by several Scandinavian governments to aid 'Nansen' refugees.

[42] See Chichester to Cranborne, December 17, 1936, FO 371/20483, W 18933/172/98.

raw material allotments available to such enterprises; early in 1938 Jewish firms were excluded, with very few exceptions, from all public contract work. Parallel with the accelerating pace of 'aryanisation', dismissals of the remaining Jewish and 'non-Aryan' members of management in large enterprises increased at the instance of Party and Government officials. The slow strangulation of the remaining Jewish enterprises, and the hopeless future for the younger generation, led to a continuing emigration throughout 1937 : some 23,500 Jews and 'non-Aryans' left Germany that year, and the tempo of departures quickened in the early months of 1938.[43]

At Geneva, Sir Neill Malcolm reported flatly to the League Assembly in September, 1937 that the final settlement of refugees had not made appreciable progress since the preceding year. Emigration prospects were adversely affected by restrictive immigration laws in many countries, and indeed several countries heretofore more generous were now adopting stricter control measures. 'Emigration prospects', the High Commissioner summarised, 'are therefore seriously affected. . . . In fact, the settlement of refugees on any considerable scale is, at the present time, ruled out. . . .'[44]

Limited as he was by his strictly circumscribed mandate, the High Commissioner perforce devoted a large proportion of his activity to measures designed to improve the legal status of refugees in the countries of their sojourn. A preliminary Convention for the protection of refugees from Germany, in most respects identical with the 1933 Convention dealing with 'Nansen' refugees, was drafted and circulated to interested governments. The British Government signified its willingness in principle to accede to this Convention, which was designed to give a more permanent form to the Provisional Arrangement of 1936.[45]

It had become all too clear that the refugee problem was not,

---

[43] See Genschel, *Verdrängung*, pp. 144–150.

[44] Report to the Eighteenth Ordinary Session of the Assembly of the League of Nations by the High Commissioner, September 1, 1937, League Publication No. XII.B. International Bureaux, 1937. XII.B.2., FO 371/21235, W 16867/61/98.

[45] Foreign Office to Secretary-General, League of Nations, July 21, 1937, FO 371/21235, W 13886/61/98.

as had been stubbornly hoped and predicted, simply fading away. Knowing that both the Nansen Office and the High Commission for Refugees from Germany were scheduled to be wound up at the end of 1938, the organisations interested in refugees redoubled their efforts to urge on the Foreign Office the importance of continuing international protection for refugees as a League function, preferably by a single League organisation. In the discussions at the League Assembly, Lord Cranborne called for continuing the League's political and legal protection of refugees, while maintaining firmly the principle that no League funds should be spent on relief or settlement. The British Government now felt it inevitable that some broad decisions of principle would have to be taken on the future of the Nansen Office and the High Commission; it held that a single League body should be established to deal with both categories of refugees.[46] The League Council was therefore requested to formulate, before the 1938 meeting of the Assembly, a comprehensive plan for international assistance to refugees.

The Home Office, for its part, expressed concern over the possible implications of a new, autonomous League refugee organisation. In a letter to the Foreign Office, it explained that such an organisation, released from some of the restraints imposed on the Nansen Office and the High Commission, might 'pursue an idealistic and adventurous policy which would not commend itself to the countries of temporary refuge'. The most practical solution of the refugee problem, the letter continued, would be a 'constructive programme of development overseas'. If a suitable country could be found, the finance necessary for settlement could doubtless be procured.[47] The Home Office was acutely aware that it was the Government department which had to bear the brunt of criticism in Parliament and the press when refugees were admitted in any conspicuous numbers to the United Kingdom, and although the volume of such criticism had been less in 1937 than in preceding years, it could at any time be evoked by reference to numbers of aliens landed at the ports, or the number of foreigners permitted to take up professional or other

[46] See Report of United Kingdom Delegate to Sixth Committee of Assembly, October 6, 1937, FO 371/21235, W 19577/61/98.

[47] See Cooper to Hayter, January 11, 1938, FO 371/22525, W 527/104/98.

F

employment.[48] On the other hand, pro-refugee organisations scrutin-
ised Home Office policy and procedure with equal care, and were
not diffident in bringing their views to the attention of officials and
Ministers.

The League of Nations Union, whose frequent calls at the Foreign
Office evoked a certain defensive weariness, was particularly
generous with advice and criticism. The Secretary of its Refugees
Committee represented to the Foreign Office that 'there appeared
to outside observers to be a certain inconsistency between our
enthusiastic support of the case of the refugees at Geneva and the
very little we actually do for them in this country'. He was told that
all the British Government had advocated at Geneva was continuance of League protection for refugees; the Government had
never promised, nor urged others, actually to admit large numbers
of refugees. In any case, the points the Secretary had raised were
'really for the Home Office'.[49]

Caution was the predominant note struck in the Home Office
brief prepared for the conference at Geneva in February 1938 for
the adoption of a convention regulating the status of German
refugees. It was emphasised that every individual refugee case had
to be 'sifted with the utmost care', and considered not merely on the
merits of each individual, but on how he might be fitted into the
economy without detriment to British nationals. The British Government had to reserve the right to decide in its sole discretion to whom
and in what measure facilities for entry, training or employment
could be granted.[50] The Convention was duly signed by the British
delegate at the conclusion of the conference, with material reservations, the principal of which was that the Convention was not to be
regarded as applying to 'persons coming from abroad who were

[48] For example, the Home Secretary was asked in May how many alien doctors
and dentists had been admitted to practice in Great Britain in the past two
years, and in replying that there were 183 doctors and 78 dentists in this class,
added that Home Office policy had been and continued to be one of restricting
closely the admission of foreign doctors and dentists to practice. 324 H.C. Deb.,
562–563, May 28, 1937. Again, in July, the Home Secretary was requested to
consider the possibility of placing further restrictions on all alien immigration.
326 H.C. Deb., 1986–1987, July 20, 1937.
[49] See Hayter, minute, January 21, 1938, FO 371/22525, W 780/104/98.
[50] See Home Office, statement, January 22, 1938, FO 371/22525, W 985/
104/98.

admitted to the United Kingdom for a temporary purpose'.[51] Most refugees, at least initially, described themselves as coming to the United Kingdom for just such 'temporary purposes'.

Shortly after the Convention was signed, the League Council's Committee on Refugees reached agreement that a 'temporary' organisation should be set up to replace the Nansen Office and the High Commission. The new organisation, under a League High Commissioner, would extend legal protection to refugees and maintain liaison with the private organisations. The main hope of solving the problem, the Committee concluded, lay in the absorption of refugees in their present countries of refuge; it was no longer feasible to contemplate mass transfers of 'Nansen' or German refugees to overseas areas. The Committee went on to recommend the establishment of an intergovernmental committee which would concern itself with the absorption of refugees in the countries represented on it. Upon receipt of the Committee's report, the Home Office raised strong objections, making clear its anxiety that if the report were adopted the Home Office might be called upon to absorb all Germans arriving in England who did not wish to or could not return to Germany. Moreover, the Home Office felt that the proposed intergovernmental committee with its vague and threatening mandate might present inadmissible opportunities for interference in the internal affairs of countries of refuge including Great Britain.[52]

1938, the year that was to have seen the orderly solution of the refugee problem, was not more than one month old before the British Embassy in Berlin reported that the entire trend of German policy was to intensify measures of discrimination against Jews and 'non-Aryans'. There were no longer illusions at the Embassy or the Foreign Office that British representations could alter the course

---

[51] See minutes of conference and Final Act, February 7–10, 1938, FO 371/22526, W 2318/104/98. The privileges granted by the Convention of sojourn and residence, as well as some limited protection against return to Germany, were never fully available to refugees from Germany even on paper: of the seven signatories to the Convention only three States actually ratified it, each of these with reservations so major as to render the ratifications virtually meaningless. See United Nations Department of Social Affairs, *A Study of Statelessness* (New York, 1949), Annex 9.

[52] Cranborne, memorandum, February 15, 1938, FO 371/22526, W 2244/104/98.

of Nazi policy, whose end-product was inexorably larger and ever more impoverished numbers of refugees. 'I need hardly tell you what you already know,' a member of the Embassy wrote to London, 'namely that nowadays our credit is exhausted and any intervention in regard to the Jews or the Church merely has the effect of exasperating the Germans both against us and the victims.'[53]

There matters stood on the eve of the Anschluss, the improvised but ruthlessly successful takeover of Austria, which had as its immediate effect another quantum leap in the numbers of those in flight from the expanding Reich.

[53] See Kirkpatrick to Strang, February 2, 1938, FO 371/21693, C 785/251/18.

4

Austrian Exodus

March — June 1938

In successive waves they came, from Germany, from Austria, from Czechoslovakia, each of Hitler's advances registered by their arrival, distant ripples of a large disturbance, swallows which made a winter.[1]

AT dawn on March 12, 1938, Austrian independence, since Versailles at best a delicate plant, was crushed out of existence as Wehrmacht formations crossed the frontier and swept on unopposed to Vienna. On March 13, while the Gestapo was already engaged in making mass arrests, and Austrian Nazis had begun their uncoordinated confiscations and looting, Austria was officially incorporated into the Reich. Protests were made by France and Great Britain, but their effect was nil in the absence of any guarantees to Austria or willingness to counter force with anything stronger than mere expostulations.

The mass flight which immediately followed the takeover far exceeded in disorganisation, haste and panic the exodus which had occurred when Hitler became Chancellor in 1933. Jews,[2] Social Democrats, civil servants who had supported the Schuschnigg government, and others who had reason to fear the Nazis headed desperately for the frontiers by train, car or on foot. A fortunate few parted with enormous sums to secure air passages on the limited number of international flights leaving Vienna. Thousands besieged foreign consulates; others who could not risk the delays that pro-

[1] Malcolm Muggeridge, *The Thirties* (London, rev. ed. 1967), p. 261.

[2] At the Anschluss, there were approximately 180,000 Jews in Austria, of whom 165,000 lived in Vienna. See Eugene M. Kulischer, *Europe on the Move* (New York, 1948), p. 199.

cedure entailed fled through the woods into Czechoslovakia, the sole neighbouring country which had not sealed its frontiers with Austria. Still others, more than one hundred a day according to contemporary reports, sought their escape in suicide.[3]

The process of driving Jews out of the economy which in Germany itself had taken years and was still far from complete, was accomplished in Austria within two or three months, by means of large-scale looting and takeover of Jewish property of all sorts, often in circumstances of the utmost brutality. The forms of sale and compensation, however derisory, which had evolved in Germany into an established 'aryanisation' procedure were largely ignored in Austria: self-appointed 'Commissars'—most of them long-standing Nazi Party members—simply took possession of houses, shops, factories and other enterprises, frequently helping themselves in addition to cash or valuables for their own private accounts. The real and movable property of all 'enemies of the people', and of émigrés, was confiscated as a matter of course for the benefit of Party and other organisations, and later for the Austrian state itself. This 'giant plundering expedition',[4] which struck a Jewish community many of whose members were already barely eking out an existence as petty traders, or who were subsisting on charity, produced more completely destitute refugees from Nazism than had hitherto appeared in the countries of increasingly reluctant asylum.

Extensive press coverage of the Austrian events, and the appearance of the first refugees at Croydon and at the ports, directed the attention of the British public for the first time to the possibility of a large-scale influx of refugees from Austria. The Home Office, in a glare of unwelcome and not always informed publicity, prepared to deal with the new problem, the most disturbing aspect of which was the anticipated arrival of many Austrian nationals holding passports which would subsequently become invalid, thus making it impossible to deport them if it should become desirable to do so. Moreover, the Home Office had been informed on March 14 by the German Jewish Aid Committee that in view of the dimensions of the Austrian situation it could no longer undertake that any Jewish

---

[3] See G. E. R. Gedye, *Fallen Bastions* (London, 1939), pp. 300–326.
[4] See Genschel, *Verdrängung*, p. 165.

refugees who might be admitted to Great Britain would not be allowed to become a public charge; an exception could be made only for those refugees who might be admitted by the Home Office after consultation with the Committee. Finally, the members of the Aliens Department at the Home Office were uncomfortably aware that any 'unnecessary or wholesale restriction' of Austrian immigration 'would give rise to a strong reaction of public opinion which would no doubt find expression in the House of Commons'.[5] Impaled on the horns of this dilemma, but convinced that additional precautions against unwanted arrivals were indispensable, the Home Office pressed the Foreign Office to consider the feasibility of urgently re-introducing the visa system for all aliens holding German or Austrian passports.

In a confidential memorandum addressed to the Foreign Office,[6] the Home Office foresaw that the pressures in Austria would cause a large increase in 'refugees of Jewish race or ancestry' seeking admission to Great Britain : although these refugees might not be individually undesirable, their uncertain numbers might 'create social and labour problems'. Referring to the German Jewish Aid Committee's inability to extend its undertaking to the new wave of refugees, the Home Office argued that there was a need for additional precautions against the admission of all aliens holding German or Austrian passports. It would however be difficult to take such precautions at the ports, where refusal of leave to land might entail great hardship; it would be much easier to institute a visa system whereby aliens could be prevented from embarking on fruitless journeys and the potential flood thus 'checked at the source'. Although a visa system would doubtless be unpalatable to British businessmen and travel agencies, since Germany would now require visas of British subjects, there seemed no alternative to its introduction. Concluding its memorandum, the Home Office reiterated its genuine alarm :

. . . from the Home Office point of view the situation is serious, and . . . without the check that a visa system affords there can be no

[5] See minutes recording conversations between Home Office and Foreign Office, March 12–14, 1938, FO 372/3282, T 3272/3272/378.

[6] Home Office, memorandum, March 14, 1938, FO 372/3282, T 3517/3272/378.

guarantee that the entry of refugees from Germany and Austria can be effectively controlled.

The Home Secretary, Sir Samuel Hoare, raised the question of refugees from Austria at the Cabinet meeting of March 16, reporting to his colleagues that many persons were now expected to seek asylum in Britain and that 'he felt great reluctance in putting another obstacle in the way of these unfortunate people'. The Home Secretary added however that

a curious story had reached him (from M.I. 5) suggesting that the Germans were anxious to inundate this country with Jews, with a view to creating a Jewish problem in the United Kingdom.[7]

The Cabinet minutes record no discussion of this particular statement : but the fear that any large inflow of Jewish refugees might lead to a wave of anti-Semitism in Great Britain was one that continued to haunt both the Home Office and the refugee organisations. The Nazi authorities for their part tirelessly and stridently propagated the view, which met with a positive response in several pro-German quarters, that Jewish refugees represented potential sources of moral and political contamination wherever in the world they might choose to seek asylum. The Cabinet agreed that a small committee composed of the Home Secretary as chairman, the Foreign Secretary, the Minister of Labour, and the President of the Board of Trade, should be formed to deal with the question of refugees from Austria. In consideration of the matter, this committee should

bear in mind the points mentioned by the Home Secretary regarding the importance of adopting as humane an attitude as possible, and at the same time of avoiding the creation of a Jewish problem in this country.

For the Home Office, the first priority in the emergency remained the institution of a visa system for Germans and Austrians. For the purpose of establishing an agreed policy on this proposed action, an interdepartmental meeting was convened on March 18, at which representatives of the Intelligence Services joined Home Office, Foreign Office, Board of Trade and Ministry of Labour officials.

[7] See Cabinet Conclusions 14(38), March 16, 1938, CAB 23/93.

After consideration of all aspects of the matter, it was agreed that a visa system should be introduced without delay. An agreement for the mutual abolition of visas had been concluded with Germany in 1928, but this agreement would have to be abrogated, although this step would of course elicit a reciprocal visa requirement from the German Government.[8]

The British Ambassador in Berlin gave formal notice on April 21[9] of the British Government's intention to terminate its abolition of visas agreement with the German Government, but the German Chargé d'Affaires in London called at the Foreign Office six days later with the counter-proposal that it might be possible to negotiate an arrangement which would obviate the necessity for imposition of visas. The Foreign Office, always hopeful of removing any potential irritant to Anglo-German relations, welcomed the German démarche, but the Home Office remained adamant in refusing to depart from its determination to demand visas of both Germans and Austrians 'so long as the Germans persist in their persecution policy with its attendant refugee problem'.[10] The Foreign Office felt unable to interpose any real objection to Home Office insistence on visas; one Foreign Office member reminded his colleagues : 'we merely provide the machinery for a policy which is primarily, if not exclusively, theirs.'[11]

The German Embassy followed its verbal representations with written proposals which the Foreign Office found sufficiently reasonable to warrant further examination, but the Home Office reacted with asperity to the prospect of any negotiations, stating that the German scheme—which contemplated that would-be émigrés should be issued with a distinctive passport—would not at all solve its problem of how to decide which individuals should properly be admitted to Britain.[12] The Home Office view was communicated to the German Embassy on May 20, but the next day, without any warning, numerous British subjects caught without German visas

[8] Foreign Office, memorandum, March 18, 1938, FO 372/3282, T 3605/3272/378.
[9] See Henderson to Halifax, April 21, 1938, FO 372/3283, T 5179/3272/378.
[10] See minutes, April 27–29, 1938, FO 372/3283, T 5565/3272/378.
[11] See Creswell, minute, April 27, 1938, FO 372/3283, T 5566/3272/378.
[12] See Holderness to Under-Secretary of State, May 20, 1938, FO 372/3283, T 6718/3272/378.

were turned back at the German frontier, to the intense annoyance of the Foreign Office, which had considered the question of visas still under discussion. Wrote one of its members :

This is typical. Obviously, while the German Embassy were imploring us to postpone our visa requirement, orders had already been given to retaliate—thus causing the maximum inconvenience to innocent people, a too favourite pastime of these people, I fear. It is perfectly useless to ask them to be considerate for people without visas.[13]

The circular of visa instructions subsequently issued to Consuls and Passport Control Officers stated that the main purpose of the visa would be to 'regulate the flow into the United Kingdom of persons who, for political, racial or religious reasons, may wish to take refuge there in considerable numbers'.[14] The circular cautioned that considerable care would be necessary to distinguish between applicants for visas who were bona fide visitors, and those whose real object was to apply after admission to be allowed to remain indefinitely. If such persons proved unacceptable as residents, it might be very difficult to deport them, both on humanitarian grounds and because the German Government might well refuse to recognise them as its nationals. The Passport Control Officers must therefore carefully investigate the intentions of all persons describing themselves as visitors, even if they might have been regular visitors in the past. The circular continued :

Such persons, especially those who appear to be of Jewish or partly Jewish origin, or have non-Aryan affiliations, should be discreetly questioned as to their family circumstances, and how their business or employment has been affected by recent events; and if it is suspected that emigration is intended, the applicant should be invited to say so frankly. He may be told that, if he does so, his application for a visa will be dealt with on its merits on that basis. If he persists that a visit only is intended, he should be told that his application will be dealt with accordingly, and that, if a visa is granted, he will be required to terminate his visit and leave at the end of the specified time. He should be required to sign an undertaking that he will do so, and he should be warned that, if he overstays the period allowed, steps will be taken

[13] Bland, minute, May 21, 1938, FO 372/3283, T 6797/3272/378.

[14] Foreign Office, Passport Control Department, Circular, Visas for Holders of German and Austrian Passports entering the United Kingdom, April 27, 1938, FO 372/3284, T 7056/3272/378.

to compel him to return to Germany or Austria, as the case may be, notwithstanding any plea to the contrary.

In the class of potential immigrants or refugees—declared or suspected—there would likely be a large number who would 'have no special claims to hospitality in the United Kingdom'; even if such individuals were not personally undesirable, the admission of large numbers of refugees without means and without definite prospects would cause serious economic and social problems. The test for admission was therefore to be 'whether or not an applicant is likely to be an asset to the United Kingdom'. In applying this test, *prima facie* unsuitable candidates would be small shop-keepers or retail traders, artisans and 'persons likely to seek employment'; agents and middlemen; minor musicians and commercial artists; and 'the rank and file' of doctors, lawyers, and dentists. A member of this class who could nevertheless demonstrate that he was in special danger and represented an exceptional case to be granted political asylum, or that he could rely on some source of support in Great Britain while arrangements were being made for his future, might have his case referred to the Home Office for instructions. Those who should not be refused visas without reference to London included leading persons in science, medicine or research; artists, architects, and designers of sufficient standing to maintain themselves by private commissions and industrialists who planned to transfer well-established businesses to Great Britain.

Visas could be granted on the spot to 'distinguished persons, i.e. those of *international* repute in the field of science, medicine, research or art'—provided there was evidence that the applicant would be assured of the hospitality of friends or colleagues in Great Britain; students of the non-refugee class 'who are known not to have any Jewish or non-Aryan affiliations'; and students who were refugees if they had been admitted to a British university or college for at least a two-year course and had adequate funds for their period of stay.

Even while the reintroduction of the visa for Germans and Austrians was still being mooted, public concern over the treatment of Austrian refugees at the ports found expression in the press and in Parliament. The *Manchester Guardian*, reporting several cases of

Austrians being turned back at Croydon and elsewhere, declared in a strongly worded leader on March 19 that many Englishmen, when noting the treatment refugees were receiving, must 'look back with shame to the days when our reputation as a country of sanctuary stood highest in Europe'. Asserting that Britain had been far less generous to refugees than France, Switzerland, the Netherlands or Czechoslovakia—a recurring theme of pro-refugee opinion—the *Manchester Guardian* called on the Home Secretary to 'give at least a breathing-space to those who have lost all by the invasion of Austria'.[15] In similar vein, the *News Chronicle*, in a leader entitled 'British Duty', urged that 'the present restrictions on the admission of aliens must be relaxed in the case of Austrian refugees'.[16]

An increasing volume of Parliamentary questions urging the Home Secretary to give Austrian refugees sympathetic consideration was climaxed by the tabling of a motion by Colonel Josiah Wedgwood, MP calling for the admission of refugees from Austria for a period of six months and the granting of British nationality to those of them who might request it. As the Home Secretary prepared for the House of Commons debate on this motion, he was also approached privately by those concerned over the refugee crisis. The Archbishop of Canterbury, Cosmo Lang, wrote to Sir Samuel Hoare on March 22, referring to the plight of Jews in Austria and the difficulties some refugees were encountering in gaining admission to Great Britain. 'No one,' wrote the Archbishop, 'knows better than I do the difficulties which might be created if any large number of Austrian Jews were permitted to enter this country. But it seems lamentable that there should be no place of refuge for these unhappy people.'[17]

Replying in the House to the Wedgwood motion, Sir Samuel Hoare made the fullest statement to date of Government refugee policy :

[15] *Manchester Guardian*, March 19, 1938.

[16] *News Chronicle*, March 19, 1938.

[17] Canterbury to Hoare, March 22, 1938, Templewood Papers. Hoare replied to the Archbishop on March 23, referring to his statement on the 22nd in the House of Commons, and asserting: 'As a matter of fact we have let in by far the greater number of the Austrian refugees who have arrived in the last ten days. Incidentally the newspaper reports on the subject have been almost entirely devoid of any foundation.'

On the one hand, there is, I am sure, a general desire to maintain the traditional policy of this country of offering asylum to persons who for political, racial, or religious reasons have had to leave their own country. On the other hand, there are obvious objections to any policy of indiscriminate admission. Such a policy would not only create difficulties from the police point of view but would have grave economic results in aggravating the unemployment problem, the housing problem and other social problems. While, therefore, it is proposed to pursue the policy of offering asylum as far as is practicable . . . it is essential to avoid creating an impression that the door is open to immigrants of all kinds. If such an impression were created would-be immigrants would present themselves at the ports in such large numbers that it would be impossible to admit them all, great difficulties would be experienced by the immigration officers in deciding who could properly be admitted, and unnecessary hardship would be inflicted on those who had made a fruitless journey across the Continent. I am anxious that admission shall not be refused to suitable applicants, including persons whose work in the world of science, of the arts or business and industry may be advantageous to this country. It must, however, be remembered that even in the professions the danger of over-crowding cannot be overlooked, whilst in the sphere of business and industry the social and economic difficulties must be taken into account. . . . As regards Austrians who have been admitted here for limited periods, sympathetic consideration will be given to applications for extensions of their stay. Each case must, of course, be considered on its merits, but the general considerations governing the policy of admissions to this country will also be applicable to the question of extensions of stay.[18]

Although pressed by further sharp questions, the Home Secretary declined to be drawn into an amplification of his statement, whose formula was indeed to be repeated frequently in the weeks and months ahead. Nor, on further questions, did the Home Secretary state the nature of the instructions he had issued to Immigration Officers concerning Austrian refugees; he revealed only that instructions had been given to refer any cases of 'special doubt or difficulty' to the Home Office for decision.[19] Following the debate, the Wedgwood motion with its sweeping proposal for wholesale admission and naturalisation of refugees was defeated.

[18] 333 H.C. Deb., 991–994, March 22, 1938.
[19] See exchange with Mr Arthur Henderson, MP, 333 H.C. Deb., 1363–4, March 24, 1938.

Press comment on the Home Secretary's statement was generally favourable, echoing the Secretary's own sympathy for the plight of refugees as well as his caution in extending a carefully measured hospitality to those who might present themselves at the ports. In its leader, *The Times* referred to the 'high and honourable' English tradition of offering asylum to refugees, and welcomed the Secretary's assurance that the tradition would be maintained. It added : 'In all the circumstances, more could hardly be expected. It is to be hoped, however, that it [the Home Secretary's statement] will be interpreted with wide liberality.[20] The *Daily Telegraph* leader asserted that the Government was 'bound to qualify sympathy with practical and prudential considerations'.[21] Taking a rather less high-minded tone, the *Daily Mail* applauded the House's rejection of the Wedgwood motion :

To be ruled by the misguided sentimentalism of those who think with Colonel Wedgwood would be disastrous . . . once it was known that Britain offered sanctuary to all who cared to come, the floodgates would be opened, and we should be inundated by thousands seeking a home.[22]

Displaying its traditionally robust and unabashed nativism, the *Daily Express* asked rhetorically in its leader 'Shall All Come In?', and continued :

We need to ask, for there is a powerful agitation here to admit all Jewish refugees without question or discrimination. It would be unwise to overload the basket like that. It would stir up the elements here that fatten on anti-Semitic propaganda. They would point to the fresh tide of foreigners, almost all belonging to the extreme Left. They would ask : 'What if Poland, Hungary, Rumania also expel their Jewish citizens? Must we admit them too?' Because we DON'T want anti-Jewish uproar we DO need to show common sense in not admitting all applicants.[23]

Although, predictably, the *News Chronicle* and the *Manchester Guardian* pleaded for the greatest possible latitude in interpreting the Home Secretary's statement, it was *The Scotsman* which expressed in its leader perhaps the most widespread opinion :

[20] *The Times*, March 23, 1938.
[21] *Daily Telegraph*, March 23, 1938.
[22] *Daily Mail*, March 23, 1938.
[23] *Daily Express*, March 24, 1938.

the policy of the fully open door is not practicable, and it is important that oppressed minorities should not assume that admission into this country is to be offered to all and sundry. . . . The problem has an international character, and it is clearly impossible for this country alone to provide the necessary refuge.[24]

It was with the international character of the refugee problem that the British Government was to be principally concerned in the spring and summer months of 1938, for the initiative of President Roosevelt in proposing an international conference to facilitate emigration of refugees from Germany and Austria lent an entirely new dimension to the refugee question, and raised in acute form the issue of what, if any, concrete contribution each government was now prepared to make toward a solution.

The United States proposal, handed to the Foreign Office in a Note on March 24, 1938,[25] asked whether the British Government would be willing to cooperate in setting up a 'special committee composed of representatives of a number of Governments for the purpose of facilitating the emigration from Austria, and presumably from Germany, of political refugees'. It was to be understood, the Note made clear, that the emigration referred to would be financed solely by private organisations; and that 'no country would be expected or asked to receive a greater number of emigrants than is permitted by its existing legislation'. The first meeting of the proposed intergovernmental committee should take place in some Swiss city, the invitation suggested.[26]

The Foreign Office greeted Washington's invitation with some scepticism. It was noted that the United States Government had no intention of revising or enlarging its own immigration quotas, and that the President's scheme seemed both vaguely phrased and so broad as to raise doubts concerning the concrete results it might achieve. Moreover, the Foreign Office felt that unless the entire matter were very carefully dealt with, the constitution of the com-

[24] *The Scotsman*, March 23, 1938.
[25] Printed in FO 371/21747, C 2460/2289/18. The proposal was sent to twenty-nine European and Latin American countries, and to Australia, New Zealand and Canada. See *FRUS*, 1938, Vol. I, 740.
[26] The Swiss Government, however, preferred not to act as host to the meeting, and it was therefore held at Evian-les-Bains, on the French shore of Lake Geneva.

mittee might in itself provoke increased persecution and a new wave
of emigration, perhaps from countries such as Poland and Rumania,
in addition to Germany.[27] The possible motives for President Roosevelt's initiative were also a subject for some speculation; it was surmised that the Administration was under increasing pressure from
'certain Congressmen with metropolitan constituencies' to do something about refugees, and that in an effort to deflect a possible campaign to liberalise the United States' own immigration laws an international solution was sought.[28] The American willingness, after
years of aloofness from League of Nations refugee work, to associate
itself with any international effort to alleviate the refugee problem
was however unreservedly welcomed in Whitehall.[29]

In replying to the United States initiative,[30] the British Government pointed out that the term 'political refugees' was used by the
State Department in a sense not hitherto applied in international
usage, i.e., to refer to persons who had not yet left Germany or
Austria, but who desired to emigrate because of persecution to
which they might be subjected on political, racial or religious
grounds. Further, it was observed that it was less difficult to facilitate
the departure of refugees than to effect their admission to countries
of refuge as permanent residents; it was with the latter question
that the proposed intergovernmental committee should primarily be
concerned. Washington was reminded that the proposed committee
would necessarily have to concern itself with refugees from both
Austria and Germany, and that it would not be possible to differen-
tiate between the two groups. The need for effective liaison with
existing international agencies was also stressed and, finally, the full
agreement of the British Government was placed on record that
any financing of emigration should be undertaken by private
organisations without reliance on governments.

[27] See minutes on FO 371/21747, C 2560/2289/18, and despatch from the
British Ambassador in Washington, April 5, 1938, FO 371/21748, C 2977/
2289/18.
[28] The available evidence appears to be ambiguous on this point. See David
S. Wyman, *Paper Walls* (Amherst, Mass., 1968), pp. 43–45, and Henry L.
Feingold, *The Politics of Rescue* (Rutgers, N. J., 1970), pp. 22–25.
[29] See Foreign Office memorandum, May 23, 1938, FO 371/21749, C 5319/
2289/18.
[30] See British Note, May 6, 1938, FO 371/21747, C 2560/2289/18.

Against a background of generally favourable public comment on the Government's acceptance of the American invitation,[31] the Foreign Office addressed itself to the more immediate proposal that the authority of the League's High Commissioner for Refugees coming from Germany should be extended to cover refugees from Austria as well. The British Government took the lead in proposing that this be accomplished by putting the question on the agenda for the May 9 meeting of the Council of the League. At this meeting, the Council accepted the British recommendation extending the High Commissioner's mandate; and also adopted a report by its sub-committee on refugees concerning the reorganisation of the Nansen Office and the High Commission into a single organisation under League auspices.[32]

As the Council was meeting, a short-lived and bizarre scheme was put forward by the High Commissioner for Refugees from Germany to meet the growing problem of stateless refugees who had no travel documents or other identity papers. Sir Neill Malcolm proposed that some small state should be created, presumably by legislative fiat, of which stateless persons could become nationals, and which would in turn issue them with the appropriate documents necessary to secure their legal status in countries of refuge. Sir Neill 'thought a minute area might be ceded for this purpose and he felt sure that he could arrange for this area to be situated in North Borneo'.[33] The Foreign Office for its part considered the notion of a fictitious state 'rather impracticable', since even if it could be called into existence it could not in any case improve the chances of refugees for emigration and settlement. The suggestion was allowed quietly to expire.

While the Foreign Office laboured to prepare for the intergovernmental conference on refugees, the situation of the victims in Austria continued to arouse grave concern. In a sombre despatch to the

---

[31] The internationalisation of the refugee burden was particularly welcomed by the press: the consistently pro-refugee *Manchester Guardian* suggested that the situation would become even more hopeful if the United States were to take the lead in removing its own restrictions on immigration. See leader, 'The Refugees', March 26, 1938.

[32] See Speaight, minute, May 20, 1938, FO 371/22527, W 6714/104/98.

[33] See Makins, minutes, May 6 and 17, 1938, FO 371/22526, W 5830/104/98.

G

Berlin Embassy[34] the British Consul General in Vienna described
the Jewish population of Vienna as 'terror-stricken, despoiled and
fearful of what the morrow may bring forth'. There was dire distress,
suicides were continuing, and there was as yet no scheme of organised
emigration; passports had in many cases been confiscated, and no
travel facilities were being granted. Reporting further the uncom-
promising hostility of officials and others in demanding the brutally
rapid expulsion of the Jews, the Consul General stated :

it would almost seem as if the manner of their going, whether by the
process of emigration to other countries or of starvation in their own,
was of little consequence to those in authority.

The despatch ended with a reference to the approximately four
million Jews of Eastern and Central Europe, and the bitter hostility they too faced in their own countries. What was needed to
solve the problem, the Consul General concluded, was 'a long-term
policy, a comprehensive scheme, the best brains, and ample finance'.

Just over one month later the Consul General again reported, this
time that 'the situation of the Jews in Austria is becoming more
desperate than ever'. He explained that it was virtually impossible
for any Jew to obtain a British visa, even for a short visit to the
United Kingdom, because as a condition of being granted a passport to leave Austria, any Jewish Austrian national had to sign an
undertaking never to return to Austria and to make over all his
property to the State; British visas simply could not be granted to
individuals thus rendered both destitute and *de facto* stateless. Furthermore, mass arrests were continuing, and when those arrested
were released, frequently after lengthy and brutal detention, they
were required to sign a declaration that they would leave Austria
within four to six weeks. 'In consequence of these measures,' the
Consul General continued,

the distress and despair amongst the Jews are appalling. This consulate-
general is literally besieged every day by hundreds of Jews who have
been told to leave the country and who come vainly searching for a
visa to go anywhere. Every consulate in Vienna is in a similar position. . . . Unless pressure from international quarters can be brought
to bear upon the Reich Government to force them to intervene in

[34] Gainer to Henderson, April 21, 1938, FO 371/21634, C 3588/1667/62.

Austria and regulate the Jewish problem along the lines obtaining in the rest of Germany, it is impossible to predict the horrors which may come about.[35]

The grim situation in the Reich, and the pressures it generated, convinced the Home Office that the many British voluntary organisations concerned with refugees would now have to concert their efforts if confusion and overlapping were to be avoided. A Co-Ordinating Committee for Refugees[36] was accordingly established at the initiative of the Home Office to form a link between the various refugee organisations, and to distribute to its appropriate constituent committees for investigation the rapidly-increasing number of immigration applications received by the Home Office or by voluntary organisations. Later, the Co-Ordinating Committee was requested by the Home Office to set up two new case work committees, one for nurses and one for domestic servants. Most importantly, however, the Co-Ordinating Committee was called into being in order to represent the collective interests of the refugee organisations vis-à-vis the British Government, especially in questions of residence, training facilities, and official approaches to Dominion, colonial or foreign governments on emigration matters. A deputation from the newly-formed Committee called on the Home Secretary in late May to ask whether certain aspects of British Government practice on the admission, training, employment and naturalisation of refugees could be made somewhat less stringent, so that the uncertainty in which many refugees were living could be minimised. The deputation hoped to establish a 'general understanding that temporary permits are renewed with a minimum of formality on the recommendation of a responsible organisation'—

[35] Gainer to Henderson, May 31, 1938, FO 371/21635, C 5609/1667/62. Sir Robert Vansittart minuted on this despatch: 'I earnestly hope that we shall give publicity to this savagery. It is a heavy load on our conscience indeed that there has been nothing outspoken, though we have the material.' Gainer's despatch was thereafter printed, and circulated to the Cabinet by order of the Foreign Secretary.

[36] Organisations represented on the Co-Ordinating Committee were: Catholic Committee for Refugees from Germany, Church of England Committee for Non-Aryan Christians, German Jewish Aid Committee, Inter-Aid Committee for Children Coming from Germany, International Student Service, Society of Friends, Society for the Protection of Science and Learning, Trades Union Congress and Labour Party (International Solidarity Fund).

and that regulations should not operate to separate members of the same family. Looking toward the forthcoming Evian conference, the deputation offered the assistance of the refugee organisations in carrying out international migration schemes, and asked in return that the 'treatment of refugees in the United Kingdom, which is at present considered very favourable, would be stabilised and would not in the future be made less generous'.[37]

Although the United States Government had suggested on May 9 that the first meeting of the proposed conference be held on July 6 at Evian,[38] the weeks slipped by without any further indication of what precisely the State Department had in mind, and what the procedure and scope of the meeting should be. The silence from Washington, followed by the bare announcement that Mr Myron C. Taylor, a former President of United States Steel Corporation but innocent of experience in international affairs, was to be the Chairman of the conference, and that his deputy would be Mr James G. McDonald, former High Commissioner for Refugees from Germany, caused considerable misgivings at the Foreign Office, where Mr McDonald was dismissed as 'not a success as High Commissioner', and his letter of resignation termed 'a very ill-advised document'. The reappearance on the refugee scene of this 'very tiresome individual' was deemed 'unlikely to help the work of the committee'.[39]

In the absence of any lead from Washington, the Foreign Office proceeded with its own attempt to assess the possible outlines of the forthcoming conference : in a lengthy memorandum R. M. Makins considered the problems likely to arise at Evian, and what the British Government's attitude might be toward them.[40] First, the evidence was that the American proposals had not been 'thought out before they were launched'; the United States Government was moreover inexperienced in dealing with international meetings and indeed 'American proposals' were 'apt to be wild and impracticable'. The

[37] See Makins, minute, May 20, 1938, FO 371/22527, W 6570/104/98.

[38] See Johnson to Halifax, May 9, 1938, FO 371/21748, C 4070/2289/18.

[39] See Makins, minutes, May 6, 1938, FO 371/21748, C 3981/2289/18 and May 23, 1938, FO 371/21749, C 5319/2289/18.

[40] Makins, memorandum, International Assistance to Refugees, May 23, 1938, FO 371/21749, C 5319/2289/18.

need for the British Government to define its own position was therefore more than usually important.

If, the memorandum continued, the Evian meeting were to restrict its work to the limited problem of Germany and Austria, some solution might be envisaged if the United States were prepared to fill up about three-quarters of its annual combined German and Austrian quota of 46,000[41] with refugees, thus leaving between 10,000 and 20,000 refugees a year to be absorbed in all other countries—assuming an annual assisted emigration of some 50,000 people a year, which the refugee organisations hoped to achieve.

On such a basis the meeting at Evian might have little difficulty in arriving at concrete results, were it not for the financial aspect. We are assured that it would be beyond the resources of private organisations to finance an emigration on a large scale.

But quite apart from the stubborn dilemma of finances, there was the far wider problem of the Jewish populations in such countries as Poland, Rumania and Hungary. Anti-Jewish measures were being steadily intensified in all these countries, and Poland in particular had been trying since 1936 'to initiate some scheme of emigration in which they look for British financial support'. Unfortunately, then, any settlement schemes agreed at Evian would likely constitute a positive incentive to these East European governments to increase pressures on their Jewish minorities, in the assurance that room would somehow be found elsewhere for their unwanted citizens. The problem was thus not merely a refugee problem, nor even one of a limited emigration; world governments were confronted with 'the prospect of a mass movement of population perhaps involving some millions of people'.

The British Government might make a contribution to the solution of the problem, either by granting extensive facilities for emigration to British colonial territory or by supporting a scheme of financing emigration through an international loan or the establishment of a revolving settlement fund. Either the territorial or the financial contribution would however require a reversal of the policy which had thus far been consistently pursued on the refugee problem—

[41] The Foreign Office figures are based on a miscalculation: the combined German-Austrian immigration quota was in fact only 27,370.

although, Mr Makins remarked parenthetically, it was true that the British Government had in the past made financial contributions toward the settlement and relief of Armenian and Russian refugees. If the British Government were nevertheless to take the lead in helping to solve the German and Austrian refugee problem, it could expect to be rewarded by securing 'the sympathy and support of world Jewry', which might help to ease its difficulties over Palestine. Solving the refugee question could also go some way toward allaying tensions in Central Europe, thus contributing generally to 'appeasement in Europe' : such an initiative would also 'have a striking effect upon world opinion and particularly opinion in the United States'.

Finally, Mr Makins mentioned two wider possible aspects of the Evian meeting. First, in convening the meeting, the United States Government had departed from its policy of non-intervention in European matters. That departure should in itself be welcomed and encouraged, but the British Government probably could not effectively do so unless for its part it were now prepared to make a greater contribution to the refugee problem than it had done in the past. Second, the Evian meeting might, if it achieved concrete results and forged an effective link with existing League refugee bodies, enhance the prestige of the League of Nations itself. 'Even in a time of unfavourable political developments' an increase in the influence of the League would be important.

Following the lead indicated in the Makins memorandum, an interdepartmental meeting was held at the Foreign Office on June 8 to discuss British policy for Evian.[42] The Foreign Office representatives at this meeting showed themselves consistently alive to the serious potential problem of mass Jewish migrations from Poland and elsewhere in Eastern Europe, and pressed both Colonial Office and Dominions Office representatives to adopt a more generous view of how the British Government might help refugees.

Considering initially the domestic scene in the United Kingdom, the meeting heard the Home Office representative, Sir Ernest Holderness, assert that although his Department's policy was to be as generous as possible in admitting refugees, it would be difficult to

[42] Record of meeting, June 8, 1938, FO 371/22527, W 8127/104/98.

give any undertaking at Evian as to numbers. The Home Office would however be prepared to consider the admission of individuals in five main classes : those prepared to start businesses, young people for training or education, professional men, academics, and certain skilled artisans.

The Colonial Office representative stated that while 'it might be possible to deal with individual cases, the colonies were not in a position to make a serious contribution to the problem'. Kenya, Tanganyika, and Northern Rhodesia seemed to offer the 'least unhopeful prospect for the admission of a certain number of refugees'; the Governors of these territories had been asked to investigate settlement possibilities and to report before the Evian meeting. That other large sub-division of the Empire, the self-governing Dominions, represented another problem, according to the spokesman of the Dominions Office. It was not likely that anything which the British Government might do would influence the Dominions' attitude, which seemed likely to be negative. Australia might admit a few refugees; Canada was unwilling to encourage even British immigrants; New Zealand could not undertake the absorption of groups or individuals; in South Africa there was anti-Semitic feeling, and she had recently tightened her immigration controls; the attitude of Eire was not known. Replying to this bleak catalogue of prospects in the Dominions, Mr Makins of the Foreign Office argued forcefully that the United States Government probably looked to the British Empire for substantial assistance on the refugee problem; the United States could legitimately 'criticise very strongly this negative response to their initiative and . . . attribute to it any blame that may accrue from a possible failure of the meeting'. It was agreed after discussion that the appropriate Ministers should consider whether the Dominion Governments should be specially invited to cooperate more actively at the Evian meeting.

There was next a consideration of the attitude to be adopted if financial contributions from governments were to be proposed at the meeting. The Treasury representatives stated that the grant of financial assistance to refugees by the British Government was 'almost out of the question', since it would create a precedent which might lead to demands of unpredictable extent and would moreover encourage other governments to increase the pressure on their minorities with the object of driving them abroad. The possible alternatives of an international loan, or subsidies to shipping lines for the transport of refugees, were not feasible under present circumstances. Mr Makins again intervened, to point out that although the invitation to the Evian meeting had assumed that finance would be found by the private organisations, the question of governmental financial assistance for emigration was 'bound to arise in the very near future and would have to be considered'.

Finally, the meeting discussed the possibility that an intergovernmental committee might be formed to continue the work of the Evian meeting. Sir Ernest Holderness of the Home Office opposed the formation of such a committee, asserting that it would be large and unwieldy and would not perform any useful function; the work of emigration was carried out by private organisations which in any case dealt direct with governments in the countries of refuge. Mr Makins suggested that the British delegation should endeavour to 'make the proposed committee as innocuous as possible'. The meeting agreed that the British delegation should work for the establishment of a committee 'which would eventually be advisory to the League High Commissioner on the emigration side'.

If the potential British share in solving the refugee problem seemed to shrink under detailed scrutiny, the American contribution, as reflected in the state of preparations for Evian, now scarcely a month away, appeared virtually invisible. Lord Bearsted of the Council for German Jewry called at the Foreign Office on June 9, to report that he had been to see the American Ambassador, and had found his ideas 'somewhat hazy'. In addition, Ambassador Kennedy had made no effort to conceal his low opinion of Myron C. Taylor, 'who had not only no knowledge of the problem, but was making no attempt to get it up'. Lord Bearsted thought that any settlement schemes devised at Evian would inevitably require financial assistance from governments. But, as far as the meeting itself was concerned, 'in default of a lead from the United States . . . the outlook for Evian was gloomy . . . the meeting would be chiefly occupied with passing the buck'.[43]

[43] See Makins, minute, June 9, 1938, FO 371/21749, C 5681/2289/18.

The Foreign Office, clearly anxious to avoid the potential criticism to which Makins had referred at the interdepartmental meeting, proceeded to urge on the Colonial Office the need for a special effort at Evian. In a personal letter to the Colonial Secretary, Lord Halifax stated frankly:

I am anxious that the attitude of our delegation should be positive, and I hope you will consider very seriously whether the Colonial Empire can offer more extended facilities for the entry of refugees than it has been possible to give hitherto. Whatever the results of the Evian meeting, I feel that it may well be a prelude to an international negotiation of great magnitude concerning the future of the Jewish population in Central Europe. I have no doubt that this problem will call for large action on international lines in which we shall be obliged to participate and in which all aspects of our policy towards the Jews including that aspect of it which is particularly exercising you at the moment [Palestine] will come up for consideration. We may thus be obliged to depart from the policy we have followed in recent years as regards the admission of emigrants to our overseas territories and as to the provision of finance from governmental sources for the settlement of refugees. It is in the light of this wide problem which looms ahead of us that I ask you to give special attention to the official letter which is being sent to the Colonial Office on the subject of the instructions for our delegation to the Evian meeting.[44]

Despite the earnest prodding of Lord Halifax, the Colonial Secretary stated in his personal reply that he could not 'hold out any hope that the Colonial Empire will be able to contribute much to the settlement of the problem'.[45] Nevertheless, the report of the possibilities offered in Kenya, Tanganyika and Northern Rhodesia was still being awaited.

If the Foreign Office had entertained any hopes that the African colonies might offer large-scale settlement possibilities for refugees, these must have been somewhat dampened by a letter from the Governor of Kenya in which he stated his opposition to the setting aside of any area of land for a large refugee settlement, since 'a

[44] Halifax to MacDonald, June 9, 1938, FO 371/21749, C 5319/2289/18.
[45] MacDonald to Halifax, June 14, 1938, FO 371/21749, C 5895/2289/18. In a letter to the Passport Control Department of the Foreign Office, dated May 21, 1938, the Colonial Office had advised the Passport Control Officer at Vienna that he 'should strongly discourage Jewish refugees from attempting to go to any of the Colonial Dependencies unless they have definite offers of employment'. FO 371/21749, C 5370/2289/18.

Jewish enclave of this kind would be an undesirable feature in a Colony which . . . should be developed on lines predominantly British'. The Governor added however that he would not object to

the carefully regulated influx of Jews of the right type—i.e. nordic from Germany or Austria—for agricultural settlement in reasonably small numbers . . . in small groups of a size not too large to become part of the general economic and social life of the community.[46]

In its official letter to the Foreign Office[47] the Colonial Office repeated that the only two territories which might possibly make any 'material contribution to the problem' were Kenya and Northern Rhodesia, in which an investigation of possible settlement in scattered holdings was still continuing, but no colonial government would in any case be in a position to make any financial contribution towards the settlement of refugees in its territory.

Having canvassed the Colonial Office, the Foreign Office next turned to the Dominions and arranged a meeting with the Dominion High Commissioners in London to discuss arrangements for the conference. It transpired that all the Dominions, with the exception of South Africa, now proposed to be represented at Evian, although each Dominion Government reserved complete freedom to consider what immigration conditions it would impose : there was therefore to be no Empire-wide policy on refugees. The Dominion High Commissioners were nevertheless unanimous on one point : opposition to any proposal which might be raised at Evian for government financial assistance for migration or settlement schemes. The Foreign Office representative at the meeting observed that the Dominions appeared to welcome the representation of South American governments at Evian, since they wished to see 'other "wide open spaces" besides themselves' at the conference. Of the several Dominions, Australia appeared to offer the largest potential contribution; all the Dominion High Commissioners expressed general scepticism as to the contribution the United States was itself prepared to make. Following a consideration of this theme, the minutes

[46] Governor of Kenya to Colonial Secretary, June 18, 1938, FO 371/22534, W 12288/104/98.

[47] Colonial Office to Foreign Office, June 30, 1938, FO 371/22529, W 8924/104/98.

record, 'a discussion supervened on the biological value of the mixture of Jewish with other stock and Mr Dulanty [High Commissioner for Eire] enquired whether the biologists "got hold of the President?" As no answer was forthcoming to this question, the meeting broke up in a good atmosphere of imperial cooperation.'[48]

British preparations for Evian were carried a step further by the appointment of Earl Winterton, Chancellor of the Duchy of Lancaster, as the head of the British delegation to the conference. The announcement of Lord Winterton's appointment was received publicly in Jewish quarters, particularly by the Zionists, with some dismay : Winterton had helped to form a pro-Arab group in the House of Commons several years previously, and had made in the course of a Palestine loan debate what had been construed as anti-Semitic remarks.[49] In private conversation however the Zionist leader Dr Chaim Weizmann found Winterton more sympathetic than otherwise. Winterton was approaching the refugee question 'very much as a newcomer', but he was able to reveal that the British Government proposed to 'try and do something to assist by relaxing Home Office regulations as far as possible, also by doing whatever they could by way of emigration to the colonies'. Winterton conceded however 'that this would not amount, in the result, to very much'. As far as Palestine was concerned, the Government's attitude had not yet been formulated, but it would probably be considered unwise to mix the Palestine problem with the general refugee question at Evian.[50]

The final memorandum of instructions for the United Kingdom delegation,[51] distilling the results of several further interdepartmental meetings, outlined the scope of the problem to be considered at Evian. Total numbers of those who desired to leave Germany and

[48] Butler, minute, June 28, 1938, FO 371/22528, W 8640/104/98.
[49] See the *Manchester Guardian* comment, June 27, 1938. Winterton himself was later to refer to the 'stubbornly unrealistic approach' of some leading Zionists to the refugee problem, in their insistence that all Jews who could escape from persecution should go to Palestine. See Earl Winterton, *Orders of the Day* (London, 1953), p. 238.
[50] See Weizmann, Note of Interview with Lord Winterton, June 24, 1938, ZA, S25/9778. Weizmann was described by one of his colleagues as returning 'extraordinarily satisfied' from this interview. See Rosenblueth to Landauer, June 26, 1938, ZA, S25/9778.
[51] July 5, 1938, FO 371/22529, W 8885/104/98.

Austria were unknown, but since the problem was 'at least 85 per cent' a Jewish one, the magnitude of the Jewish population in these countries would be some indication. There were believed to be some 350,000 Jews left in Germany, and 200,000 in Austria; estimates of 'non-Aryans' were 500,000–1,000,000 for Germany and 300,000–600,000 for Austria. In addition, there were some 20,000–30,000 German refugees in European countries who would need to seek permanent homes overseas.

The delegation was cautioned that the work of the Evian meeting was linked closely with the wider problem of Jewish populations in Eastern Europe. Anti-Jewish measures were being intensified in Poland, Rumania and Hungary; the Polish and Rumanian Governments were 'hoping for the assistance of other countries in disposing of part of their Jewish population'. It could certainly be assumed that interested governments would be following the Evian deliberations closely, and it would be

desirable that the results of the meeting should not act as an incentive to these governments to increase the pressure on their Jewish minorities, and at the same time create an inconvenient precedent for dealing with the results of such pressure.

The British delegation was urged to bear this problem constantly in mind, and to avoid giving the impression that such facilities for emigrants would be created at Evian as would permit countries 'with impunity' to force sections of their populations into exile.

The British Government for its part had always had a traditional policy of offering shelter to those persecuted for their political or religious beliefs or their racial origins; the Government had nevertheless to consider the fact that the United Kingdom was 'not a country of immigration, and to recognise that for demographic and economic reasons this policy can only be applied within narrow limits'. Within those limits the Government was prepared 'on the ground of humanity' to adopt an even more liberal policy than hitherto on admission and employment of refugees, and would be willing after Evian to consider applications for admission to Britain from persons without means desiring to take up employment, if the Co-Ordinating Committee for Refugees could find jobs for them. Individuals with capital who were prepared to start businesses in

Great Britain; students who would emigrate after their education; and academics for whom the Society for the Protection of Science and Learning could find positions were others who might now be admitted. Although the numbers of doctors and dentists had perforce to be limited, applications from professional men could be entertained, as well as from those who would be trained in Britain with a view to emigration. The Government could not specify in advance any total figure for annual admissions, nor for numbers within any particular class, but would be prepared to 'adopt a liberal attitude in the matter of admissions'.

As to the Empire, the delegation should if possible avoid all references to the possibilities of immigration into Palestine: that question presented 'special problems and special difficulties' and could not therefore be 'usefully dealt with in connexion with the more general considerations with which the Evian Conference is concerned'.[52] Furthermore, any possibility of Jewish immigration into the colonies in the West Indies, British Honduras, or British Guiana[53] should be kept out of the discussions; prior consideration for settlement in these territories had to be given to excess populations in several West Indian islands. With the exception of Palestine, there were no general restrictions on the entry of Europeans to colonial territories, but intending immigrants would have to demonstrate definite prospects of employment, or other means of subsistence; there would in any case be few openings in the colonies for town dwellers engaged in commerce and industry—the category to which most German and Austrian refugees belonged. Investigations were still proceeding as to the possibility of settling refugees trained in agriculture. Only Kenya and Northern Rhodesia appeared to be feasible for this purpose, but even in these territories, any 'project which may emerge is unlikely to envisage the settlement of

[52] The memorandum reminded the delegation however that 32,754 German Jews had been admitted to Palestine in the years 1933 to 1936. In Palestine itself, a technical commission was at work attempting to devise a partition scheme on the basis of the recommendations of the Peel Commission. See Royal Institute of International Affairs, *Great Britain and Palestine 1915–1945* (London, 1946), pp. 108–112. The presence of the partition commission (Woodhead Commission) in Palestine did little to damp down a wave of violence in the country, which abated only after military government had been imposed.

[53] British Guiana was later to be proposed as the location of a large-scale refugee agricultural settlement.

more than a few hundred families'. The British Evian delegation should therefore exercise the greatest caution to avoid raising false hopes or encouraging any 'exaggerated publicity which might seriously embarrass the Colonial Office and the two Colonial Governments'.

The British delegation was next reminded that if the financial aspect of emigration were raised at Evian, it should hew closely to the line that the conference had been convened on the basis that no financial assistance from governments would be forthcoming; if the United States delegation should now make proposals for such assistance, the British delegates should seek further instructions.

It was probable, the instructions continued, that the question of an approach to the German Government to urge a modification of its practice of expropriating refugees before their departure would arise at Evian. The Foreign Office did not consider that representations to Berlin along these lines would be likely to be effective, and they would certainly be resented by the German Government. On the other hand, the principle that 'the country of origin should make a contribution to the solution of emigration problems' should be established at Evian; if refugees were to be rendered destitute, the problems of settlement became almost insoluble. The principle was moreover important for the future : it should be borne in on 'other Central European Governments that, if they wish to get rid of their Jewish populations, they will be required to make a contribution to that end'. In the circumstances, the British delegation should not encourage any proposals for representations, but if the United States Government decided to take the initiative in making representations in Berlin, the British Government would be willing to support such a move.

The appointment of a committee to continue the work of the Evian meeting was not essential, in the British Government's estimation, but 'from the point of view of public opinion it may well prove necessary to give a clear indication that the work of the meeting will be pursued'. If the Evian meeting thus set up an intergovernmental committee, the British delegation should try to press for a small committee which would function in an advisory capacity to the League High Commissioner for Refugees from Germany;

it should also be made clear that the proposed committee, which should not be obliged to meet frequently, would confine its attention solely to emigration from Germany and Austria.

The carefully considered refugee policy that was reflected in these instructions was under vehement attack even before the delegates departed for the Continent. Miss Eleanor F. Rathbone, MP launched a campaign on May 23 to have the Government appoint a committee to formulate a 'national, imperial and international' refugee policy, which would involve the provision of government financial assistance for large-scale settlement. In a hostile exchange with the Prime Minister in the Commons, Miss Rathbone's proposal was turned down, to the accompaniment of interjections from other Members deploring any proposal to give public money away to 'these refugees from other countries' while British unemployed were still awaiting relief measures.[54] Miss Rathbone claimed, in the House and elsewhere—as did other pro-refugee individuals and groups—that the British Empire contained vast unoccupied spaces which could easily absorb a population of many thousands if only the political will and the financial assistance of the Government were to be mobilised on a scale sufficient to cope with a problem demonstrably far beyond the present capacity of any private organisations. 'If,' Miss Rathbone wrote in the *Manchester Guardian*, 'the British Government feels itself too weak to be courageous, at least it might show itself merciful.'[55]

The clash of pro-refugee and anti-refugee opinion in Britain, as reflected in Parliament and in the press, formed a counterpoint to the diplomatic minuet which was about to proceed at Evian, a minuet which concealed one basic unpalatable fact: no country, in any part of the world, wanted to add to its population destitute and demoralised outcasts. For such many of the refugees had become. Expelled from their countries of long residence, reduced to beggary, and labelled with the by-now pejorative collective title of 'refugees', the fugitives wandered aimlessly on a planet which appeared quite simply to have no room for their kind.

---

[54] See 336 H.C. Deb., 834–836.
[55] *Manchester Guardian*, May 23, 1938.

5

The Waters of Evian

July — September 1938

The world seemed to be divided into two parts—those places where the Jews could not live, and those where they could not enter.[1]

As the British delegation prepared to depart for Evian, efforts were made by the Foreign Office to convey the hint to Berlin that an orderly solution of the refugee problem lay largely in the hands of the German Government. The British Ambassador, Sir Nevile Henderson, was authorised at his discretion to 'mention' the forthcoming meeting to Foreign Minister von Ribbentrop, and without making any formal representations to express the concern of the British Government at the 'difficulties which will be created if the present restrictions on the export of Jewish property are maintained'.[2] It was acknowledged at the Foreign Office that even if the Evian conference resulted in a relaxation of certain countries' immigration laws, these countries would nevertheless find it impossible to admit totally destitute refugees.

Complying with his instructions, Henderson 'mentioned' the Evian conference to Ribbentrop, who reportedly 'knew nothing about it' [sic!] and asked Henderson to explain what its purpose was. Ribbentrop thereupon expressed fear lest Evian be used as a forum for Jewish propaganda against Germany, to which Henderson replied that this would be inevitable but 'might be mitigated' if Germany were prepared to let Jewish emigrants take some of their property with them. Henderson found the German Foreign Minister 'not

[1] Dr Chaim Weizmann, quoted in the *Manchester Guardian*, May 23, 1936.
[2] Halifax to Henderson, July 2, 1938, FO 371/22528, W 8733/104/98.

unsympathetic' but 'clearly perplexed as to what could be done to co-operate in this matter'. Taking Ribbentrop's disingenuous expression of puzzlement at face value, the Ambassador went on in his despatch for London to express his personal concern that the Evian meeting might do more harm than good : attacks on Germany would only worsen the situation of those being persecuted. Henderson advised that the best policy for the British delegates at Evian would be to make the reception of German and Austrian Jews in England dependent on the amounts of property they were permitted to export; this would act as an incentive to the German Government, which strongly desired to get rid of its Jews, to relax its stringent capital export laws. 'In general', the Ambassador concluded,

I would deprecate too dogmatic an attitude by British delegates as regards German policy towards Jews. However uncivilised and deplorable, it is, in the Chancellor's eyes, Germany's own business, even though she will probably be the greatest sufferer for it in the end.[3]

Lord Winterton was apprised of Henderson's views, and assured the Foreign Secretary that he and the other delegates would bear in mind the need to avoid provoking the Reich Government. Winterton added however that he felt the Evian conference should put on record that the German Government's policy of despoiling and expelling its Jewish population raised 'questions of world-wide importance', toward the solution of which the German Government itself should make some contribution.[4]

The prognosis for Evian, guarded at best in the Foreign Office, became even gloomier after informal meetings with the United States representatives in advance of the conference. R. M. Makins attended a small dinner on July 1 to meet Mr James G. McDonald, at which leaders of the British Jewish community were present.[5] Makins reported McDonald's confirmation that the idea of the Evian conference had been an 'intuitive' proposal of President

---

[3] See Henderson to Halifax, July 4, 1938, FO 371/22529, W 8887/104/98.
[4] Winterton to Halifax, July 8, 1938, FO 371/22530, W 9531/104/98.
[5] See Makins, minute, July 2, 1938, FO 371/22528, W 8829/104/98. Besides Makins and McDonald, those present at the dinner were : Sir Osmond d'Avigdor Goldsmid, Lord Bearsted, Lord Samuel, Lord Reading, Sir A. Waley Cohen, and Sir Cosmo Parkinson of the Colonial Office.

Roosevelt's, and had not been thought out in advance : some of the President's advisers had considered the time opportune for a ' "Napoleonic" approach to the problem through finance for a great scheme of settlement on a semi-commercial basis'. Those present at the dinner showed little enthusiasm for these large-scale settlement schemes; it was generally thought that the only hope of even a partial solution lay in a change of attitude by the German Government to permit refugees to take some of their possessions with them. McDonald had urged that President Roosevelt and Mr Myron C. Taylor should not be discouraged : 'it was as much a personal and psychological matter as a question of concrete proposals.' Makins concluded his report pessimistically :

I derived the strong impression that the United States were much embarrassed by the difficulty in which their initiative had placed them and were looking to the British Empire as the likeliest scapegoat. Mr McDonald was essentially negative, and the outcome of the discussion was that on the basis proposed for the meeting little progress could be expected.

Commenting on the Makins note, R. A. Butler summarised the Foreign Office view of McDonald's revelations : ' "Intuition", "Napoleonic gestures" are always dangerous, especially when buried in the convenient sand of private organisations which have no money.'

In other meetings with the American delegation, Foreign Office representatives found the Americans most anxious that the Evian conference should have at least one result : the setting up of an inter-governmental body apart from the League to explore refugee immigration possibilities. Although the British delegates argued that such an organisation would be bound to duplicate work already being done by the League High Commission, the Americans remained insistent; after comparing notes, the French and British delegations concluded that 'public opinion in the United States' was forcing the creation of the new body.[6] Although disappointed at the dogged American persistence in advocating establishment of a committee of whose possible utility they were unconvinced, the British delegates remained anxious to encourage any United States initiatives

---

[6] See Palairet, minutes, FO 371/22528, W 8851/104/98.

toward an international solution of the refugee question. This 'forth-coming attitude' on the part of the American representatives seemed to Lord Winterton and his colleagues to have 'implications of wider scope than the actual proceedings at Evian'.[7]

The conference itself was opened with minimum formalities in the Hotel Royal at Evian on the afternoon of July 6, 1938. Some 200 delegates,[8] members of the press and observers from private organisations—who had not been officially invited—were welcomed by the head of the French delegation as host.[9] Mr Myron C. Taylor made the opening address of the conference, announcing that his Government had taken steps to consolidate the German and former Austrian immigration quotas, thus enabling a total of 27,370 immigrants to enter the United States in any one year. He further urged the establishment of a permanent intergovernmental committee to continue the work of the conference.[10]

Lord Winterton followed Taylor, carefully confining himself to his instructions, but adding that no orderly solution of the refugee problem could be envisaged unless 'the country of origin, on its side, will equally assist in creating conditions in which the emigrants are able to start life in other countries with some prospect of success'. In a clear hint to the Polish and Rumanian Governments, each of which had sent an observer to the conference, Winterton deplored any attempt to consider a possible wider emigration from countries other than Germany and Austria. 'The limited problem before us', he asserted,

> will tax, even in favourable circumstances, the goodwill of the States represented here to the full, and it will only raise false expectations

---

[7] Winterton to Halifax, July 8, 1938, FO 371/22529, W 9166/104/98.

[8] The British delegation was the largest any government sent to Evian. It consisted of: Lord Winterton, Chancellor of the Duchy of Lancaster; Sir Charles M. Palairet, Minister Plenipotentiary; Sir John Shuckburgh, Deputy Under-Secretary of State, Colonial Office; J. G. Hibbert, Principal, Colonial Office; E. N. Cooper, Principal, Home Office; R. M. Makins, Assistant Adviser on League of Nations Affairs, Foreign Office; and, as Private Secretaries to Lord Winterton, T. B. Williamson of the Home Office and Captain Victor Cazalet, MP.

[9] *Proceedings of the Intergovernmental Committee*, Evian, July 6 to 15, 1938, Verbatim Record of the Meetings of the Committee, Resolutions, and Reports (London, 1938); hereafter *Proceedings*.

[10] *Proceedings*, pp. 12–13.

if it is believed that a policy of pressure on minorities of race and religion can force other countries to open their doors to its victims.[11]

R. M. Makins, in separate talks with the Polish and Rumanian observers, told them privately that the German and Austrian refugee problem seemed difficult enough; on purely practical grounds therefore it would be impossible to discuss other emigration problems at Evian. Makins thereafter reported laconically to London that 'M. Sokolowski [Poland] did not betray any great concern and seemed to understand the position . . . M. Crutesco [Rumania] . . . seemed to be more interested in his golf handicap than the refugee problem.'[12]

Winterton did not mention Palestine by name, but referred only to overseas territories under British jurisdiction where 'local political conditions hinder or prevent any considerable immigration'. His silence on Palestine was strongly criticised by the Jewish organisations and the press, particularly in the United States, and Winterton returned to the subject on the last day of the conference, explaining the acute problems which had arisen in Palestine necessitating a temporary restriction on Jewish immigration designed to maintain 'within reasonable limits the existing balance of population', pending an investigation of partition possibilities. He stated in conclusion that

the question of Palestine stands upon a footing of its own and cannot usefully be taken into account at the present stage in connection with the general problems that are under consideration at this meeting,

a clear warning that other governments should not concern themselves with a problem for which Great Britain as the mandatory power bore sole responsibility.[13]

The representatives of France, Belgium, Switzerland, the Netherlands and the Scandinavian countries each emphasised the vast numbers of refugees they had already admitted, and referred to their inability to absorb further fugitives, except for those in transit to overseas countries. The South American governments,[14] anxious not

[11] *Proceedings*, p. 15.
[12] FO 371/22528, W 8851/104/98.
[13] *Proceedings*, p. 42.
[14] Argentina, Bolivia, Brazil, Chile, Colombia, Costa Rica, Cuba, Dominican Republic, Ecuador, Guatemala, Haiti, Honduras, Mexico, Nicaragua, Panama, Paraguay, Peru, Uruguay, and Venezuela.

to offend the United States, expressed eloquent sympathy with the plight of the refugees, but pointed out that their laws made it impossible to contemplate any large intake of immigrants. Only the Dominican Republic indicated willingness to grant 'specially advantageous concessions to . . . agriculturists with an unimpeachable record'.[15]

The representatives of the British Dominions made similar speeches signifying their willingness to collaborate in studying and suggesting solutions to the refugee problem, but confirming that any modification of their existing immigration laws and practices was unlikely in the prevailing circumstances.

These statements in public session by representatives of thirty governments seemed to most observers unhelpful, repetitious, and designed largely for domestic consumption. The actual work of the meeting was referred to two sub-committees : a Technical Sub-Committee which was to hear in confidence statements of the immigration law and practice of individual governments, and the numbers of immigrants each might be willing to receive; and a Sub-Committee for the Reception of Organisations concerned with the Relief of Political Refugees. The Technical Sub-Committee had little work to do; most governments had already included as much information as they cared to make available in their formal statements to the plenary sessions.[16]

The British memoranda submitted to the Technical Sub-Committee were a straightforward recitation of British Government refugee policies and their implementation, and as such aroused little comment.[17] The statement on admission to colonial dependencies,[18] on the other hand, unleashed considerable speculation in the press and elsewhere, although it made clear that an intending immigrant would have to show definite prospects of employment or other means of subsistence before he could be admitted to any of the colonies.

[15] *Proceedings*, p. 32.

[16] See S. Adler-Rudel, 'The Evian Conference on the Refugee Question', *Leo Baeck Institute Year Book*, XII (London, 1968), 251–253.

[17] See Conference Documents Nos. E.I.E./C.T. 3, July 8, 1938 and FO 371/22529, W 9330/104/98, and C.I.E./C.T. 15, July 11, 1938, FO 371/22530, W 9465/104/98.

[18] Conference Document No. C.I.E./C.T. 5, July 8, 1938, FO 371/22530, W 9332/104/98.

The statement did however repeat the revelation that a preliminary investigation 'of the question of the admission of a limited number of refugees into certain East African territories' was under way, cautioning that the outcome of such investigation was still uncertain and that any project which might result could involve only a limited number of selected families.

This hint, vague though it was, of a possible settlement in East Africa, was greeted with intense interest by the press, other delegations, and the refugee organisations. Lord Winterton, eager to be in a position to give more positive information by the end of the conference, sent a private and personal telegram to Lord Halifax urgently requesting more information on the Colonial Office attitude to Northern Rhodesia and Kenya settlement possibilities, arguing that if the British Government could 'make a fairly positive announcement other countries may be led to do likewise'. He added :

I am most apprehensive of criticism in debate on this meeting which is likely to arise in the House of Commons if we cannot make more definite statement in regard to settlement in East Africa.[19]

Winterton was however authorised only to repeat that in Kenya the possibility of a small-scale settlement of a number of families on individual holdings was being explored, but that there was no further information available. As to Northern Rhodesia, the matter had not yet been discussed with the elected members of the Legislative Council, and in the circumstances the British delegation should avoid further announcements on possible settlement there.[20]

The Sub-Committee established to hear the representatives of the thirty-nine separate refugee organisations registered with the Secretariat of the conference organised its proceedings so as to hear in private session twenty-four representatives, each of whom was given up to ten minutes to speak, a procedure which precluded any coherent presentation. In addition, almost all of the thirty-nine organisations submitted memoranda summarising their activities and observations on the refugee problem. Despite strenuous efforts, the refugee bodies proved unable to form a unified representation,

[19] Winterton to Halifax, July 10, 1938, FO 371/22529, W 9222/104/98.
[20] See telegrams to Winterton, July 13, 1938, FO 371/22530, W 9415/104/98, and July 14, 1938, FO 371/22530, W 9462/104/98.

or to agree on some limit to the number of memoranda or statements submitted to the conference;[21] the confused and repetitious sessions which resulted had the predictable effect of irritating the Sub-Committee members and disheartening the representatives of the refugee organisations, dismayed at the lack of response to their often anguished appeals.[22]

In its closing session, the Evian meeting unanimously adopted a resolution recommending the establishment in London of an Intergovernmental Committee to continue and develop its refugee work.[23] George S. Rublee, a seventy-year-old American with extensive international law experience, was appointed Director of the Committee, which had in addition a Chairman and four Vice-Chairmen representing France, Great Britain, the Netherlands and the United States. The Director was to 'undertake negotiations to improve the present conditions of exodus and to replace them by conditions of orderly emigration'. Establishing 'conditions of orderly emigration' was meant to imply an effort to persuade the Reich Government to permit refugees to bring with them a portion of their property, thus rendering them at least minimally acceptable as potential immigrants in countries of ultimate settlement. To persuade these countries to enlarge their view of what constituted acceptable numbers of immigrants, the Director was also to 'approach the Governments of the countries of refuge and settlement with a view to developing opportunities for permanent settlement'. The new Committee was also to maintain liaison with the existing refugee services of the League. Although those concerned with refugee affairs recognised that the new Intergovernmental Committee, with its authority to negotiate with the German Government, represented a potential advance on the League refugee bodies, they were agreed that the Evian conference had signally failed to find what was most needed : places in which refugees could actually be settled. 'Evian', some refugee wits pointed out wryly, was merely 'naive' spelled backwards.

[21] Rivalries between Zionist and non-Zionist organisations blocked attempts to unify a Jewish delegation under the leadership of Dr Chaim Weizmann. See Goldmann and Ruppin to Landauer, July 12, 1938, ZA, S25/9778.
[22] See S. Adler-Rudel, 'Evian Conference', p. 255.
[23] *Proceedings*, Annex IV, p. 55.

In a report to the Cabinet[24] following his return to London, Lord Winterton betrayed no such disappointment. He told his colleagues that it had been possible at Evian to 'reach a conclusion which was not only unanimous, but which was more satisfactory than seemed likely at the outset'. The majority of the delegates had shown 'great goodwill and a disposition to modify their immigration practice so as to admit a greater number of emigrants from Austria and Germany'; an intergovernmental committee was to meet in London to 'continue and develop' the work of the Evian conferees; there were 'already some indications that the German Government may not be indisposed to come to an arrangement'. As far as the British contribution was concerned, Winterton said that his statement on a possible Kenya settlement had 'had an excellent effect', and he hoped it would be possible to issue a similar statement shortly about Northern Rhodesia. Winterton added that he had made his pronouncement about Palestine at the close of the meeting 'in order to counter possible criticism of the fact that Palestine had not been mentioned at the meeting at all' : this statement too had 'had a good effect'.

The question of possible emigration from countries other than Germany and Austria, which the United States had wished to raise at Evian, would have meant 'biting off more than it was possible to chew' and would have raised false expectations on the part of 'other governments', presumably those of Poland and Rumania. The American delegation had nevertheless given way 'quite easily' on this matter, and the London committee could occupy itself with this larger question if it chose to do so. The Dominions representatives, Winterton continued, had 'all made sympathetic speeches even though they could not promise much in the way of performance'. Winterton concluded by asserting the desirability, for general policy reasons, of encouraging the United States Government to continue to interest itself in the refugee question, and for the British Government to do all it could to make a success of the London committee.

One of the difficulties experienced at Evian, Lord Winterton revealed in the confidential remarks to the Cabinet which were not

[24] See statement prepared at the Foreign Office for Lord Winterton's report, July 19, 1938, FO 371/22531, W 9747/104/98.

included in his official report,[25] was over the proposed intergovernmental committee's relationship with the League refugee bodies: the American representatives considered the League a moribund institution. An accord had nonetheless been reached with the British delegation to recognise the need for close collaboration between the League and the new committee. Another difficulty arose from the fact that the United States and German Governments were on bad terms with one another. 'This, perhaps,' Lord Winterton surmised, 'was not unconnected with the fact that the Jewish vote in the United States was a large one'; the Americans had wanted some denunciation of the German Government, but this had successfully been resisted by the British delegation. A point of considerable importance was the new interest of the United States Government in a European problem: Mr Taylor, who was a close personal friend of President Roosevelt, had confided the President's conviction that 'if ever war came the idea that any single country could escape from its effects was a delusion'. Although the primary purpose of the new intergovernmental committee would be to 'try and get in touch with the German Government in order to promote and regulate the emigration of Jews from Germany', this activity ought also to 'promote Anglo-American cooperation and assist oppressed peoples'.

At the Cabinet meeting which received Winterton's report, the Colonial Secretary thanked him for 'the skill with which he had looked after the colonial interests involved at Evian', and then summarised the prospects for 'Jewish settlement' in the Colonial Empire by saying that apart from Kenya and Northern Rhodesia, in which settlement of some hundreds rather than thousands of refugees might be feasible, there was little prospect of alleviating the refugee problem in the colonies.

Commenting on Winterton's report, the Home Secretary warned the Cabinet that 'while he was anxious to do his best, there was a good deal of feeling growing up in this country—a feeling which was reflected in Parliament—against the admission of Jews to British territory'. The Home Secretary hoped nevertheless to 'go on quietly considering individual cases on their merits'. The Government had

[25] See Cabinet Conclusions 33(38), July 20, 1938, CAB 23/94.

not long to wait before a full-scale Parliamentary debate was launched on the outcome of the Evian conference and British refugee policy generally.

On July 27, 1938, after private notice to the Home Office and the Foreign Office,[26] Bishop Bell of Chichester tabled a motion in the House of Lords calling attention to the seriousness of the refugee problem and asking for information on the results of the Evian meeting and on British Government refugee policy generally.[27] While paying tribute to what had already been done by the British Government, Bishop Bell called for the Government now to 'give a generous lead and show that they really mean to find a solution', principally by increasing facilities in Britain for training of young Germans and Austrians and by stating with 'more precision' the extent to which the colonies would be opened to refugee settlers, 'something more than a purely general statement about Kenya or Northern Rhodesia', which latter territory the Bishop felt could absorb a considerable number of European settlers—'perhaps 50,000 or 100,000'.

Bishop Bell was followed by other speakers emphasising the necessity for German concessions to enable refugees to take with them some of their property and asserting that the British Empire, covering one quarter of the earth's surface, would be compelled to respond to the challenge of the refugees by thinking in terms of large-scale settlement rather than the gradual infiltration of individuals. Summing up for the proponents of the Bell motion, Lord Marley, who had been at Evian, challenged the Government to 'make a far greater contribution in the future than was outlined at the Evian Conference'.

The Earl of Plymouth, Parliamentary Under-Secretary at the Foreign Office, replied for the Government by referring to the three conditions on which invitations to the Evian conference had been extended: countries participating would not be asked to modify their existing legislation, finance for new settlement schemes should remain the concern of private organisations, and there should be no interference with the work of existing refugee agencies. Lord Plymouth emphasised the necessity for 'countries of origin' to cooperate

---

[26] See correspondence and minutes on FO 371/22531, W 10196/104/98.
[27] Chichester motion and debate in 110 H.L. Deb. 1206–1249, July 27, 1938.

in enabling 'involuntary emigrants' to remove enough of their property to permit them to settle elsewhere, and refused to give more precise information on possible Kenya or Northern Rhodesia settlement schemes, pointing out that the inhabitants of these territories must be given 'reasonable time' for the consideration of any refugee admissions policy. The Government would look into the possibility of expanding training facilities for refugees in transit to countries of permanent settlement, but a 'policy of the open door' would not commend itself to the Government, nor would the unrestricted admission of German and Austrian refugees be favoured by the voluntary organisations; a total of approximately 2,800 visas had however been granted in the months of May and June, and visas were being issued at the same rate in July. Lord Plymouth assured the House finally that the British Government would continue to promote international action to relieve the sufferings and dislocations attending the refugee problem. The Bishop of Chichester thanked Plymouth for his sympathetic answer, and thereupon withdrew the motion he had tabled.

If the House of Lords debate had been inspired from a position of pro-refugee sympathy, such was not the case in less rarefied circles, where the discussion on refugees and on the results achieved at Evian frequently revealed considerable anxiety as to the effects of any large refugee influx into Great Britain. Even the *Manchester Guardian*, which had characterised the Home Secretary's March 22 statement of Government refugee policy as 'a cautious idealism diluted by the desire not to offend',[28] warily approved Lord Winterton's position at Evian. The *Manchester Guardian* referred to the disquiet of Members of Parliament, especially from Lancashire constituencies, over the unrest caused in their districts by 'so-called "immigrant labour" '.[29] The Home Secretary had indeed been bombarded in the House by hostile questions suggesting that he was threatening British trades union and professional standards by proposing to let too many refugees into Britain.

The concern of the professional groups came to a head over the question of admitting Austrian doctors. The British Medical Associa-

[28] *Manchester Guardian*, July 5, 1938.
[29] Ibid., July 14, 1938.

tion adamantly refused to agree to the admission of more than a very limited number of the refugee doctors, some of world-wide repute, streaming out of Vienna, and set up a committee to advise the Home Secretary on the conditions under which such refugees were henceforth to be allowed into Great Britain.[30] That committee was able later to report to the meeting of the British Medical Association that it had achieved a 'severe limitation on the admission of refugees'; each individual applicant would have to undergo very careful scrutiny and would be obliged to undertake at least two years of clinical study before admission to practice.[31] Even this carefully limited hospitality was attacked by the *Daily Express*, which asserted in a leader entitled 'The Open Door' that there were already far too many alien doctors, dentists and psychoanalysts in Great Britain, and that the British Medical Association had let down the 'little men' of the profession in agreeing to the admission of any alien doctors.[32]

Public misgivings could only have been increased by a leader in the *Observer* stating baldly that if a further accretion of perhaps 100,000 Jews came into Britain, the danger of anti-Semitic feeling could not be averted. The *Observer* concluded that the problem could not be solved 'unless every great country takes her proportionate share'.[33]

The Jewish refugee organisations were acutely aware of the dangers posed by the growing number of Austrian refugees who were admitted to Britain on the strength of invitations—sometimes bogus—from relatives or friends, without having first been vetted by the refugee committees, and who were then discovered to be without means, unsuitable for employment in Britain, and in many cases incapable of being trained for emigration elsewhere. Alarmed

[30] The Home Secretary recalled in his memoirs that he personally 'would gladly have admitted the Austrian medical schools *en bloc*', but that his humanitarian sentiments had received 'an unpleasant shock' when he encountered the massive resistance of the British medical profession, who assured him that 'British medicine had nothing to gain from new blood, and much to lose from foreign dilution'. Viscount Templewood, *Nine Troubled Years* (London, 1954), p. 240.

[31] See *Manchester Guardian*, July 16, 1938.

[32] *Daily Express*, July 5, 1938. The leader went on to ask, as it transpired prophetically: 'Who will be next? The Czechs?'

[33] *Observer*, July 31, 1938.

at the prospect that many new arrivals might become a permanent charge on their rapidly dwindling funds, the refugee organisations found it necessary in late July to insist on a formal guarantee of maintenance from any applicants to them who wished to bring friends or relatives to Britain. Moreover, the Co-Ordinating Committee for Refugees officially advised the Home Office that its constituent committees could only assume responsibility for those refugees whose circumstances they had previously investigated.[34]

At a meeting on August 5 between representatives of the refugee organisations and the Home Office, it was agreed that the organisations should establish an office in Vienna to investigate visa applications from refugees, and to select domestic servants from among the flood of applicants, many of whom had been found to be completely unsuitable for this work upon their arrival in England. The Home Office for its part undertook to authorise a visa, provided the Passport Control Officer in Vienna had no objection, if the appropriate committee was prepared to sponsor a refugee.[35] In order to eliminate past abuses in the permit system for female domestics, an agreement was reached in late August between the Home Office and the Ministry of Labour stipulating that any employer wishing to engage a servant from Austria should apply initially to the Co-Ordinating Committee for Refugees, which after completing its investigation in Vienna would submit a recommendation to the Home Office, thus bypassing the normal entry procedures through the Ministry of Labour.[36]

On August 19, as the climax to a number of cases where aliens had smuggled themselves into England, three refugees were sent to prison by a London magistrate for landing without leave. Not content with imposing the sentence, the magistrate, Mr Herbert Metcalfe, declared that

it was becoming an outrage the way in which stateless Jews were pouring in from every port of this country. As far as he was concerned, he intended to enforce the law to the fullest extent.[37]

[34] See Ormerod to Holderness, August 4, 1938.
[35] See Cooper, memorandum, August 10, 1938.
[36] See Gee to Cooper, August 19, 1938.
[37] See *The Times*, August 20, 1938.

Press comment on Metcalfe's remarks was largely unfavourable : the *News Chronicle*, for example, suggested that the magistrate might try to 'hound homeless and helpless refugees' with 'less obvious pleasure'.[38]

The *Daily Express*, however, which had for some time been reporting darkly the existence of an 'underground railway' smuggling refugees into Britain, launched a full-scale campaign whose theme was that it was much too easy to get into the country. The Metcalfe case afforded an opportunity for a series of articles on smuggling techniques, and gibes at Lady Violet Bonham Carter, Josiah Wedgwood, MP, and others who had publicly attacked Metcalfe.[39] The *Daily Express* ended its series with a leader entitled 'The Wandering Jew', whose light ironies were doubtless not entirely lost on readers of its other editorial comments on the refugee question :

dreadful, dreadful are the afflictions of the Jewish people. . . . Every warm heart must sympathise deeply with them in their plight. . . . Certainly there is no room for the Jews in Britain, where we have 1,800,000 of our own people out of work and biting their nails. But places must be found for the Jews. There are plenty uninhabited parts of the world where, given a touch of the Christian spirit, they may yet find happy homes.

Perhaps more disturbing to pro-refugee organisations than the predictable fulminations of the *Daily Express* was the evidence of a groundswell of protest by those hitherto sympathetic to refugees. The columns of newspaper letters to the editor reflected this protest, and typical of the genre was a letter written by six trades unionists to the *Daily Herald* to complain of that newspaper's pro-refugee position. The unionists wrote :

we appreciate that often the refugees have committed no crime against the country that harries them; but charity begins at home, and we shall never . . . keep the standards that have been won for us, if the influx of aliens goes on unchecked.[40]

At a more exalted level, Nancy Viscountess Astor, MP revealed similar feelings, perhaps typical of a number in her set, transmitting

[38] *News Chronicle*, August 20, 1938.
[39] See *Daily Express*, August 23, 1938.
[40] *Daily Herald*, August 25, 1938.

to R. A. Butler of the Foreign Office a letter of appeal concerning a German refugee, with the postscript: 'However I personally feel too many Jews coming to England a mistake!'[41]

While public disquiet over refugee immigration continued to preoccupy the Home Office, the Foreign Office was concerned in the weeks following Evian with the establishment of the new Intergovernmental Committee and assuring its liaison with the existing League refugee organisations. The first order of business was the appointment of a new High Commissioner for Refugees to replace Sir Neill Malcolm, and then the consideration of the future organisation of League refugee services, since both the Nansen Office and the High Commission for Refugees from Germany were scheduled to be wound up at the end of 1938.

The French and other governments made it known to the Foreign Office that they would welcome the appointment of an Englishman as the new High Commissioner, and the establishment of the High Commission itself in London, especially in view of the presence there of the Intergovernmental Committee. Reappointment of Sir Neill Malcolm might have been considered, but the Foreign Office was told that he had alienated the Americans at Evian and that the refugee organisations were unanimous in their desire not to see him reappointed. Moreover, Lord Duncannon, Sir Neill's assistant, informed the Foreign Office that Sir Neill would be willing to stay on as High Commissioner only if 'he were allowed to devote a third of his time to North Borneo, where he has business interests'. This revelation served to harden the Foreign Office view against his reappointment.[42]

Sir John Hope Simpson, whose preliminary refugee survey[43] had been acclaimed at Evian and elsewhere as a definitive statement of the dimensions of the refugee problem, was the obvious choice for

[41] The appeal letter had been addressed to Lady Astor on August 17 by Mrs Charles Roden Buxton and Miss Margery Fry of the Quakers, asking her to interview a refugee recently interned in Buchenwald so that she might verify his story for herself and then try 'to influence the German authorities in favour of more humane treatment'. FO 371/22534, W 11865/104/98. W. G. Hayter minuted on September 5: 'I am not sure why Lady Astor passed this on to us, particularly in view of her pencilled postscript'.
[42] See Hayter, minute, September 2, 1938, FO 371/22533, W 11768/104/98.
[43] *Refugees, Preliminary Report of a Survey* (London, July 1938).

an English High Commissioner, but the Foreign Office was disturbed at his 'unnecessarily critical' views on British Government refugee policies and felt that if he persisted in these views 'they might lead to a difference of opinion with us'.[44] Hope Simpson stood out so prominently however that the Foreign Office anticipated criticism if it 'tried to run another English candidate'. Nevertheless, the India Office was requested to supply the name of an ex-Indian civil servant who might be considered, and Sir Herbert W. Emerson, who was about to retire from the Governorship of the Punjab, was suggested. Sir Herbert called at the Foreign Office and made a favourable impression, thus clearing the way for his official nomination at the forthcoming League Assembly in September.[45]

The retiring High Commissioner's report to the members of the League[46] estimated that 35,000 German and more than 15,000 Austrian refugees were present in European countries at the beginning of September 1938: this situation was described as 'most precarious', since virtually none of them had been able to take with them means to support themselves for any length of time, or to make them eligible for emigration and settlement elsewhere. Calculating that there were still some 550,000 Jews left in Germany and former Austria, and that Catholics, 'non-Aryans', Legitimists and others in the hundreds of thousands might be forced out of the expanded Reich, the report concluded that the private organisations were now finding it 'quite impossible to cope with the situation'.

The report of the League Council's committee on the reorganisa-

[44] See Makins, minute, July 22, 1938, FO 371/22531, W 10261/104/98. Hope Simpson had written, in the *Spectator* of July 8, 1938: 'It is somewhat humiliating to compare French treatment of refugees with that of Great Britain. In this country selection is carefully exercised. . . . The Home Office is entirely sympathetic, but is tied by the provisions of the Aliens Act. . . . Right of asylum as such has ceased to exist in Great Britain since 1914.' An extract from this article was minuted: 'it is a pity that his [Hope Simpson's] public utterances have not been rather more restrained. His description of Mr McDonald's letter of resignation as "noble" is very ill-applied.' July 25, 1938, FO 371/22531, W 9713/104/98.

[45] See minutes August 2, 1938, FO 371/22532, W 10389/104/98, and August 12, 1938, FO 371/22532, W 10993/104/98.

[46] Report submitted to the Nineteenth Ordinary Session of the Assembly of the League of Nations, August 22, 1938, League Document No. A.25.1938.XII., FO 371/22534, W 11910/104/98.

tion of League refugee services[47] was also submitted to League members in late August, and provided for the establishment of a single organisation to replace the Nansen Office and the High Commission for Refugees from Germany. The High Commissioner of the new body was to exercise functions of a consular and legal character for refugees coming under the protection of the international conventions of October 1933 and February 1938, and in addition to coordinate relief measures and 'assist the Governments and private organisations in their efforts to promote emigration and permanent settlement'. The League would make a financial contribution to the High Commission's administrative expenses, but not for relief or resettlement.

The Home Office and Foreign Office were agreed that the Council's view of the functions of the new League High Commission was acceptable, but the Home Office took care to emphasise that the new High Commissioner and the Director of the Intergovernmental Committee should arrive at a clear demarcation of their respective fields of activity before the two organisations embarked on their tasks. Looking ahead moreover, the Home Office opposed any suggestion that Spanish, Italian and other refugees might be brought within the scope of the new League High Commission.[48]

When the new Intergovernmental Committee on Refugees (IGC) held its first meeting in London on August 3, it concerned itself principally with the question of approaching the German authorities to obtain permission for emigrants to export some part of their property. Sir Nevile Henderson had reported from Berlin that although there was some evidence of a German desire to 'regulate the position of the Jews and perhaps thereby diminish the universal dislike of Germany to which her present policy is exposing her' it was important to avoid giving the Germans the impression 'they were being rushed'.[49] Despite elaborate precautions designed to make clear to the Wilhelmstrasse that the refugee problem was to be

---

[47] Report of the Council Committee appointed to draw up a Plan for International Assistance to Refugees, adopted by the Council on May 14, 1938, League Document No. A.27.1938.XII. FO 371/22534, W 12121/104/98.

[48] See Cooper to Hayter, September 7, 1938, FO 371/22534, W 12040/104/98.

[49] Henderson to Halifax, August 1, 1938, FO 371/22532, W 10295/104/98.

I

approached entirely as a humanitarian concern 'without any political *arrière pensée*'[50] the British Ambassador informed the Foreign Office that he and his United States colleague agreed that so long as the question of Czechoslovakia remained critical the time was not propitious for the proposed visit of the IGC Director to Berlin. The most that could be envisaged was a 'quite unofficial visit' of the sub-Director, who could 'take soundings through minor officials'.[51] Henderson, who had returned to London for consultations on the Czech crisis, subsequently told Lord Winterton that even a visit by the sub-Director would be unlikely to do much good, and should in any event be deferred until October.[52] The staff of the IGC thereupon decided that an immediate approach to the German Government was out of the question.[53]

Although the developments in Czechoslovakia overshadowed the entire question of an approach to the German authorities, the members of the IGC did display lively concern over possible public criticism arising from the Committee's apparent torpor. Myron C. Taylor pressed Lord Winterton strongly for a concrete indication of what steps the British Government was taking to deal with 'the heart of the matter': places for actual settlement of refugees.[54] Taylor was told that a statement would shortly be made by the British Government on immigration; although no figures could be specified, the numbers which could be admitted to Great Britain were 'in effect limited only by the arrangements which can be made by the voluntary organisations, with which the Departments concerned are in the closest touch, to establish them in this country'. Meanwhile, Lord Winterton felt too pessimistic a view of the situation ought not to be taken, since the 'involuntary migrants' were moving all the time—in small numbers, to be sure—to Great Britain and other countries. The object of the IGC's efforts should therefore be to 'widen, accelerate and regularise the flow of the stream'.[55]

[50] Makins, minute, August 5, 1938, FO 371/22532, W 10572/104/98.

[51] Henderson to Halifax, August 12, 1938, FO 371/22532, W 10945/104/98.

[52] See Hayter, minute, August 30, 1938, FO 371/22533, W 11759/104/98.

[53] See record of IGC meeting, August 31, 1938, FO 371/22533, W 11782/104/98.

[54] Taylor to Winterton, September 13, 1938, FO 371/22534, W 12948/104/98.

[55] Winterton to Taylor, September 18, 1938, FO 371/22534, W 12948/104/98.

The unremitting American pressures on the British Government to do more for refugees may well have occasioned some cynicism in Whitehall, where the fact was duly noted that as the Czech crisis became more acute the Director and staff of the IGC were enlisted by the United States Ambassador, Joseph P. Kennedy, in the task of arranging for the repatriation of United States citizens in the event of war. A member of the Home Office reported on September 28 that the Director was 'now devoting almost the whole of his time to this task'—which could hardly be described as assisting in the settlement of refugees from Germany and Austria.[56]

The official Home Office letter to the IGC on the contribution of the United Kingdom to the refugee problem[57] set forth essentially the same points as had been made by the British delegation at Evian, adding that Medical and Dental Advisory Committees had been established to consider applications from refugees and report to the Home Secretary how many doctors and dentists would be permitted to settle in Great Britain. Further, there were openings for some refugees in nursing, domestic service and in training schemes for agricultural workers and for students; such programmes were limited only by offers of hospitality and funds at the disposal of the private organisations.

The Home Office and not the Ministry of Labour was now dealing with applications for refugee employment, and would grant its consent to such employment if it were satisfied that the foreigner's engagement would not 'prejudicially affect the employment of any British subject', would be 'reasonable in the circumstances', and would conform to standard British wages and conditions.[58] Moreover, refugees with capital who were permitted to set up enterprises in Great Britain would be allowed to bring with them a certain number of their employees who might be without means. The report revealed that some 185 factories had been established by aliens in Britain between April and July 1938; the extent to which it was

[56] See Williamson to Coulson, September 28, 1938, FO 371/22534, W 13048/104/98.

[57] Cooper to Under-Secretary of State, September 8, 1938, FO 371/22534, W 12173/104/98.

[58] This arrangement was an extension of the agreement between the Home Office and the Ministry of Labour on the entry of refugee domestic servants. See Home Office to Ormerod, September 12, 1938.

possible to continue this development would 'depend almost entirely
upon the readiness of the German Government to allow refugees
leaving the territory of the Reich to take a sufficient amount of
capital with them to finance the enterprise'.

The prospects that refugees could rescue any fraction, however
minuscule, of their property were in any case becoming steadily
dimmer as the German Government began with increasingly
accurate methods to extrude Jews and 'non-Aryans' entirely from
the German economy. On April 26, an ordinance[59] was passed
requiring every Jew to declare the entirety of his assets to the financial authorities : such assets included all household goods, jewellery,
securities, pension rights and other intangibles; only property under
the value of RM 5,000 was exempted from the requirement. On
June 20, Jews were excluded from the stock and commodity
exchanges; on July 6, they were forbidden to engage henceforth in
a wide variety of occupations, such as those of real estate agent,
travel agent, sales representative, or broker of any kind.[60] The last
Jewish doctors were forbidden to engage in general practice from
September 30; as from November 30, the remaining Jewish lawyers
were excluded from the Bar. Only a limited number of Jewish
doctors and lawyers were to be permitted to care exclusively for the
needs of the Jewish community.[61] The effect of all these and other
measures was to drive thousands who had managed thus far pre-
cariously to maintain themselves on to the relief rolls of the hard-
pressed charitable organisations—and, with increasing desperation,
into the queues which besieged the foreign consulates in Berlin and
other major cities.

The pace of 'aryanisations' had also very sharply quickened since
the Anschluss; in January–February 1938, only two 'aryanisations'
of large enterprises were announced in the *Jüdische Rundschau*;
this number rose to forty in May, thirty in June, sixty in July,
seventy-five in August and 235 in September. Not counted in these
totals were the takeovers or the forcing out of Jewish proprietors in
twenty-two 'non-Aryan' banks, among them such famous and long-

[59] *Verordnung über die Anmeldung jüdischen Vermögens, RGBl, I*, 414.
[60] See Genschel, *Verdrängung*, p. 167.
[61] Ibid., p. 173.

established houses as S. Bleichröder & Gebr. Arnhold, Behrens & Söhne, Wassermann, and M. M. Warburg & Co.[62] Similarly not included were the scores of smaller enterprises whose fate went unrecorded by the *Jüdische Rundschau*, or the hundreds of firms simply liquidated or taken over unofficially under the *'wilde Kommissarwirtschaft'* in Austria which continued despite the protestations of the tidy-minded Berlin bureaucracy.

There was a recrudescence of violent anti-Jewish incidents in Vienna in August 1938, and the despair of those still trapped in the city led to turbulent scenes outside the foreign consulates, as hordes of would-be emigrants competed frantically for places in queues from which the Gestapo and Nazi Party functionaries would occasionally make random and brutal arrests. British refugee organisation workers reported with horror that conditions in Vienna had become completely chaotic, with corruption rampant in all official circles. Everything was for sale, at grotesquely inflated prices : identity documents, travel tickets, Latin American passports and visas, priority numbers for queues outside foreign consulates; there was even evidence that forged British visas could be bought. The Gestapo established in August a Central Bureau for Jewish Emigration in Vienna, which under the administration of its bureau chief, Adolf Eichmann, inaugurated a system of taking bus and train-loads of refugees and simply dumping them over the nearest frontier, despite the furious protests of the neighbouring countries, all of which tightened their border controls in a vain effort to stem the flood of unwanted aliens. The central body of the Jewish community, utterly demoralised by constant Gestapo raids and threats, was forced to accelerate the pace of emigration regardless of the consequences.[63]

Bitter accusations, from which the British Passport Control Office and the Consulate General were not exempt, were made by refugees of indifference, slowness, favouritism and even anti-Semitism on the part of hard-pressed consular and clerical staffs. What was con-

[62] See Genschel, *Verdrängung*, pp. 174–175. Genschel estimates the total of enterprises 'aryanised' from the property declaration ordinance of April 26 to November 1938 at 4,000.

[63] See Eliahu ben Elissar, *La diplomatie du IIIe. Reich et les Juifs, 1933–1939* (Paris, 1969), pp. 244–245.

firmed, at least in the British case, was the overwhelming pressure of thousands of applications which at times threatened a breakdown of the entire visa system, both in the over-worked Consulates within the Reich, and at the Home Office itself. The British Consul-General in Vienna, defending his staff against charges of inefficiency and favouritism voiced by Sir Walter Citrine to the Foreign Secretary, wrote :

Considering the immense numbers of persons dealt with daily and the very trying nature of the duties involved in such dealings, the number of complaints is infinitesimal . . . Kendrick [the Passport Control Officer] tells me that his staff are so overwrought that they will burst into tears at the slightest provocation and every means must be found of easing their burden. The same applies to my own staff. . . . In order to conduct the work of the Passport Office as applicants desire, we should need a staff of 40 people and a building like the Albert Hall—but why should we incur such a burden?[64]

The introduction, under German pressure, of racial legislation into Italy in September 1938 had the effect of rendering liable to expulsion about 15,000 Jews and 'non-Aryans', of whom more than two-thirds were Germans or Austrians who had sought their first refuge in Italy.[65] Yet another source of refugees was the Free City of Danzig, where the position of Jews and 'non-Aryans' was rapidly becoming untenable under Nazi pressures, despite the League's guarantee of the Constitution which safeguarded the position of minorities there. The potential exodus from Danzig particularly embarrassed Great Britain since it was felt that refugees from Danzig would have a special claim to generous treatment in view of the British delegate's position as head of the Council of Three appointed by the League to deal with Danzig affairs. But the difficulty of doing anything even for the Danzig refugees was vividly illustrated when Lord Halifax felt it necessary to intercede personally with the Home Office, requesting as a special concession the admission of three Jewish doctors from Danzig to Great Britain. The Home Secretary replied that although the British Medical Association had opposed such admission he would be prepared to authorise it,

---

[64] Gainer to Hutcheson, August 2, 1938, FO 372/3284, T 10774/3272/378.
[65] See Perth to Ingram, September 24, 1938, FO 371/22534, W 13050/104/98.

'always provided that the other Powers concerned agree to afford similar facilities'.[66]

Even as the tide of refugees from the Reich mounted, ominous and increasingly strident threats were heard offstage from the Polish Government, which since the death of Marshal Josef Pilsudski in May 1935 had openly espoused an anti-Semitic policy whose goal was a radical decrease in Poland's Jewish population.[67] In pursuit of that policy, an internal offensive against Jewish participation in the economy was coupled with measures to force the pace of Jewish emigration; but in this enterprise the Warsaw regime had encountered a studied lack of cooperation from other governments. The Polish Government, which since the death of Marshal Josef Pilsudski in Polish Jews' : the Foreign Minister, Colonel Beck, told the American Ambassador in Warsaw that he, Beck, 'would have to try what could be done to induce the League to interest itself in this question'.[68]

Despite the demonstrably huge and growing need, it was moreover becoming increasingly evident that the spaces of British colonial territory, so vast on the world map, in fact contained virtually no room for refugees. The Colonial Office, in its official reply to the Foreign Office concerning an inquiry from the IGC, explained that the total number of settlers in the proposed Kenya scheme would not exceed 150, and that there appeared to be little prospect for refugee settlement elsewhere in the Colonial Empire.[69] Lord Winterton intervened personally with the Colonial Secretary in an attempt to secure a more favourable reply—Mr Myron C. Taylor had consistently been pressing for a full statement of the colonies' potential contribution—but none was forthcoming, beyond a reiteration of

[66] See Mallett to Under-Secretary of State, August 26, 1938, FO 371/21635, C 8415/1667/62, and Cooper to Under-Secretary of State, September 3, 1938, FO 371/21636, C 9300/1667/62.

[67] See Edward D. Wynot, Jr., ' "A Necessary Cruelty" : the Emergence of Official Anti-Semitism in Poland, 1936–1939', *The American Historical Review*, Vol. 76, No. 4 (October, 1971), pp. 1035–1058.

[68] See minutes, September 6, 1938, FO 371/22534, W 12004/104/98.

[69] Howard to Under-Secretary of State, September 10, 1938, FO 371/22534, W 12178/104/98. This letter was minuted at the Foreign Office on September 16 : 'This is most unhelpful. The tiny contribution of the Colonies to the refugee problem would only be emphasised if we cannot give the Committee more information than this.'

the assurance that the refugee question was engaging the Colonial Secretary's 'constant attention' and that 'certain projects' aside from the Kenya scheme were now being examined. The Dominions, with the exception of Australia, were equally non-committal. Australia let the Dominions Office know that she was prepared to accept up to 5,000 Jewish immigrants per year, although if they proved unable to bring with them some capital, they might not be able to qualify as immigrants under the applicable statutes. The Foreign Office was told that 'the last thing the Australian Government desired was that their good intentions should become public property'.[70]

In all the frenzied alarums and excursions which attended the Munich talks over Czechoslovakia, a suggestion transmitted by Mr Rublee of the IGC that Prime Minister Chamberlain raise the refugee question with Hitler was brushed aside after brief consideration. The proposal emanated from Myron C. Taylor, whose personal friendship with President Roosevelt brought his submission to the immediate attention of Lord Halifax. It was felt however that a reminder to Hitler 'that justice be done to the refugees in the matter of their property' would be 'quite impracticable, at any rate at the moment'. The moment was the eve of Mr Chamberlain's departure for Godesberg.[71]

The refugee organisations, for their part, were acutely aware that with the signing away of the Sudeten areas many thousands of potential refugees had come within the expanded borders of the Reich. That a German-Czechoslovak Commission was to secure the right of those leaving the Sudetenland to remove their property, and that the British representatives in Prague and Berlin would 'no doubt use their influence against any discrimination in the arrangements which may be made', was of scant comfort to the relief committees, reeling under the experience of a mass flight whose present scale already exceeded their worst forebodings.

[70] See Makins, minute, August 28, 1938, FO 371/22533, W 11092/104/98.
[71] Rublee to Winterton, September 20, 1938, FO 371/22534, W 12604/104/98.

6

A Far Away Country
September — November 1938

A fairly high percentage of the continent's population had
become quite accustomed to the thought that they were outcasts.
They could be divided into two main categories: people doomed
by the biological accident of their race and people doomed for
their metaphysical creed or rational conviction regarding the
best way to organise human welfare.[1]

THE multinational Czechoslovak state, whose position since the
Anschluss had appeared increasingly precarious, was buffeted
throughout the spring and summer months of 1938 by waves of
extremist demands from the Germans of the Sudetenland, whose
National Socialist leader, Konrad Henlein, orchestrated his violent
separatist campaign in close cooperation with Berlin. In Britain,
Prime Minister Chamberlain remained unconvinced that Czechoslovakia could in any event be defended against Germany, and
throughout the course of negotiations with Prague and Berlin British
policy was motivated by the desire 'to be done with a tiresome and
unjust source of friction and to proceed with business as usual'.[2]
Ambassador Sir Nevile Henderson, consistently exceeding his instructions in his eagerness to justify and if possible accommodate
German policy aims, undermined whatever moral authority the
British Government might still have retained by making it quite
clear to the Wilhelmstrasse that Britain would not fight to save
Czechoslovakia.

The intense German propaganda campaign of the summer

[1] Arthur Koestler, *Scum of the Earth* (London, 1968), p. 102.
[2] See Christopher Thorne, *The Approach of War, 1938-9* (London, 1967),
p. 61.

months and the steady erosion of the minimal resolve of France and Great Britain were climaxed on September 29 when a conference was held in Munich between Hitler, Mussolini, Daladier and Chamberlain. The terms agreed at Munich, after discussions conducted without agenda or minutes, in an atmosphere of indecent haste, provided for German occupation of the Sudeten area within the first ten days of October, to a frontier to be established by an International Commission composed of representatives of the conferring governments. Plebiscites were to decide the allegiance of other German-speaking areas, and concessions were also to be made by the Czechs to the Poles and Hungarians. On October 1, after intense pressures from the French and British representatives, the Czechs capitulated to the German demands and Chamberlain returned in triumph to London, having persuaded Hitler at the conclusion of their talks to sign a meaningless declaration of Anglo-German friendship, the declaration which was to have secured 'peace in our time'.

Helpless in the face of threats from her smaller neighbours who now swooped down for their share of the spoils, Czechoslovakia was forced in October and early November to cede Magyar areas in Slovakia and Ruthenia to Hungary, as well as the Teschen region—containing valuable industrial plant and coal mines—to Poland. The International Commission which was to decide questions arising out of the Munich settlement was dominated throughout its brief existence by the German Government; plebiscites which were to determine the actual frontier were never held, and by means of further threats the Reich ultimately was ceded an area almost identical with the maximum originally demanded by Hitler before Munich.

Although the extent of economic and strategic loss caused by the dismemberment of Czechoslovakia was dimly perceived at Munich, the scale of the potential exodus of new refugee groups was not. The plight of thousands trapped behind the new German frontiers—anti-Nazi Czechs and Sudeten Germans, Jews, and refugees from Germany and Austria—was simply not raised by the French and British representatives throughout the course of negotiations, and could hardly have concerned Hitler or Mussolini themselves.

When the occupation of the Sudeten areas by German troops

began on October 1, large numbers of refugees hastily fled and converged on Prague, to the alarm of the Czech authorities who feared that the presence within their shrunken frontiers of any sizeable number of German-speaking people might serve as an excuse for further intervention and territorial demands from Berlin. Thousands of anti-Nazi Sudeten Germans, whose loyalty to the Czech Republic had been publicly demonstrated, were therefore sent back to their homes in the Sudetenland despite their consequent exposure to reprisals from Henleinists and the Gestapo. Czechs who had fled from the annexed areas were accepted, though their absorption seemed doubtful after the disappearance of so many industrial enterprises and farm lands which had formerly provided their employment. A third category, composed of Jews—most of them German-speaking—who had lived in the Sudeten areas, sometimes for generations, was in a position more precarious even than that of the Sudeten Germans : their expulsion into Reich territory would mean their subjection to the entire discriminatory regime which had been the lot of their co-religionists in Germany. In most danger, however, were the approximately 5,000 refugees from Germany and Austria who had been resident in Czechoslovakia, some since 1933.[3] Many of them, as well-known Social Democrats or members of other left-wing groups, figured prominently on the wanted lists of the Gestapo, and expulsion into German territory would have been equivalent to a concentration camp sentence, or worse; others of this group were Jews or 'non-Aryans', who laboured under the disabilities of this status as well.

The refugee problem in rump Czechoslovakia was complicated and intractable not merely by reason of the confusion caused by several classes of refugees all competing for scanty relief and settlement possibilities, nor the unremitting threats from Berlin, but also because even if visas were forthcoming, and definite settlement offers made, it was frequently impossible to make the necessary travel arrangements to remove refugees from danger. The Czech railway system had been grossly mutilated by the annexations; the Polish Government was hostile and frequently made difficulties over transit

[3] See Hope Simpson, *Refugees, A Review of the Situation Since September, 1938* (London, 1939), pp. 35–40.

facilities; and travel over German-controlled roads or railways was unthinkable. Air passages, moreover, were exceedingly scarce and correspondingly expensive. Above all, what was lacking was time: the pressures on the defenceless Czech state to deliver wanted individuals to the Germans were relentless, and few refugees—particularly those who had already escaped once from the jurisdiction of the Gestapo—could rely on more than a very temporary refuge in a country which threatened daily to disintegrate altogether.

Of these several classes of refugees, the one that earliest preoccupied the British Government was composed of anti-Nazi Sudeten German Social Democrats. As early as September 21, Wenzel Jaksch, the leader of the Sudeten Social Democratic Party, appealed to the French and British Governments to come to the assistance of his followers, whose existence would be threatened by German occupation of the Sudetenland: they could not remain under a Nazi regime, and there would be no room for them in what was left of Czechoslovakia. This appeal went unheeded at Munich in the general anxiety to avoid any conflict with Germany; such issues as the fate of Sudeten anti-Nazis were among the minor points to be settled by the International Commission which was meant to oversee the detailed application of the Munich Agreement.

Jaksch came to England at the beginning of October, and with the support of Clement R. Attlee of the Labour Party addressed an appeal to the Prime Minister, asking the British Government to use its influence to have the amnesty which was granted to Sudeten German political prisoners in Czechoslovakia extended reciprocally to Sudeten German Social Democrats in areas occupied by Germany.[4] Jaksch saw Malcolm MacDonald, the Dominions and Colonial Secretary, on October 5, and pleaded that sympathetic consideration be given to the possibility of settling in the Dominions or the colonies some of the 15,000 to 20,000 refugees of his Party who he estimated would have to emigrate from Czechoslovakia. MacDonald convened a meeting of the Dominions High Commissioners[5] that same afternoon and requested them to explore with

[4] Halifax to Attlee, October 10, 1938, FO 371/21583, C 12071/11896/12.
[5] A representative of the Foreign Office was also present. See record of meeting, October 5, 1938, FO 371/21583, C 11953/11896/12.

their governments the possibility of assisting these refugees, about half of whom were skilled agricultural workers. He told the High Commissioners that

he could not help feeling that in some ways all those concerned with the recent settlement in Czechoslovakia had a greater responsibility in the matter than fell upon them, for example, in respect of the Jewish refugees in Germany and Austria.

The High Commissioners reacted cautiously to MacDonald's appeal, however, asking that the extent of the problem be further explored and pointing out that each of the Dominion governments had also to consider the problem of German and Austrian refugees.

Jaksch, who had in the meantime sent further appeals to the Prime Minister and to Sir Robert Vansittart, was told on October 6 that although the matter was of course entirely one for each Dominion Government to consider, if the magnitude of the new refugee problem could be ascertained and some machinery set up to deal with individual applications the Dominions would doubtless give would-be emigrants their sympathetic consideration.[6] When asked by the Foreign Office for his views, the British Minister in Prague responded pessimistically, stating that there were likely to be many more than 15,000 Sudeten Social Democrats who might wish to emigrate. He recommended moreover that each Dominion Government would do well to

examine each individual case with utmost care before admitting any German refugees, no matter what particular ideology they may at the moment be professing. For their herd instincts and racial instincts are liable to remain strong and provide a seeding ground for future trouble.

He went on to suggest that the United States Government be invited to help solve the problem, and asked, finally, whether the Soviet Union might not be sounded as to its willingness to 'receive Sudeten Germans into their spiritual home'.[7]

The Newton telegram, when communicated to the Dominions

[6] See Devonshire to High Commissioners, October 7, 1938, FO 371/21583, C 11953/11896/12.

[7] Newton to Foreign Office, October 8, 1938, FO 371/21583, C 11896/11896/12. Newton also suggested that Mexico might be an appropriate home for some of the Social Democrat refugees.

Office, perceptibly cooled the interest of that department in promoting any large settlement schemes for Sudeten refugees in the Dominions. A member of the Foreign Office remarked indeed that 'if it ever became known in the Dominions what line Mr Newton was taking there would be very little chance of them agreeing to take any Sudeten settlers at all'.[8] The Foreign Office felt for its part that little more could be done for these refugees until the Dominions had reacted to the proposals for settlement, proposals which the Dominion High Commissioners appeared to be forwarding to their governments without 'any marked alacrity or enthusiasm'. The Minister's suggestion that the Soviet Union be approached was rejected, since the large majority of Social Democrats 'would be almost as unhappy in Russia as in the Reich'. The United States might be involved in the solution of the problem, the Foreign Office decided, but only if the Sudeten refugees were eventually brought within the jurisdiction of the Intergovernmental Committee on Refugees.

Confusion over the numbers and status of Sudeten refugees was compounded by persistent press reports that the Czech Government, under pressure from Berlin, was going to require all non-Czech refugees—including Sudeten Germans, German and Austrian refugees, and many Jews—to return to the Reich. The alarm over these reports was sounded by Jaksch's secretary, who called on Sir Robert Vansittart on October 10 to beg that the British Ambassador in Berlin be instructed to try to dissuade the German Government from enforcing its demands for the return of refugees. Similarly, the Prague Government was to be urged to suspend its expulsions. The course of emergency action suggested had the unqualified endorsement of Vansittart, who wrote : 'it would really be a terrible piece of inhumanity and would cause wide scandal here if such a revengeful demand were to be made and the Czechs were forced to comply even with that'.[9] The British representatives in Prague and Berlin were thereupon urgently instructed to ascertain the facts, and to do everything possible to dissuade both the German and Czech authorities from proceeding with forcible return of refugees, pending the

[8] Speaight, minute, October 11, 1938, FO 371/21583, C 11896/11896/12.
[9] Vansittart, minute, October 10, 1938, FO 371/21583, C 12094/11896/12.

outcome of efforts in London to find a solution.[10] Ambassador Henderson was also instructed to press for an early agreement on the procedure by which residents in the ceded areas could opt for national status, so that non-Nazi Sudeten Germans, as well as Czechs, could choose Czech nationality if they so desired.[11]

The Foreign Office was meanwhile bombarded with letters from the National Council for Civil Liberties, the Labour Party, and other sources imploring the Government to do everything feasible to stop the forcible return of Sudeten refugees to the occupied areas. A deputation from the National Council for Civil Liberties called on the Foreign Secretary on October 19 to urge strongly that the British and Dominion Governments 'make immediate arrangements for removing large numbers of refugees from Czechoslovakia with adequate financial provision for large-scale schemes of settlement'.[12] Lord Halifax told this deputation that 'the British Government are doing everything in their power to deal with this difficult problem'.

In the bitter atmosphere of post-Munich Prague, however, what might remain in the British Government's power to alter was doubtful in the extreme. General Jan Syrovy, who had succeeded as Chief of the Czech State on October 5, clearly indicated his determination to collaborate with Germany, since no credence could henceforth be given to Anglo-French guarantees. Sir John Wheeler-Bennett, who arrived in Prague on October 10 as member of a refugee relief mission, recalled that his plea to Syrovy to grant political refugees a fortnight's immunity from expulsion so that emergency arrangements might be made for their departure, was met with stony refusal :

'Not fifteen days, not fifteen minutes,' he said. 'The Germans have asked for them and back they go.' Then, rising to his feet and bringing the interview to an end, he said. . . . 'In this affair, messieurs, we have been willing to fight on the side of the angels, now we shall hunt with the wolves.'[13]

---

[10] See Foreign Office memorandum on Sudeten German refugees, October 13, 1938, FO 371/21583, C 12240/11896/12.

[11] See Halifax to Henderson, October 13, 1938, FO 371/21583, C 12330/11896/12.

[12] The deputation consisted of Miss Eleanor Rathbone, MP, Sir Norman Angell, Sir John Hope Simpson, Mr H. G. Wells, and Mr Ronald Kidd. See communiqué, October 19, 1938, FO 371/21583, C 12337/11896/12.

[13] See Wheeler-Bennett, *Munich, Prologue to Tragedy* (London, 1948), p. 198.

The specific forms British Government assistance might take were raised by two other deputations which called at the Foreign Office on October 13. One, from the League of Nations Union, was received by the Foreign Secretary;[14] the other, of the National Council of Labour, met with R. A. Butler, Parliamentary Under-Secretary.[15] Both delegations pleaded in the strongest terms that the Czech Government should be pressed not to expel Sudeten German refugees, and the German Government not to demand their return; similarly, both stressed the inescapable moral responsibility of the French and British Governments, as parties to the Munich Agreement which led to the hasty surrender of so much Czech territory, for the safety and welfare of the refugees thus inevitably created. The National Council of Labour in addition requested that some sort of commission be established to take temporary charge of anti-Nazi Sudetens pending the development of a constructive emigration plan, and argued further that the British Government should take action in Berlin which would ensure that all the inhabitants of the Sudeten areas, whether Czech or German, should be granted the right to opt for Czech nationality. The League of Nations Union deputation went beyond this point to hold that the British Government should if necessary provide funds to maintain the refugees until they had found permanent homes. In a memorandum left at the Foreign Office, presumably drafted with the concurrence of the major refugee organisations, the League of Nations Union also recommended that temporary places of refuge in Britain, such as disused Army camps, be made available to refugees, and that they be transported out of Czechoslovakia with the assistance of the British Government. The memorandum stressed that the Government should in addition use its good offices with the Dominions to

[14] The deputation consisted of Lord Lytton, Lord Cecil and Mrs Blanche Dugdale, and represented all the major refugee organisations united in the Co-Ordinating Committee for Refugees. Record of meeting, October 14, 1938, FO 371/21584, C 12485/11896/12.
[15] This group was composed of Mr George Dallas, Chairman of the Executive Committee of the Labour Party; Mr Arthur Greenwood, MP; Mr H. V. Tewson, Acting Secretary of the General Council, Trades Union Congress; Mr J. Marchbank, Secretary of the National Union of Railwaymen; and Mr J. S. Middleton, Secretary of the Labour Party. The Duke of Devonshire and a colleague from the Dominions Office were also present. Record of meeting, October 14, 1938, FO 371/21583, C 12250/11896/12.

ensure the reception of as many refugees as possible, and should 'make their transport and settlement materially possible by a substantial financial grant'.

Lord Halifax instructed his staff to examine carefully all the points raised by his visitors, 'with a view to our rendering as much assistance and protection to these refugees as may be possible since we may be held to be under a certain moral obligation to them'. Reacting sharply to this suggestion however, R. M. Makins wrote on October 17 :

I suggest that we should not admit that His Majesty's Government has any responsibility, legal or moral, for the future of refugees from the occupied areas or from Czechoslovakia itself.[16]

The assertion that the British and French Governments bore at least some moral responsibility for the fate of the refugees from Czechoslovakia was nevertheless one that was to be repeated by virtually every one of the many groups interested in these refugees, and as the dimensions of the problem began to be grasped the Government was to find it increasingly difficult to reject this notion out of hand.

Intimately connected with the issue of moral responsibility was the entire question of financial assistance to the truncated Czech state. Many ordinary people at least had no doubt that they had been spared the horrors of war at the expense of the Czechs : they flocked in thousands to contribute to a fund established on October 5 by the Lord Mayor of London to relieve distress among those forced to leave the areas ceded to the Reich, or to the National Council of Labour's fund which was launched on October 4. The British Government for its part offered in early October to advance £10 million to the Czech Government; this sum represented a counter-offer to the Czech request immediately after Munich for a £30 million loan.[17] It was recognised in Whitehall that the advance of £10 million, which was to be repaid out of the proceeds of a loan to be subsequently floated, would enable the Treasury to insist that the money be used for purposes which the British Government

---

[16] See FO 371/21584, C 12485/11896/12.

[17] See Ian Colvin, *The Chamberlain Cabinet* (London, 1971), p. 170.

K

regarded as 'permanent and constructive', including the resettlement of refugees from the Sudeten areas.[18]

When a Czech financial mission arrived in London to discuss British aid, its members were told by Sir Frederick Leith-Ross of the Treasury that although the purposes of the £10 million advance were not limited solely to refugee relief, 'from the point of view of sentiment—and sentiment appeals to Parliaments—the thing that gets support for an advance is the humanitarian desire to help the refugees'.[19] This desire could be 'fitted in' with the Czechs' natural wish to improve their budgetary and monetary position as rapidly as possible, and to rebuild their mutilated communications network and industrial plant. Leith-Ross stressed that there should be no political or racial discrimination by the Czechs in assisting refugees from the Sudetenland, and that the Czechs should agree to maintain and not to expel such refugees 'for the two, three or four months perhaps' during which emigration outlets for them would have to be sought. The head of the Czech delegation assured the British representatives that his Government had no intention of discriminating against any class of refugees and that no decision of principle had been taken to expel Sudeten Germans, but that certainly the Czechs would be 'anxious to reduce the minorities' within their shrunken frontiers. The Czechs further acquiesced in a recommendation that they maintain Sudeten refugees for the time being, but they firmly resisted the notion that they should also make grants for emigration of refugees, pointing out that they had need of every penny of the proposed advance for their urgent reconstruction requirements, and that grants to emigrants on the scale required— estimated at a minimum of £800 per family—would swallow up a large sum which could have settled some four to five times as many Czech-speaking refugees within Czechoslovakia as German-speaking refugees overseas. The Czechs proposed therefore that if the British Government insisted that funds be provided for emigrants out of

[18] See memorandum of interdepartmental meeting on financial assistance to Czechoslovakia, October 7, 1938, FO 371/21575, C 11972/2320/12.

[19] Record of meeting, October 15, 1938, FO 371/21575, C 12939/2320/12. The meeting was attended by officials of the Treasury, Department of Overseas Trade, and the Foreign Office. The Czech delegation was composed of members of the National Bank and other major Czech banks, and the Commercial Counsellor of the Czech Embassy in London.

the advance, the British should treat such expenditure as a 'free grant' to the Czech Government. The Czechs were told that they could not be given any assurances on this point, but that 'if and when' the amount of emigration expenditure were more accurately known, their Government could raise the question again.[20]

In Prague itself meanwhile, a series of unofficial British emissaries had arrived to assess the dimensions and urgency of the Sudeten refugee problem. From the Labour Party and the Trades Union Congress came William Gillies and David Grenfell, MP, who were authorised to offer that if any of the refugees most endangered by German repatriation demands could instead be evacuated to England, their maintenance would be guaranteed by the Labour Party and TUC until their further emigration.[21] The Lord Mayor of London, accompanied by John Wheeler-Bennett and Sir Neill Malcolm—acting in a purely private capacity—flew to Prague on October 10 to investigate the situation on behalf of the Lord Mayor's Fund. They reported that about 40,000 refugees from the Sudeten areas had already fled, and that others were arriving in Czech territory at the rate of 1,500 per day. Most urgent was the question of what should be done with the German-speaking refugees, many of them Social Democrats, who despite assurances to the contrary were in many cases being expelled into German-held territory by the Czech Government. Sir Neill Malcolm wrote :

. . . it is only fair that one should recognise the extraordinarily difficult position in which the Czechoslovak Government has been placed. Broadly speaking, their attitude to me was, 'It is your nation that have placed us in this appallingly difficult position, and now you come asking us not to deal with it in the only way which we believe to be possible'. I admit that I found this a little bit difficult to answer.[22]

It was recognised in London that the danger to certain of the German refugees was now very acute, and that the British Government's standing to press the Czechs not to send refugees back into German territory was at least dubious in the absence of more con-

[20] Leith-Ross to Sargent, October 17, 1938, FO 371/21584, C 12569/11896/12.
[21] See Newton to Foreign Office, October 12, 1938, FO 371/21583, C 12135/11896/12.
[22] Malcolm, report. October 13, 1938, FO 371/21583, C 12266/11896/12.

crete steps to aid the casualties of the Munich Agreement. Following a meeting in London between Lord Halifax and David Grenfell, MP, it was decided to instruct the British Minister in Prague, while continuing to urge the Czechs to keep their German refugees, also to grant three-month British visas for up to 250 individuals in demonstrable danger, but not to members of their families. In deciding on the suitability of applicants for these visas the Minister was to be guided by Jaksch, the head of the Sudeten German Democratic Party, and his colleague Taub, the Secretary of the German Trades Union movement, who had already made a selection of priority cases from among the main body of refugees.[23] Maintenance of those refugees who came to Britain under this scheme was to be guaranteed by organisations represented on the National Council of Labour, and Mr Grenfell returned to Prague on October 19 to assist in organising the departure of refugees from Czechoslovakia. A further 100 visas were placed at the disposal of Sir Walter Layton for individuals whose immediate departure from Czechoslovakia was necessary for their protection; maintenance of these 100 was guaranteed by a fund launched by the *News Chronicle*.

In addition to making these exceptional 350 visas available, the British Government decided to attach an officer to the Legation staff in Prague, whose duties would be to 'keep in touch with the Czechoslovak authorities in regard to the expenditure of the advance made to them . . . more especially on refugee relief work', and to try to compile reliable statistics on the number of refugees.[24] The officer appointed, R. J. Stopford of the Treasury, a former member of the Runciman Mission to Czechoslovakia, was instructed to pay particular attention to the observance of the Czech Government's undertaking not to discriminate among the several classes of refugees. He was further told that since opportunities for large-scale emigration were 'virtually non-existent and the most that can be hoped for is the admission of a small number of carefully selected cases', the influence of the British Government would be 'most usefully directed to securing the settlement of as many refugees as possible in Czechoslovakia and to arranging for the return home

[23] Halifax to Newton, October 15, 1938, FO 371/21583, C 12266/11896/12.
[24] Halifax to Newton, October 20, 1938, FO 371/21583, C 12341/11896/12.

of any who are willing to go back to the Sudeten areas'.[25] The
£10 million advance from the British Government was to be
regarded as available to meet the transport costs of emigrants and
to provide them with capital sufficient to qualify them for entry
into countries which required the possession of means. It was emphasised, finally, that Stopford was not intended to have executive
control over the expenditure of the advance; his function in Prague
would be that of an 'observer' only.

One of the reasons which led to the appointment of a British
liaison officer in Prague was the difficulty of ascertaining whether
in fact German-speaking refugees were being sent back against their
will to German-occupied areas. Intense public and Parliamentary
interest in this issue had continued unabated[26] and Minister Newton
was repeatedly requested to watch the position and to report immediately if he had evidence that Germans, particularly Social Democrats, were being expelled from the new Czechoslovakia.[27] In Berlin,
Ambassador Henderson was instructed to raise the question with
the German authorities. The German Foreign Ministry denied 'most
indignantly' that the German Government had any desire to insist
on the return of any individual who did not freely wish to come
back to the Reich, and Henderson informed London that he personally had 'no doubt whatsoever . . . that this in fact represents
Herr Hitler's attitude', and that he, Henderson, was 'at a loss to
understand insistence of Herr Jaksch and others at Prague to the
contrary'. 'It is possible', the Ambassador conceded,

that German secret police may be running some stunt of their own in
respect to certain individuals or there may be some genuine misunder-

[25] See Treasury letter of appointment to Stopford, October 29, 1938, FO 371/
21575, C 13088/2320/12.

[26] In addition to a stream of Parliamentary questions from Eleanor Rathbone,
MP and others, the Foreign Office and the Prime Minister were peppered with
letters and memoranda from the League of Nations Union, the Committee for
Intellectual Liberty, and the various Labour groups. Typical of these appeals
was a letter from the Committee for Intellectual Liberty to Lord Halifax, referring to the 'moral responsibility' of Great Britain and France for the fate of
non-Nazi Sudeten Germans, and urging a special grant of public funds to
re-establish these refugees, as well as arrangements for their safe transport out
of Czechoslovakia. October 14, 1938, FO 371/21584, C 12565/11896/12.

[27] See Halifax to Newton, October 26, 1938, FO 371/21583, C 12341/
11896/12.

standing such as confusion between willingness of German Government to take back those refugees who may wish to return and insistence on their return—a very different matter.[28]

Yet another factor complicating efforts in Whitehall to grapple with the Czechoslovakia refugee crisis was the firm opposition of the Dominions Office to any British Government financial assistance to refugee migrants, on the grounds that direct financing by the United Kingdom of foreign settlement in the Dominions would be giving aliens more favourable treatment than that accorded to British migrants under the Empire Settlement Acts. The Dominions Office was highly sensitive to letters of protest it had already received from individuals in Britain whose lack of resources prevented their migration to Dominions even with assisted passages, and who objected strongly to any use of Treasury funds as a grant to facilitate emigration from Czechoslovakia.[29]

Reviewing the entire Czechoslovakia refugee problem for his colleagues on October 18, R. M. Makins of the Foreign Office wrote[30] that there had been 'a great deal of emotional assertion about these refugees' but a shortage of verified facts. Makins recommended that the class of Czechs from the occupied areas should be left to the care of the Czech Government and of private charity; Germans from these areas, both Sudetens and Jews, were 'on the same footing as refugees from Germany and Austria, and probably in a more favourable position than for example the Jews in Germany'. Those refugees, Jews and others, who had taken refuge in Czechoslovakia from Germany and Austria, and whose extradition was being demanded—or whom the Czechs wished to expel—should properly be looked after by the League High Commission for Refugees from Germany. Makins stated further :

I presume that it is not the intention to make a public admission that HM Government have taken any responsibility for the main-

---

[28] Henderson to Halifax, October 17, 1938, FO 371/21583, C 12406/11896/12.

[29] See Wiseman to Waley, November 5, 1938, FO 371/21586, C 13603/11896/12.

[30] See memorandum, Refugees in and from Czechoslovakia, October 18, 1938, FO 371/21584, C 12487/11896/12.

tenance, settlement, or future of any of these categories of refugees. To do so would be to assume a commitment of unknown dimensions.

The League of Nations Union's contentions of British responsibility for refugees appeared to be 'quite inadmissible'. Summarising his conclusions, Makins suggested among other courses of action that the refugees from Czechoslovakia should be treated 'on the same lines as other refugees and should not, as far as possible, be placed in a privileged position' : the Sudeten refugees should be assimilated to other refugees from Germany and dealt with by the IGC, while those refugees from Austria and Germany who had previously fled to Czechoslovakia should be cared for by the League High Commission. Further, until the number and type of the Sudeten refugees was accurately known, the British Government should refrain from entering into any further undertaking on their behalf, including making representations to the Dominions. Since mass emigration was unlikely, the British Government should use its influence to secure that as many refugees as possible were either 'sent home' or found homes elsewhere in Czechoslovakia.

Alluding to the special arrangements with the leaders of the Sudeten Social Democrat Party and with Sir Walter Layton, Makins advocated that visas should not henceforth 'be put at the disposal of private individuals'. The Czechs for their part should continue to be urged to allocate as much as possible of the £10 million advance to refugee relief and settlement and 'no further financial commitment should at present be accepted by HM Government in respect of refugees in Czechoslovakia'. Those refugees who were 'in imminent peril through German demands for extradition' should be allowed to enter Britain temporarily, but only if each case were individually considered and maintenance guaranteed during the stay of each refugee. 'There should not be many cases of this kind', Makins concluded.

As the Foreign Office had feared, the exceptional grant of 350 visas for refugees in special danger proved a contentious and fateful departure from previous policy. Despite this concession, the League of Nations Union continued to insist on more generosity, arguing that the number of people in immediate danger was in fact 500 and that a list of 'only slightly less urgent' cases contained 1,500 more names.[31] When queried as to whether there was any substance in the League of Nations Union's contentions, Minister Newton confirmed that at least 1,700 to 1,800 men and their families, in addition to the original list of 450[32] names compiled by Jaksch, were in 'latent' if not immediate danger of expulsion from Czechoslovakia, although at the moment the Czech Government was honouring its word not to proceed with that step. Newton added that it was impossible to estimate how long the Czechs would be able to keep these refugees, commenting that it was

hardly fair or fitting to ask Czechoslovakia which has paid such a crippling price for the peace of the world to do more in the name of humanity than we are prepared to do ourselves.

'Equally, however', Newton concluded, there seemed no reason why the British Government 'should assume more than their fair share of what should clearly be an international liability'.[33]

As the Foreign Office attempted to deal with pressures to admit more refugees from Czechoslovakia—and in particular the families of the threatened 350 men—an added difficulty arose in the form of some fifteen to twenty Communist deputies and senators who appeared on Sir Walter Layton's list. The Passport Control Officer in Prague refused to issue visas to the Communists, and was accused of obstructionism by Layton's representative in Prague; when queried, the Home Office and the Passport Control Department of the Foreign Office were all reluctant to override his objections. It was finally decided to instruct the Passport Control Officer not to exclude Communists merely on the grounds that they were Communists, but the Government did wish to retain the liberty to reject undesirables such as 'violent extremists or known agitators and propagandists'; the Passport Control Officer was therefore to refer all doubtful cases to London for instructions.[34]

[31] See Dugdale to Cadogan, October 21, 1938, FO 371/21584, C 12777/11896/12.

[32] 100 refugees from this list had been accepted by France and Finland, leaving the balance of 350 to be admitted to Great Britain.

[33] Newton to Halifax, October 25, 1938, FO 371/21584, C 12903/11896/12.

[34] Makins to Jeffes, October 25, 1938, FO 371/21585, C 12904/11896/12.

A way out of this dilemma presented itself when the British Legation in Prague learned that some eighty-two Jewish refugees, among them women and children, were marooned in desperate conditions in the no-man's-land between the occupied Sudetenland and the new Czech frontier, and that neither the Czechs nor the Germans would admit them to their respective territories Although Minister Newton expressed the fear that one result of British Government assistance for these unfortunates might be to encourage the Germans to expel further Jews across the frontier, the Passport Control Officer succeeded in persuading Sir Walter Layton's representative that some of these most urgent cases should be substituted for names on the *News Chronicle* list of 100. This course of action was approved in London, where it was noted that if it were clearly understood that no increase beyond 100 visas would be permitted, some of the no-man's-land cases could be accommodated, and thus the British Government would 'be spared the necessity for bringing in the Communists . . . to many of whom we should probably have had to object'.[35]

Once it had been decided who the recipients of the precious 350 visas were to be, discussion arose as to responsibility for their maintenance in England. Sir Walter Layton called at the Treasury on October 26 to ask if the Government could help by providing funds for the maintenance of these refugees, since both the *News Chronicle* fund of £40,000 and the Lord Mayor's Fund of some £220,000 had been collected primarily to assist the Czechs, and there was some doubt—particularly on the part of the Lord Mayor—as to how far the subscribers would wish to see their money spent on refugees who had already left Czechoslovakia. Sir Walter followed this move by writing to Lord Halifax to ask urgently for a decision on British Government financial assistance.[36] Commenting on the entire constellation of issues presented by the 350 admissions, R. M. Makins wrote on October 27 :

. . . it is now being argued that because HMG have let in 350, they have thereby accepted special responsibility in the case of Czech refu-

[35] See Newton to Halifax, October 26, 1938, and Makins, minute, October 27, 1938, FO 371/21585, C 12986/11896/12.

[36] See Leith-Ross, note, October 26, 1938, FO 371/21585, C 12940/11896/12, and Layton to Halifax, October 28, 1938, FO 371/21585, C 13136/11896/12.

gees and they may therefore be pressed (1) to contribute to the maintenance of the 350 and (2) to admit further groups of refugees in the same manner and to maintain them. This argument will be reinforced by the fact that there has been trouble in the Co-ordinating Committee largely owing to shortage of funds . . . the Home Office doubt whether further funds will be forthcoming from private sources, or whether the charitable organisations will be prepared to extend their commitments to include refugees from Czechoslovakia. They will say that this is a political question in which HMG has, or ought to have, assumed responsibility. I agree with the Home Office in thinking that such an attitude should be firmly resisted. If we once depart from the principle that public money is not to be spent on the relief and the settlement of aliens a precedent will have been set for a commitment of unknown magnitude. There is no reason for treating Czech refugees differently from German, Austrian or Basque refugees, or from other groups of refugees who may wish to come from other countries to England in the future. It will moreover reasonably be objected that public money is being expended on aliens which should be expended on our own people. We have sailed very near the wind in requesting the Czechs to allot part of the £10,000,000 advance to refugee relief and settlement, though this case is distinguishable on the ground that the advance will become a loan and therefore Czech money. Apart, therefore, from our efforts to promote emigration and the special measures which have been taken, i.e. (1) admission of urgent cases; (2) £10,000,000 advance; (3) appointment of Mr Stopford, I do not consider that we ought to be driven, by the pressure of a small number of individual organisations, to depart from the policy which has been pursued in the case of Austrian and other refugees, or from the practice that public money cannot be made available for the relief and emigration of aliens. . . .[37]

Public concern, which was not confined exclusively to the 'small number of individual organisations' to which Makins referred, found repeated expression in Parliament, where Harold Macmillan, MP took the lead in forming a group of Members concerned with refugees from Czechoslovakia, and sheltered some forty refugees in his Sussex home.[38] A series of Parliamentary exchanges culminated in a debate on November 1, in which the Prime Minister, in an effort to meet the growing clamour for extra generosity, announced that the Government would now be willing to admit the families of the

[37] FO 371/21585, C 12940/11896/12.
[38] See H. Macmillan, *Winds of Change, 1914–1939* (London, 1966), p. 587.

350 refugees temporarily permitted to enter Britain, if guarantees for their maintenance could also be obtained. Despite the interjection from Miss Rathbone of 'Why only 350?' Mr Chamberlain went on to refer to the despatch of Mr Stopford to Prague and the advance of £10 million to the Czech Government as additional positive steps and he invited the assistance of other governments in solving a question which concerned 'the world as a whole'. 'Great Britain', he concluded, was 'not a country which has the area or the opportunity for settling a large number of emigrants'.[39] The Prime Minister's statement was to define for some months the outer limits of British Government effort on behalf of refugees from Czechoslovakia.

The public debate over assistance to refugees from Czechoslovakia tended to overshadow a full-scale crisis which had meanwhile arisen behind the scenes in relations between the Home Office and the major refugee organisations. These bodies, overwhelmed by the magnitude of their task and the inadequacy of the resources available to deal with it, now threatened to collapse entirely under the strain.

On October 18, the Co-Ordinating Committee for Refugees addressed a memorandum to the Home Office stating flatly that

in recent months it has become absolutely clear to all the bodies doing case work that there has been a complete breakdown, on the official side, of the policy of selected immigration through the approved voluntary organisations.[40]

As evidence for this assertion, the memorandum revealed that the German Jewish Aid Committee alone had over 1,500 visa applications pending at the Home Office, some dating back to June 1938, and that meanwhile many visas had been granted to refugees on the strength of invitations to visit or offers of employment which often proved short-lived, thus causing the refugees ultimately to fall back on the voluntary organisations for maintenance. The Co-Ordinating Committee warned that it could no longer perform its present functions unless given a Government grant to enable it to augment its staff, and to support the case work committees for

---

[39] See 340 H.C. Deb., 66–79.
[40] Ormerod to Winterton, October 18, 1938.

domestic servants and nurses which it had established at the request of the Home Office; it could not in any event establish a Vienna office without Government subsidy. The Committee urged further that the Home Office issue a clear statement of policy on the admission, absorption and employment of refugees, and that it adhere to its original undertaking to act through the Co-Ordinating Committee on refugee visa applications.

Following upon this step, Mrs Mary Ormerod, Secretary of the Co-Ordinating Committee, Mr Otto M. Schiff, and Lord Bearsted of the Council for German Jewry met at the Home Office on October 20 with Lord Winterton, Sir Ernest Holderness and a colleague.[41] The representatives of the refugee organisations outlined the dimensions of the crisis—the German Jewish Aid Committee alone had 3,000 Austrian refugees on its relief rolls, of whom only 10 per cent had been sponsored by an approved committee before their admission to Britain—and reiterated their inability to plan for the future of refugees whose circumstances had not previously been investigated by them. Winterton replied frankly that 'the Home Office was in a desperate position owing to the great flood of applications which were pouring in daily to the Aliens Department'; under these circumstances arrears in work had become inevitable, but there had not been a breakdown on the official side, as alleged by the Co-Ordinating Committee. Winterton cautioned that some refugee applicants would still have to be considered without consultation with the refugee organisations, particularly where Members of Parliament wrote personally on their behalf : 'it was a constitutional necessity to deal with these cases as speedily as possible.'

Turning to the question of the proposed Vienna refugee office, Schiff stated that such an office was entirely necessary but that the Co-Ordinating Committee simply could not afford to establish it out of its own resources; Mrs Ormerod went further to assert on behalf of all the bodies represented on the Co-Ordinating Committee that 'they were not prepared to allow their funds to be used for administrative purposes but only for direct relief'. Lord Winterton thereupon declared unequivocally that a Government grant in

[41] See Williamson, memorandum, October 25, 1938.

aid for the Committee's work would be 'a political impossibility'. Parliament would have to approve such a grant, there would be public discussion and

an immediate outcry from all anti-alien and anti-Semitic elements in this country that the Government were subsidising the admission of aliens at a time when there was widespread unemployment and economic distress among our own people;

one danger which must at all costs be averted was that of 'stirring up anti-alien and anti-Semitic feeling in the United Kingdom'. Although the refugee committee representatives concurred in this view, Mrs Ormerod warned again that without a Government grant the Co-Ordinating Committee might break down.

Shortly thereafter, on October 26, the Co-Ordinating Committee returned to the Home Office a mass of correspondence dealing with visa applications, thus compelling the Aliens Department to modify its procedures and henceforth to sift applications itself for despatch to the appropriate case-work committees, instead of forwarding them *en bloc* to the Co-Ordinating Committee for classification.[42] The Co-Ordinating Committee took steps, several days later, to restrict its activities, advising the Home Office formally that it would not be able to establish a Vienna office, nor henceforth to make preliminary enquiries into visa applications such as the Home Office had for several months been referring to it. The Committee made it plain that it was taking this action only because it had become impossible for it to finance its extended activities in the absence of a Home Office grant.[43]

The official withdrawal of the Co-Ordinating Committee from assisting in the complex task of vetting candidates for admission to Britain from among thousands of applicants added inevitably to the burdens of the Aliens Department, already struggling with massive arrears in its work. But worse was to come : on October 29, Mr Otto M. Schiff and his Vice-Chairman called at the Home Office to report that the German Jewish Aid Committee was reaching the danger point of near-collapse.[44] The Committee had for

[42] See Cooper, minute, October 27, 1938.
[43] See Ormerod to Winterton, October 28, 1938, and Winterton to Ormerod, October 31, 1938.
[44] See Cooper, minute, October 29, 1938.

some time been registering some hundred new cases a day, of whom eighty-five to ninety were refugees from Austria, many destitute or nearly so, who could neither be employed in Britain nor emigrated overseas; the Committee had been paying out approximately £3,000 weekly in relief and £1,000 a week for emigration work, and was nearing the end of its physical and financial resources. The Committee representatives suggested that the time had come for a temporary halt in admission of refugees to Britain, until those in the country had either been assimilated or emigrated. This proposed course would doubtless distress Mr Rublee of the Intergovernmental Committee, but 'the breathing space thus afforded would enable the Home Office and the Committees to examine the whole problem afresh'; admissions could be resumed later 'provided a definite policy were worked out'. Schiff considered that his Committee could most hopefully concentrate its efforts on the admission of children for education, young people for training with a view to emigration, domestic servants and nurses, and industrialists with capital, together with selected skilled artisans they might bring with them. Schiff declared emphatically in conclusion that his Committee could not in any circumstances accept responsibility for refugees from Czechoslovakia; this new refugee problem had in his view been created largely through British Government policy, and he suggested that refugees of every category coming from Czechoslovakia should apply for help to the newly-formed British Committee for Refugees from Czechoslovakia.

Faced with this situation, the Home Office reluctantly contemplated the imposition of a visa requirement on holders of Czech passports, for the same reasons as had earlier prompted the requirement for holders of German and Austrian passports: the need somehow to regulate the flood of refugees at the source.[45]

Manifestly, Great Britain alone could not expect to solve the problem of refugees from Czechoslovakia. In efforts to inter-

---

[45] See Holderness to Mallett, November 2, 1938: 'My Department is so overwhelmed with cases of Austrian and German refugees that further work which might arise from a visa requirement for Czechs is dreadful to contemplate but I feel that this requirement is more or less inevitable and must be faced'. FO 371/21586, C 13325/11896/12. The visa requirement was imposed on holders of Czech passports on April 1, 1939.

nationalise a possible solution, the Foreign Office noted that Sir Neill Malcolm, High Commissioner for Refugees from Germany, was authorised only to intervene on behalf of those Germans or Austrians who had originally taken refuge in Czechoslovakia and now had again to leave; refugees from the Sudetenland did not come within his mandate since they had never held German citizenship. Any question of extending the High Commissioner's powers to deal with refugees from the Sudeten areas would depend on arrangements made for the exercise of the nationality option under the Munich Agreement; this issue could not in any event usefully be raised before the January 1939 meeting of the League Council. It was also observed at the Foreign Office that the High Commissioner was experiencing growing difficulties in making any representations whatsoever on behalf of refugees. R. M. Makins ascribed the High Commissioner's decreasing effectiveness to growing anti-Semitism and a decline in the authority of the League itself. He concluded that the increasing pressures on Jews in Central and Eastern Europe and the resistance of governments to any intervention on questions which they regarded as strictly internal were to be regarded as 'inevitable consequences of the Munich Agreement' and were 'hardly susceptible of treatment through action by HMG or the League, unless and until the process of appeasement has developed rather further than it has at the present moment'.[46]

The Director of the Intergovernmental Committee on Refugees proposed for his part on October 26 that refugees of German origin from the Sudeten areas be assimilated to other German and Austrian refugees, thus coming within the scope of the IGC's activities.[47] This suggestion was under discussion throughout the month of November, but was cast into the background by the far more important issue of Rublee's hoped-for visit to Berlin to discuss with the German authorities emigration schemes and their financing.

Concern over possible offence to German sensibilities led to the elaborate consideration in a series of meetings with Foreign and Home Office officials of the precise form an approach to Berlin

[46] See Makins, minute, November 8, 1938, FO 371/22536, W 14815/104/98.
[47] See IGC Memorandum No. L.I.C. 13, October 26, 1938, FO 371/22536, W 14354/104/98 and Butler to Malcolm, November 18, 1938, FO 371/22536, W 14816/104/98.

might take, and which intrepid explorer from the IGC would first attempt the descent on Berlin.[48] President Roosevelt's impatience over the lack of IGC action was reflected in a personal telegram he sent to the Prime Minister on October 5, reminding Chamberlain that his 'personal contact with Chancellor Hitler' gave Chamberlain an opportunity to raise the possibility that the German Government would permit refugees to take with them some of their property.[49] Replying, the Prime Minister assured Roosevelt that he shared his anxiety over the refugee problem, and suggested that the American and British Ambassadors in Berlin should approach the German Government and jointly take soundings on the possibility of an early visit to Berlin by Mr Rublee.[50] The substance of the President's telegram was transmitted to Ambassador Henderson, but Henderson's response after he had called on the German Foreign Ministry was discouraging in the extreme : the State Secretary at the Wilhelmstrasse had seen little point in establishing contact with a body such as the IGC 'in a world where every country was a producer and none a consumer of Jews'.[51] Henderson was nonetheless instructed, provided his American colleague received similar ininstructions, to return to the charge lest the German Government take a final decision not to receive Rublee. The German authorities continued to procrastinate, however, even going so far as to hint that their reluctance to grant Rublee an audience was connected with doubts as to the purity of his Aryan descent. Even after the British Embassy was assured that Mr Rublee 'judging by his known ancestry and his appearance is unquestionably of good Anglo-Saxon stock . . . his mother was called Hopkins', and presumably transmitted this crucial information to the Wilhelmstrasse, the German authorities refused to budge from their stubborn insistence that 'reports were being awaited from the competent Government departments'. [52] There the proposed Rublee visit was to rest until the

[48] See note of meeting, October 5, 1938, FO 371/22535, W 13305/104/98.

[49] Roosevelt to Chamberlain, October 6, 1938, FO 371/22535/W 13303/104/98.

[50] Chamberlain to Roosevelt, October 7, 1938, ibid. Copies of the exchange of telegrams were sent to all the Dominion Prime Ministers.

[51] Henderson to Halifax, October 18, 1938, FO 371/32535, W 13860/104/98.

[52] Ogilvie-Forbes to Halifax, November 7, 1938, FO 371/22536, W 14859/104/98. See also Wilson to Hull, *FRUS*, 1938, Vol. I, 824.

entire situation turned disastrously worse following the organised pogrom of November 9–10.

In the absence of any evidence from Berlin that its Director would actually be permitted to negotiate an orderly migration from Germany, the IGC occupied itself with elaborating capital transfer schemes, and with pressing its member governments without signal success for statistical statements of their willingness to accept refugees. A bizarre note was added to discussions between the Treasury, Board of Trade, and the IGC on capital transfer possibilities when a Lieutenant-Commander Godman of the Royal Naval Reserve inserted himself as uninvited intermediary, on the strength of his alleged important contacts in Nazi circles, particularly with Göring, to whose first cousin he was reportedly married. Although the Berlin Chancery reported on October 4 that Godman was a man of 'forthright, not to say violent temperament' and remarked that the IGC should be able to find 'a more reliable and level-headed intermediary', he appears not to have been eliminated from his self-appointed rôle until November 7, when he turned up in Berlin with a scheme to entertain Rublee and Dr Hjalmar Schacht in his Berlin flat, and produced a photograph of himself with Sir Oswald Mosley to demonstrate his *bona fides* to the incredulous British Embassy.[53]

The substance of the scheme which ultimately emerged from intensive IGC–Treasury talks was a proposal that emigrants should be permitted to export German goods to Great Britain and receive the sterling proceeds from the sale of these goods, which would be outside the Anglo-German Payments Agreement. This scheme foundered however on the unyielding opposition of the Board of Trade, which pointed out that the proposal would discriminate against British holders of blocked marks in favour of refugees. A personal appeal by Lord Halifax to Oliver Stanley, President of the Board of Trade—made at the urgent request of Lord Winterton, who was

---

[53] See Kirkpatrick to Makins, November 7, 1938, FO 371/22536, W 14808/104/98. Godman was nevertheless paid £200 for 'expenses' he incurred in trying to arrange Rublee's visit to Berlin. In February 1939, Godman demanded a further £500 from the IGC, threatening suit if his claim were denied: after taking legal advice Lord Winterton rejected Godman's demand. See correspondence on FO 371/24101, W 3232/3232/48.

L

being harried by Rublee for evidence of concrete British initiatives
to help release refugees' property—failed to budge the Board, even
though Halifax argued overriding political considerations, including
the strengthening of Anglo-American relations, and went so far as
to suggest that the British Government by playing its part in the
Evian meeting and the formation of the IGC had 'assumed at any
rate partial responsibility for finding a solution to the problem'.[54]

Since the Board of Trade continued its refusal to countenance
the export scheme, the IGC Director himself evolved a plan
in which the international Jewish boycott of German goods would
be lifted if the Germans agreed to apply to the transfer of refugees'
property 50 per cent of the foreign exchange proceeds of the increased German exports which it was estimated would result from
withdrawal of the boycott. Although this proposal struck the
Treasury as 'Utopian and impracticable', in the prevailing crisis
atmosphere it was seriously considered along with other schemes
only marginally less unlikely.[55]

Through its Director the IGC also exerted consistent pressure on
the British Government, as a great colonial power, to explore settlement possibilities on a scale commensurate with refugee needs, and
to state the numbers of refugees it would be prepared to receive,
assuming that the problem of financing refugee migration could be
solved.[56] Lord Winterton wrote personally to the Colonial Secretary
on October 18 to convey some notion of the pressures to which
Rublee was subjecting him in their continuing series of discussions
on 'the subject of numbers': Rublee considered that as far as
colonies were concerned, the British contribution—Palestine always
excepted—had been very poor, and Winterton confessed that he
felt himself 'superficially, though not actually' in 'a somewhat weak
position having regard to the vast amount of colonial territory
under the administration of the Colonial Office'.[57] In a rejoinder
of some asperity, the Colonial Secretary assured Lord Winterton

[54] See Halifax to Stanley, November 3, 1938, FO 371/22535, W 13673/
104/98, and Stanley to Halifax, November 22, 1938, FO 371/22538, W 15482/
104/98.

[55] See Waley to Pinsent, November 9, 1938, FO 371/22536, W 14806/104/98.

[56] Rublee to Winterton, October 7, 1938, FO 371/22535, W 13405/104/98.

[57] Winterton to MacDonald, October 18, 1938, FO 371/22535, W 13882/
104/98.

that his department was doing its utmost to induce colonial governments to make the maximum possible contribution toward a solution of 'this overwhelming and almost insoluble problem'. Many colonies however were unsuited climatically to European immigration; others, such as the West Indies, were already over-populated. In Africa, the existence of large native populations made any large settlement of aliens undesirable. There was a small experimental settlement in Kenya; but in Northern Rhodesia, news of such a proposed scheme 'aroused very strong feeling amongst the Unofficial Members of the Legislative Council', feeling which had now abated only because the Unofficial Members had 'the impression that the project is dead'. The Colonial Office for its part regarded the scheme as merely 'in abeyance' pending the result of the Kenya experiment, and would shortly recircularise colonial governors, who were being encouraged to take 'as sympathetic a view as possible of the situation'. Finally, as far as Palestine was concerned, immigration on a restricted scale of about 12,000 per year was to be permitted for another six months; what would happen at the end of that period it was 'quite impossible to say'.[58]

The Dominions, whose interest in refugees from Czechoslovakia threatened to recede entirely in face of the difficulties of selecting and transporting migrants, were also pressed by the IGC to indicate specifically how many refugees they would receive. In London, the Dominions Office would only reiterate its willingness to act as a channel of communication between the Dominions themselves and the various organisations attempting in Prague and elsewhere to organise emigration. Rublee was compelled to content himself with collecting a file of repeated assurances of Dominions sympathy and of the British Government's readiness to use its good offices vis-à-vis the Dominions in the refugee cause.[59]

While the IGC and the League High Commission continued to elaborate emigration plans which had ever more tenuous connections with the inescapable reality—that doors all over the world were

[58] MacDonald to Winterton, November 9, 1938, FO 371/22536, W 14805/104/98.
[59] A spokesman of the Dominions Office told R. M. Makins on October 27 that the Dominions 'were only interested in Germans, not in Jews or Czechs'. See Makins, minute, October 27, 1938, FO 371/21585, C 13106/11896/12.

firmly shut to anyone without means—the position of Jews and 'non-Aryans' in German territory drastically deteriorated. Mr Wilfred Israel, a representative of the Jewish community in Germany, told the British Embassy on October 14 that the position of the community was 'rapidly becoming desperate'; a general breakdown was inevitable unless 100,000 individuals could be emigrated each year in the next four years. He expressed the opinion that the septuagenarian Mr Rublee had insufficient energy or initiative to cope with the crisis; what was urgently required was an 'energetic personality' to come directly to Berlin and organise the proposed migration. The British Government could help by making available camps for temporary asylum pending further emigration. In response to his urgent pleas, Israel was told that no immediate action could be taken on his proposals in advance of the planned Rublee visit to Berlin.[60]

Pressures on the British Government mounted, meanwhile, from yet another quarter : from the Polish Government. The Counsellor of the Polish Embassy called at the Foreign Office on October 28 to insist that the Jewish question for Poland was more than pressing : 'it was becoming intolerable.' Although the Counsellor was informed that immigration possibilities in the British colonial Empire were distinctly limited, he repeated that the Polish Government was compelled to keep approaching the British authorities on this subject, since for Poland 'the question of finding an outlet for her Jews was one of vital necessity'.[61] The Polish Government refused however to wait for other governments to indicate willingness to accept its 'surplus' Jews : it moved unilaterally to deprive of their Polish nationality thousands of Poles, mostly Jewish, who were resident outside Poland.

By a decree of October 6, 1938, all Polish passports were recalled for inspection, and the stamp validating them for return to Poland was liable to be withheld if the passport holder had lost Polish citizenship or had given some cause for his denationalisation. This sweeping decree and its designedly illiberal interpretation by Polish consular officials abroad confronted thousands of Polish Jews living

---

[60] Makins, minute, October 14, 1938, FO 371/22535, W 13823/104/98.
[61] See Bagallay, minute, October 28, 1938, FO 371/21636, C 13206/1667/62.

outside Poland, many of them in Germany, with the threat of statelessness. The Berlin authorities swiftly seized this opportunity to rid themselves of unwanted *Ostjuden*—some of them resident in Germany since World War I or before—by ordering them summarily to return to Poland. After more than 6,000 Jews had reluctantly returned to Poland, where they faced the bleak prospect of subsistence on the charity of the impoverished local Jewish community, some 15,000 of those who had not moved of their own accord were arrested and then simply dumped at the Polish frontier after mass train transports had delivered them to the limits of Reich territory. The Polish Government refused however to admit more than a portion of this group on the grounds that they had forfeited their Polish nationality, and flung them back into the no-man's-land on the Polish-German border. Over 7,000 of those expelled from both countries lived for months in disused stables, tents and cellars in the no-man's-land hamlet of Zbonszyn, their bare existence sustained by a meagre trickle of foodstuffs which had to be smuggled across to them by charitable organisations.[62]

Among those deported to Zbonszyn were the parents of a seventeen-year-old Polish Jew named Herschel Grynszpan. His deranged quest for revenge led him on November 7 to shoot and fatally wound the Third Secretary of the German Embassy in Paris. This deed was the signal and official excuse for the organised pogrom which swept Germany and Austria on November 9–10—*Kristallnacht*, as it came to be called—and triggered the final desperate pre-war wave of flight from the Reich.

[62] The Polish Government reluctantly admitted those who had survived the rigours of Zbonszyn only in July 1939. In the meanwhile, a fortunate few of the children had been rescued and permitted to enter Britain, among other countries. See *Survey of International Affairs*, 1938, II, 330–331.

7

Kristallnacht and After
November 1938 — March 1939

The Pogroms in Germany and the persecutions there have
roused much indignation everywhere. I must say Hitler never
helps, and always makes Chamberlain's task more difficult.[1]

In the course of November 7, 1938, young Herschel Grynszpan
called at the German Embassy in Paris and fired with a concealed
pistol at the first German diplomat to receive him : Third Secretary
Ernst vom Rath. Attended by Hitler's personal physician, vom
Rath survived only until November 8. His death was seized upon
by the Nazi press as tangible proof of the existence of a wide-
ranging international Jewish conspiracy against Germany. Inspired
by the propaganda outcry, groups of Nazi enthusiasts made relatively small-scale and uncoordinated attacks on Jews and Jewish property in Kurhessen and Magdeburg-Anhalt in the evening of November 8. The following evening, Propaganda Minister Goebbels told a
group of Nazi Party leaders in Munich that Hitler had decided that
if riots continued to spread throughout the Reich, they were not
to be interfered with. The Party leaders, who had for years been
chafing under the official restraints against 'wilde Aktionen', required
no further encouragement to orchestrate and set into operation the
systematic violence which became notorious as Kristallnacht, the
night of broken glass.

In the night of November 9–10, SA and other formations, working with great speed, stormed Jewish synagogues, dwellings and
business enterprises all over the Reich. Shops were plundered and

[1] Sir Henry Channon, Chips, The Diaries of Sir Henry Channon (London
1967), p. 177.

smashed, schools and charitable institutions attacked, thousands of individuals assaulted, and 20,000 arrested, of whom most were sent to concentration camps. Ninety-one persons were killed. The material results of *Kristallnacht* were 177 synagogues destroyed, 7,500 shops plundered, and insured damage amounting to RM 25 million. The total of property destroyed was estimated at several hundred millions of Reichsmarks. The damage to window glass alone was estimated at RM 3 million; replacing all the smashed glass would have required purchase of half the entire annual production of the Belgian glass industry, a fact which considerably upset Göring, who remarked that he wished two hundred Jews had been killed rather than have so much property destroyed.[2] By the evening of November 10, Goebbels issued a proclamation calling a halt to the pogrom, and warning that the final answer to the 'murderous Jewish assault in Paris' would be given the Jews by means of legislative decrees.

A conference was convened under the chairmanship of Field-Marshal Göring on the morning of November 12, at which detailed measures for the elimination of Jews and 'non-Aryans' from the Reich economy were agreed.[3] Recognising that the effect of these measures would be the complete impoverishment and isolation of the Jewish community, Göring speculated at the end of the conference that in the event of war a final 'settling of accounts with the Jews' would have to be carried out. Hitler would then be in a position to say to those countries which had continually raised the Jewish question : 'What are you always talking about the Jews for? Take them!'[4]

In the three weeks following the Göring conference, a series of decrees was issued which succeeded in achieving the goal of segregating and expropriating the Jewish community. The first, issued on November 12, levied a collective fine of one billion Reichsmarks

[2] See Genschel, *Verdrängung*, p. 183, and Lionel Kochan, *Pogrom, 10 November 1938* (London, 1957).

[3] Present at the conference were Economics Minister Funk, Propaganda Minister Goebbels, Finance Minister von Krosigk, Foreign Ministry, SS and other officials as well as representatives of the German insurance companies. For a detailed description of the meeting, see Genschel, *Verdrängung*, pp. 180–186.

[4] Göring also suggested that rich Jews could buy some large territory in North America or elsewhere for their co-religionists. Ibid., p. 185.

(approximately £84 million) on the German Jewish community, to 'expiate' the crime of vom Rath's murder. Another regulation of the same date directed Jewish owners or occupants to repair at their own expense all damage done to their shops and houses; their insurance claims were declared forfeit to the State. The terms of a further ordinance, for the elimination of Jews from the German economy,[5] forbade Jews and 'non-Aryans' to function from January 1, 1939 as managers of businesses, agents or artisans.[6] Any Jews remaining in managerial positions could be dismissed at six weeks' notice, without further claim to pension or other rights. In swift succession, other discriminatory decrees were issued forbidding Jews to frequent places of public entertainment; withdrawing permission for them to own or operate motor vehicles; depriving them, with but few exceptions, of any rights to public assistance; and, finally, empowering local authorities to impose regional curfews and limitation of physical movement on Jews.[7]

The most important of the post-*Kristallnacht* measures was the decree of December 3 on the use of Jewish property,[8] which laid down in concrete terms the policy merely hinted at in the April 1938 decree concerning registration of Jewish property. The December 3 decree established the basis for 'aryanising' all remaining Jewish property, by empowering the 'aryanisation' authorities to demand the winding up or alienation of any Jewish-owned enterprise on terms which might at the discretion of the authorities include the payment of a special levy to the Reich. Pending a complete removal of the Jewish owner, an 'Aryan' trustee could be installed, at the owner's expense, to preside over the liquidation of the enterprise. Further regulations under this decree established rules for the sale of Jewish-owned agricultural land, other real estate, and such intangible property as patent rights, capital participations or rights to rental income. Jews were further required,

---

[5] *Verordnung zur Ausschaltung der Juden aus dem deutschen Wirtschaft,* *RGBl,* 1938, I, 1580. Text in Genschel, *Verdrängung,* p. 300.

[6] Jewish employers were ordered nevertheless to continue paying their employees until December 31, 1938, when all businesses would be taken over by 'Aryan' managers.

[7] See Genschel, *Verdrängung,* pp. 187–188.

[8] *Verordnung über den Einsatz jüdischen Vermögens, RGBl,* 1938, I, 1709. Text in Genschel, *Verdrängung,* pp. 301–306.

within a week from publication of the decree, to deposit all their securities, jewels or art objects in designated banks; such properties were henceforth to be sold only to Reich purchase agencies, and solely with official approval.

It was recognised by foreign observers that these decrees and regulations were clearly designed to grind Jews and 'non-Aryans' down to a bare subsistence level, if that. Moreover, the wave of Gestapo raids and arrests was continuing, and thousands of potential victims were wandering about the streets or hiding in the woods afraid to return to their homes. Sir George Ogilvie-Forbes reported from Berlin on November 16 that hundreds of Jews, in desperation, were smuggling themselves over the frontiers, and that the suicide rate had 'alarmingly increased'. Summarising his observations, Ogilvie-Forbes stated that

the civilised world is confronted with the sight of over 500,000 people deliberately excluded from all trades and professions, and consequently unable to earn a living. They dwell in the grip and at the mercy of a brutal oligarchy which fiercely resents all humanitarian foreign intervention. Misery and despair are already there, and, when their resources are either denied to them or exhausted, their end will be starvation.[9]

The climate of terror throughout the Reich was in fact paralleled only by that which had obtained in Vienna in the first days following the Anschluss.

Aware of this background, George Rublee of the Intergovernmental Committee on Refugees reported to Washington that the refugee situation had worsened dramatically since his Committee had been called into being. So many refugees had illegally crossed the frontiers of countries bordering Germany that the local authorities of those countries had resorted to *refoulement* on a large scale, shipping refugees indiscriminately back to Germany, where many were immediately arrested and sent to concentration camps. As far as countries of final settlement were concerned, the United States continued to maintain its rigid quota, and Great Britain was admitting immigrants at a monthly rate equal to the one at which immigrants were being admitted to the United States. The damaging

[9] See Ogilvie-Forbes to Halifax, November 16, 1938, *DBFP*, III, 277.

nature of this admission, in view of the disparity in size between the United States and Great Britain, appears to have been overlooked in Washington.[10] But throughout the world doors had been 'systematically closed' since the Evian meeting. Rublee added that he had discussed possible openings with representatives of the Dominions, of Latin American countries and of the large colonial empires, but had met everywhere with negative answers. He concluded bleakly :

new laws and decrees are going into effect each week which render the position of the involuntary emigrant more difficult. The process of infiltration is wholly arrested in many places where it was active previously. New places of settlement have not been opened up, with certain exceptions so limited as not to be worthy of being taken into consideration . . . the only constructive indication I have received is that some of the governments of the countries of settlement might be willing to reconsider the situation should I be successful in persuading the German Government to permit the involuntary emigrants to leave with substantial amount of property.[11]

Reactions in Britain to the events of *Kristallnacht* and after were swift, and virtually unanimous in condemnation of the persecution. Detailed press reports of violence, destruction of property, and the threat of massive expulsions, led to a widespread anti-German response in which there was little difference between those who were supporters or opponents of the Government's appeasement policies.[12] Although the British Government was well aware of the unfortunate effect of the persecution on Anglo-German relations, the Foreign Office advised that any intervention or public protest could only make matters worse, both for the German Jews and for British Jews with interests in Germany, whose rights would be difficult enough to protect under the circumstances. In a minute written on November 10, R. M. Makins stated that any possible British Government action seemed limited to 'a vigorous declaration that Jews who are British subjects and their property will be protected'. Discussing the

[10] By the spring of 1939, the United States quota for immigrants of German and Czech origin was filled for from four to six years ahead. See Wyman, *Paper Walls*, p. 37.

[11] Rublee to Hull, November 14, 1938, *FRUS*, 1938, I, 821.

[12] See Andrew Sharf, *The British Press & Jews Under Nazi Rule* (London. 1964), pp. 171–174.

refugee question, Makins observed that the German Government's measures had served to make Jewish immigrants 'from the economic point of view less acceptable', and that the countries of both temporary refuge and settlement were in any case less disposed than ever to accept Jewish refugees. 'It is very doubtful,' he added, 'whether an increase in the number of Jewish immigrants into the United Kingdom would be welcomed by the Home Office.'[13]

The limitations on British Government action were also recognised by the Jewish organisations and others concerned with refugees. These groups were nonetheless convinced that the acute emergency required departures from certain policies which were now clearly inadequate to meet the threatened mass exodus from the Reich. On November 15, a deputation from the Council for German Jewry[14] called on the Prime Minister to stress the heightened anxiety which was felt for the fate of the German Jewish community. Acting as spokesman, Viscount Samuel acknowledged that diplomatic action 'was probably neither feasible nor likely to be effective'. As to the possibility of admitting more refugees from Germany to Great Britain, ' the Council recognised the difficulties of the Government, and they would not think of suggesting that the doors should be widely thrown open'. Nevertheless, in the present emergency the Council was urging the Government to consider permitting the entry into Britain of children and young people up to the age of 17. The Jewish organisations would give a collective guarantee that no public funds would be expended on these children, who would be educated and trained with a view to ultimate re-emigration. Samuel also suggested that extra staff be engaged at both the Home Office and British Consulates throughout the Reich to diminish the serious delays occasioned by the massed backlog of visa applications awaiting disposition. As far as settlement was concerned, the Council 'hoped that territory might be found in which settlement would be possible', although mass settlement in the Empire was bound to be a most difficult and expensive proposition. Dr Weizmann then made

[13] Makins, minute, November 10, 1938, FO 371/21636, C 13661/1667/62.
[14] Te deputation consisted of Viscount Samuel, Viscount Bearsted, the Chief Rabbi of Great Britain, Mr Neville Laski, Mr Lionel de Rothschild and Dr Chaim Weizmann. Record of meeting by Prime Minister's Private Secretary, November 16, 1938, FO 371/22536, W 15037/104/98.

a plea for the admission to Palestine, despite the difficult conditions there, of 6,000 young men presently confined in concentration camps, and of 1,500 children. Finally, Viscount Bearsted and Mr de Rothschild addressed themselves to the financial aspects of the problem; Bearsted pointed out that it cost at least £100 to evacuate one person, and that the total required to bring out of the Reich the 300,000 individuals considered fit for emigration would therefore amount to a minimum of £30,000,000. In view of these enormous sums, he asked whether consideration could not be given to the notion of British Government assistance—or international government aid—in the raising of a settlement loan. Without such a loan, Mr de Rothschild asserted, it would be impossible to accomplish the removal from the Reich of the 300,000.

In reply, the Prime Minister affirmed that the Government was deeply concerned about the refugee problem and anxious to give whatever assistance was possible; he saw no chance however of the British Government exercising any effective influence in Berlin to diminish or stop the persecution. As to settlement, 'the prospects of solid achievements by the Evian organisation were not encouraging'. Nor could Mr Chamberlain say that 'the prospects of obtaining concessions from the German Government [on capital transfers] were at all hopeful'. Mass settlement in some part of the Empire could only be envisaged in British Guiana, where the grant of a large tract of land might be a possible Government contribution; but though this proposal would be examined sympathetically, 'the Council must recognise . . . that development would involve a large expenditure of capital and the time factor would operate'. The suggestion of a refugee loan was regarded by the Prime Minister as 'premature and hardly worth discussing at this stage'; before such a loan could even be considered some 'clearly defined plan' for the use of the loan proceeds would have to be presented. As to the points raised by Viscount Samuel about extra Government staff, and by Dr Weizmann concerning admissions to Palestine, the Prime Minister would give his 'benevolent interest' to proposals which should be taken up with the Home, Foreign and Colonial Offices on these matters. Mr Chamberlain reminded his callers, in conclusion, that 'while the world had the strongest sympathy with the

Jews in their unhappy plight, this was not purely a Jewish problem, but part of a larger question—the refugee problem'.

The entire constellation of issues raised by the Council for German Jewry was discussed by the Cabinet at its meeting of November 16,[15] where it was recognised that the rather negative tone of the answers Mr Chamberlain had given the Council for German Jewry deputation would have to be altered in the light of serious public concern not merely in Britain, but in the United States as well, where the refugee question now threatened to cast a shadow over Anglo-American relations.

Opening the Cabinet discussion, Viscount Halifax remarked that he had been 'much impressed by the powerful repercussions all over the world' of Germany's action against the Jews. He described a talk he had just had with the United States Ambassador, who had called on him shortly before the Cabinet meeting to report that American opinion, outraged by *Kristallnacht*, 'was tending to conclude that the policy of working for peace with Germany was mistaken and was consequently becoming generally less sympathetic to His Majesty's Government'. Halifax had responded sharply to Kennedy's statement, asserting that he 'was at a loss to understand why American opinion should blame His Majesty's Government because German Government persecuted the Jews, especially as United States did not show much desire to do anything substantial themselves'.[16] The Foreign Secretary also told his colleagues that he had received a letter signed by many of the undergraduate clubs at Oxford, condemning the Government for taking insufficient action on the question of Germany's persecution of its Jews. Turning to possible courses of action which might be open to the British Government, Halifax stated that Britain's position in American public opinion, which was 'now about as critical as it could well be', could be restored if Britain 'would give a lead which would force the United States in turn to take some positive action'. He expressed the hope that the Government might lend its support 'to fairly wide promises of help to the Jews'. Such help might be an under-

[15] See Cabinet Conclusions 55(38)5, November 16, 1938, CAB 23/96.
[16] See Halifax to Lindsay, November 16, 1938, FO 371/21637, C 13900/1667/62.

taking to make some area in the Empire available for settlement. The Foreign Secretary declared that wider aspects of the refugee problem must not be permitted to interfere with immediate action, and he emphasised in conclusion the great importance he attached to the entire matter 'from the political point of view'.

The Colonial Secretary agreed that the Government ought to give 'as generous promises of help in the near future as were practicable, even if those promises had to be subject to some degree of qualification', but felt nevertheless that possibilities of settlement in the colonies ought not to be exaggerated. Reviewing these possibilities, Mr MacDonald said that it would probably not be feasible to increase substantially the present volume of settlement in Kenya, which amounted to some twenty-five families a year. Proposals for Jewish settlement in Northern Rhodesia had encountered the unanimous opposition of the Unofficial Members of the Legislative Council : but it might be the Government's 'duty to override it'. As to Tanganyika, the Colonial Secretary hoped he might be able 'to effect something'. British Guiana was a more hopeful proposition; large areas there could be made available for survey by the Jewish organisations. Mr MacDonald remarked that although 'it was clear that British Guiana did not offer opportunities for the settlement of very large numbers of Jews, at any rate at once . . . the proposal to give them an area in British Guiana was one which would be important politically'.

Lord Winterton and the Home Secretary intervened at this point to stress the importance of making some concrete territorial offer, and the Prime Minister concurred, suggesting that the British Government should give Jewish settlers in British Guiana not a freehold, 'but a long lease on a peppercorn rent, in order to retain some measure of control'. Mr Chamberlain went on to report the Council for German Jewry's view that time was of the essence; anything that the Government could do to promote permanent settlement would therefore have to be 'accompanied by some effort to find a temporary resting-place for refugees while arrangements were made for their permanent reception'.

Lord Winterton then spoke of the Evian-born Intergovernmental Committee over which he presided. He characterised the IGC as 'a miniature League of Nations' in which there were 'the usual cross-currents of opinions and interests'. Moreover, the Director, Mr Rublee, was 'an elderly American, who was thought by many people not to make rapid progress'. The United States Department of State had for some time been expressing the view—which was 'quite untrue'—that Great Britain was not doing enough to solve the refugee problem. In the Dominions, Australia was taking in 5,000 refugees a year, 'due partly to the pressure which had been brought to bear upon her'; New Zealand was admitting 'a few'; it was hoped to 'induce the Canadian Government to take some helpful measures'; but South Africa was admitting no refugees at all. The United States for its part was permitting 25,000 immigrants from the Reich to enter each year; that number represented merely the normal combined quota for Germany and Austria. Winterton ended his *tour d'horizon* by predicting that Guatemala and certain other South American countries would take positive action if Great Britain 'could show them a good example'. Finally, however,

the crux of the whole question . . . was whether Jews were to be allowed to take money out of Germany. This was a question which must be discussed with the German Government, but that Government had burked discussion of it for months. No large-scale emigration could be effected unless this problem could be solved.

Giving his views, the Home Secretary asserted that the United States

was the key to the problem, but that the only way to open the door into the United States would be that we should take action in regard to, say, British Guiana, Kenya and Northern Rhodesia, which would influence opinion in the United States.

Such action would also 'be of importance on the financial side'. Sir Samuel Hoare next reported that 1,000 applications for entry were being received each day at the Home Office; these applications were sent to the Co-Ordinating Committee for Refugees, and 'broadly speaking, only cases which were recommended by the Jewish representatives were admitted'. The Jewish representatives were however

averse from allowing very large numbers of Jews to enter this country or from allowing the entry of Jews whom they had not themselves approved, since they were afraid of an anti-Jew agitation in this country. For the same reason they were unwilling to give definite figures as to the number of Jews admitted, since they were afraid that any number published would be attacked from both sides as being too big or too little.

More generally, the Home Secretary stated that the Government was 'going as far at present as public opinion would allow; and it was important to retain a check on individual immigrants'. A number of young men could nonetheless be admitted for agricultural training with a view to settlement elsewhere, and a number of Jewish women might be brought in as domestic servants to replace the German domestics who had left at the time of the Munich crisis.

In the general discussion which followed, Sir Thomas Inskip, the Minister for Co-ordination of Defence, asked how the Government could get credit for what was already being done unless some immigration figure were publicised. Other Ministers debated this point, and the Home Secretary undertook to consider whether some figure could be communicated privately to Washington. The Prime Minister suggested that if in addition to offering some territory in the Empire the Government would permit Jewish refugees to come to Britain as a temporary refuge, that would represent a 'considerable contribution towards the problem'; the Home Secretary agreed to consider this possibility. Discussing other action, the Dominions Secretary said he hoped it might be possible to induce the Dominions to admit more refugees : the Australian High Commissioner felt his Government might increase admissions to 6,000 or 7,000 refugees a year and had also agreed that the time had perhaps come to make that figure public; it 'compared very favourably with the scale of the effort in the United States'.

Winding up the discussion, the Prime Minister urged that a statement—to be drafted by the Foreign Secretary, the Home Secretary, the Colonial Secretary and Lord Winterton—should be prepared as soon as possible to set out what action the Government 'proposed to take immediately to deal with the Jewish problem'. The Cabinet so agreed, but before the meeting ended, Lord Halifax added a special plea on behalf of the older Jews in Germany, asking if it were possible to launch an appeal in Britain to induce people 'to make themselves responsible for the support of individual elderly Jews who would otherwise be left to an appalling fate in Germany'. The Prime Minister commented that this suggestion 'might be considered later'.

As the various Ministers concerned proceeded with the formulation of the Government's response to the refugee crisis, the Foreign Office moved to avert the danger that the entire question might come to envenom relations with the United States: the British Ambassador in Washington was instructed to raise with the State Department the suggestion that part of the unused British quota for immigration into the United States be made available instead for refugees from Germany.[17] In his call on Under-Secretary of State Sumner Welles, Sir Ronald Lindsay volunteered that he

did not believe that this instruction had been considered by the British Cabinet or was other than a *démarche* on the part of the British Foreign Office alone and that it seemed to him in the nature of an offer by his own Government of something which the British Government did not control.[18]

Following the lead suggested by Lindsay's half-hearted representations, Welles declared that quotas granted by Congress

were not the free property of the nations to which they were granted, nor could the terms of the law be modified because of some other government's willingness to modify or to relinquish the quotas which might be granted to its nationals by this law.

Welles added that there were thus 'insuperable obstacles from the strictly legal aspect' and that there would be policy objections as well. To the Ambassador's surprise, Welles revealed that the British proposal

would be most distasteful to Jewish leaders in America who fear any open and avowed increase of Jewish immigration because it would have the effect of increasing anti-Semitic feeling in America.[19]

Lindsay's despatch to London did not report the tone of his approach to the State Department, nor that he had asked Welles

[17] Only 4,000 British immigrants had arrived in the United States in 1938. See Arthur D. Morse, *While Six Million Died* (New York, 1967), p. 234.

[18] See Welles, memorandum, November 17, 1938, *FRUS*, 1938, I, 829–831.

[19] See Lindsay to Halifax, November 17, 1938, FO 371/21637, C 14092/ 1667/62.

M

if Welles 'really thought it necessary to bring this to the President's attention'. Lindsay was told that Welles 'did not see that the Secretary or I could avoid laying this matter before the President', and Lindsay thereupon undertook to 'see to it that no publicity was given to the suggestion made'.[20] The proposal was allowed to lapse, although American preoccupation with the potential contribution of the British Empire—and particularly Palestine—toward a solution of the refugee problem continued to concern and occasionally irritate the Foreign Office.

In the crowded days following *Kristallnacht*, the columns of letters to the editor in the British press reflected widespread concern by ordinary members of the public over the apparent lack of response by the British Government to the panicky flight from German territory. Many letters commented on Home Office delays in processing visas and suggested measures to speed up procedures. Others, in increasing numbers, dealt with the possibility of settlement in various corners of the Empire.

Organised political pressures on the Government were also mounting. A deputation from the Liberal Party executive called at 10 Downing Street on November 16, to tell the Prime Minister that 'the generous instincts of the British people were being grievously misrepresented by men whose sole object appeared to be to protect certain alleged economic interests' and that the British Government would have widespread popular support in offering asylum to large numbers of refugees from the Nazi regime.[21] The Labour Party too was active, pleading at the Foreign Office on behalf of a group of refugees marooned in the no-man's-land between the German and Dutch frontiers.[22] The League of Nations Union, weighing in with its traditional detailed memorandum, pressed the Government in strong terms to take the lead in finding a rapid solution to the emergency; such a solution would include the raising of an international settlement loan guaranteed by central banks, and Government sponsorship of organised refugee migration to the colonies and Dominions. Above all, a clear interdepartmental policy on refugees should be

---

[20] See Welles, memorandum, November 17, 1938, *FRUS*, 1938, I, 830.
[21] See *Manchester Guardian*, November 17, 1938.
[22] See Makins, minute, November 17, 1938, FO 371/22537, W 15292/104/98.

adopted by the Prime Minister and Cabinet; no progress could be made 'if each Department of Government is left to make its own decision or to adopt towards the problem of the refugees the attitude dictated by its own preoccupations'.[23]

Confronted with these pressures, the Prime Minister used the occasion of a Parliamentary question on the morning of November 21 to make the first public statement of the Government's refugee policy in the light of the new emergency. Replying to a general question on what progress had been made since the Evian conference by the IGC, Chamberlain reported that the Government had again reviewed the refugee situation.[24] Reaffirming the principle that 'the country of origin should make its contribution to this problem of migration by enabling intending emigrants to take with them their property and possessions', he revealed that the United Kingdom had since 1933 permitted some 11,000 refugees to enter, in addition to 4–5,000 who had subsequently emigrated elsewhere. Turning to the colonial Empire, the Prime Minister reviewed the small-scale schemes being explored in Kenya, Northern Rhodesia and Nyasaland, and indicated that there were larger settlement possibilities in Tanganyika and British Guiana. The Government would invite the voluntary organisations to survey territories in these colonies, and if the results of these surveys were favourable the Government would be prepared to lease large areas of land 'on generous terms'; in the case of British Guiana, such an area would be not less than 10,000 square miles. Palestine had been 'making its contribution': at least 40 per cent of the Jewish immigrants to Palestine within the past year had come from Germany. The Prime Minister emphasised in conclusion that 'however great may be our desire and that of other countries to assist in dealing with this grave situation, the possibilities of settlement are strictly limited'.

In the evening of November 21, Philip Noel-Baker, MP, of the Labour Party, opened a full-scale House of Commons debate on refugee policy by tabling a motion noting with concern the 'deplorable treatment suffered by certain racial, religious and political

---

[23] League of Nations Union, memorandum, November 17, 1938, FO 371/22537, W 15251/104/98.
[24] See 341 H.C. Deb., November 21, 1938, 1313–1317.

minorities in Europe' and calling for the adoption of 'an immediate concerted effort amongst the nations, including the United States of America, to secure a common policy'.[25] Noel-Baker called for a clarification of Government refugee policy and for representations in Berlin to stop the persecution. Citing the example of the resettlement of Greek refugees, he advocated large-scale settlement in Palestine—including the admission of 10,000 children whose support the Jewish Agency had undertaken to guarantee—and settlements in the Dominions and elsewhere in the Empire coordinated by a strong High Commission for Refugees and financed by loans to be guaranteed by the British Government. Noel-Baker's points were echoed by other speakers as well.

Replying for the Government, the Home Secretary spoke with feeling 'as a convinced believer in the possibility of Anglo-German friendship' of the 'suffering inflicted upon thousands of men and women as the result of a crime with which they had no connection whatever'. More practically, Hoare reaffirmed the British Government's view that the problem was an international one, to be solved by all the countries which were members of the Evian committee: active consultations were going on among these members, and a meeting of the IGC was to take place in London within ten days. As to the British Empire, the Dominions 'must speak for themselves', but a substantial number of refugees were in fact being admitted to Dominion territories. Colonial territories were being surveyed with a view to refugee settlement; Palestine however represented another problem: the particular difficulties there precluded 'anything like mass immigration at the present time'.

Turning to the situation in the United Kingdom, the Home Secretary reminded the House of the still large numbers of unemployed, and referred to 'an underlying current of suspicion and anxiety, rightly or wrongly, about alien immigration on any big scale'. 'It is a fact,' he continued, 'that below the surface . . . there is the making of a definite anti-Jewish movement.' Mass immigration would lead to a growth in this movement, and thus a careful check on individual immigrants had to be maintained, although inevit-

---

[25] See 341 H.C. Deb., 1428–1483.

ably such a check entailed delays. Sir Samuel told the House that refugee cases were referred to the Co-Ordinating Committee, which made the necessary inquiries, and that when the Committee informed the Home Office that a refugee could maintain himself or had friends who could guarantee him, the refugee would 'almost invariably—I think I may say invariably' receive a visa and be allowed to enter. Moreover, the 11,000 refugees who had thus far settled in Britain had been instrumental in employing 15,000 British workers in new enterprises they had established. The Home Secretary conceded that the machinery of both the Home Office and the British Consulates in Germany and Austria had been 'strained to breaking point' in face of thousands of applications a day; the administrative staff was however being greatly expanded, although there would continue to be delays. In response to an interjection by one member asking if a limit would be put on the number of refugees to be allowed into Britain, Sir Samuel stated his opposition to anything in the nature of a quota : 'Many people might think it was too big and many people might think it was too small.' It was preferable for the Home Office, working in close contact with the Co-Ordinating Committee, to 'treat individual cases on their merits and not to be bound down by a numerical figure'.

Although the capacity of Britain to absorb permanent settlers was limited, Hoare continued, the Government was now prepared to offer temporary asylum to certain refugees pending their migration elsewhere. Other refugees could be admitted for purposes of training to fit them for permanent settlement in other countries. In addition, the Home Office would give the necessary visas to facilitate entry for all child refugees whose maintenance could be guaranteed, either through their own funds or by other individuals. The Home Secretary warmly endorsed this last proposal, recommending it to the country as 'a chance of taking the young generation of a great people' and 'mitigating to some extent the terrible sufferings of their parents and their friends'. In his final words, Sir Samuel stated that the proposed international loan was a question that could only be dealt with internationally, and that it would doubtless be considered by the IGC. The British Government would be prepared to take its 'full part with other nations of the world in helping solve the refugee problem'. At the conclusion of debate, the Noel-Baker motion was adopted by the House.

The press had for the most part anticipated the debate by stressing the need for Government haste in meeting the emergency. *The Times* leader, for example, stated 'one would like to hear . . . of some immediate measure of relief'.[26] The *Daily Express* however deplored the entire notion of a Parliamentary debate on refugees, complaining that

the Jews are always in the news. Each morning we get another account of Jewish pogroms, here, there and everywhere. . . . We have already accepted our full quota of foreign Jews. We cannot assimilate any more. Shall we open the Crown Colonies to the Jews? Of course. . . . But will the Jews go to these outlying countries? Of course not. . . .[27]

After the debate there was general press approval for the statement of Government policy. The *Daily Mail* leader echoed the Home Secretary's emphasis on the international nature of the problem, and affirmed that shelter in Britain could not be given to masses of immigrants, although there was 'room elsewhere'.[28] The Government's financial wariness met with the approval of several leader writers. More critical were the *Spectator*, which urged the Government to take the initiative in providing temporary homes for refugees,[29] and the *Daily Herald*, which asserted that the Government was 'not yet sufficiently alive to its duty'; nor would it have discharged that duty until the 'emigration of whole families on a large scale' had been arranged.[30]

If the British press had shown sensitivity to the extreme urgency of the post-*Kristallnacht* situation, the same could also be said of the Foreign Office, which had received a telegram from the Berlin Embassy reporting a dramatic plea that the British Government do everything possible to help those who had actually been driven from their homes, numbering from 10,000 to 15,000, for whom temporary camps no matter how primitive would at least represent

[26] *The Times*, November 21, 1938.
[27] *Daily Express*, November 21, 1938.
[28] *Daily Mail*, November 22, 1938.
[29] *Spectator*, November 25, 1938.
[30] *Daily Herald*, November 22, 1938.

asylum and a way-station on the road to further emigration.[31] Another report, emanating from a British Consul on leave who had gone to Germany to rescue a friend from Dachau and had interviewed a senior member of Hitler's Chancellery, stated chillingly that the German official had 'made it clear that Germany intended to get rid of her Jews, either by emigration or if necessary by starving or killing them, since she would not risk having such a hostile minority in the country in the event of war'. The official had added that Germany 'intended to expel or kill off the Jews in Poland, Hungary and the Ukraine when she took control of those countries'.[32]

Following the House of Commons announcement that the Government would facilitate the entry of child refugees to Great Britain, the Home Office agreed to dispense with the formalities of passports and visas for the children; in their place a single form was devised bearing the few particulars of each child.[33] The Movement for the Care of Children from Germany[34] under the joint chairmanship of Sir Wyndham Deedes and Viscount Samuel, organised the emigration and allocation of the children in cooperation with over 100

---

[31] Ogilvie-Forbes to Halifax, November 17, 1938, FO 371/21637, C 14083/1667/62. The plea was made on behalf of the German Jewish community by Mr Wilfred Israel, whose British-German citizenship enabled him to have access to the British Embassy at a time when some 30,000 male Jews, including most of those prominent in the German Jewish community, had been arrested by the Gestapo.

[32] Foreign Office minute, November 21, 1938, FO 371/21638, C 15078/1667/62. The German official suggested that if Britain provided a home for the Jews in Tanganyika, or another African territory, a general Anglo-German agreement might be envisaged, within which Germany would then be prepared to renounce her claim to the return of her former colonies. The British Embassy in Berlin was instructed to let it be known that the British Government would be prepared to discuss concrete proposals only with representatives 'who were able to speak with the full authority of the German Government'. See Strang to Ogilvie-Forbes, December 8, 1938, ibid.

[33] There was a precedent for this procedure in the admission *en bloc* in May 1937 of 3,800 Basque children, refugees from the Spanish Civil War. They were distributed to hostels or homes throughout the country, and their support guaranteed by private organisations. The Government had admitted these children only on condition that they not be allowed to establish themselves in Great Britain; they were therefore repatriated in small numbers almost as soon as they had arrived. By May 1938, some 2,000 of the children had been returned to their parents. See Hope Simpson, *Refugee Problem*, p. 343.

[34] A merger of the British Inter-Aid Committee for Children from Germany and Austria with other groups interested in child refugees.

local committees throughout Britain which made themselves responsible for maintenance of the children in hostels pending their placement with families. Foster-parents in their turn undertook to maintain and educate the children until they were old enough to be self-supporting or could rejoin their parents. The central committee of the Movement maintained a system of inspection, and guaranteed to the Home Office that the children would not become a public charge and would either be emigrated in due course or absorbed in Great Britain in ways approved by the Government. All this machinery was set up in a few weeks, and the first party of 200 children landed at Harwich on December 3.[35]

The arrival of the first child refugees, and the poignancy of the scenes which accompanied their separation from their parents—all of which were extensively reported in the press—brought into sharp relief the financial dilemma of the refugee organisations. Despite the raising of approximately £5 million between 1933 and November 1938[36] by the Jewish organisations alone, the problem had become too huge for the private agencies. The pressures for a Government grant, or for a Government-guaranteed refugee loan, increased as relentlessly as the numbers of refugees fleeing the Reich : the Jewish organisations, the Quakers, and others were agreed that only substantial Government financial assistance could offer a hope of establishing refugees in countries of settlement. An all-party committee of MPs was established on December 6, under the chairmanship of Captain Victor Cazalet, with Miss Eleanor F. Rathbone as Secretary, to press the Government for pro-refugee action, including financial assistance.[37]

On December 8, the former Prime Minister, Earl Baldwin, made a broadcast appeal to launch the Lord Baldwin Fund for Refugees, an appeal deliberately cast in the widest possible terms and made with the support of the Archbishop of Canterbury, Cardinal Hinsley, Lord Rothschild, and the Lord Mayor of London. Baldwin's speech

[35] See *The Times*, December 3, 1938. For an account of the children's movement, see Karen Gershon (ed.), *We Came as Children* (London, 1966).

[36] See Brooks, minute, December 7, 1938, FO 371/22539, W 16410/104/98.

[37] See *News Chronicle*, December 4, 1938. Other sponsors of the Parliamentary Committee for Refugees were Vernon Bartlett (Independent); Lord Marley (Labour); Major Gwilym Lloyd George (Liberal); Harold Nicolson (National Labour); David Grenfell (Labour).

was cleared in advance with the Home Office and the Foreign Office, which interposed no objection to Baldwin's speaking strongly so long as his words could not be 'misrepresented as an attack by a British statesman on the Nazi regime as such'. When consulted, Lord Winterton expressed his concern that the more funds were raised for Jewish refugees

the less Germany and other countries with large Jewish populations will feel inclined to help and the more they will adopt the attitude that the problem is one for other countries to solve. . . . These countries will also be apt to draw the conclusion that the best method of forcing other countries to take their Jews is that of persecution. . . .

Winterton thereupon asked Baldwin to emphasise that however generous the response to a fund-raising appeal might be, it would

do no more than touch the fringe of the problem of the emigration of refugees from Germany, and . . . this problem can only be solved if the country which creates the refugees will co-operate, and will make it possible for them to depart in a condition, both physical and economic, to start fresh lives elsewhere.[38]

When *The Times* opened its own subscription list for the Lord Baldwin Fund, it noted pointedly that 'private charity cannot take, and must not be asked to take, the responsibilities which belong to the Government'.[39]

The Treasury for its part summarised Government policy on refugee financing as follows:

. . . the Government do not wish to commit themselves on the question of financial assistance at this stage; . . . to consider the question of financial assistance before there is any concrete plan for dealing with the position would be regarded as premature; . . . the Government would expect the other Governments represented at Evian to participate in any financial assistance.

The notion of a guaranteed loan could only be considered, the Treasury asserted, when the probable cost of settlement schemes had been examined at their own expense by the refugee organisations, and then 'everything will depend on the attitude of the Governments concerned *as a whole*'. In conclusion, 'the Jews must

[38] See Makins to Fry, December 5, 1938, FO 371/22539, W 16100/104/98.
[39] See *The Times*, December 9, 1938.

not count upon any loan but must be content to leave the question for future decision'.[40] The question of Government financial support for refugees was not to be permitted to rest there, however.

On December 7, the League of Nations Union sent a detailed memorandum to the Foreign Office, rejecting 'categorically and unanimously' on behalf of the voluntary refugee organisations the notion that these organisations must assume the total financial burden of maintaining refugee children admitted to Britain, the temporary camps for adult transmigrants which it was proposed to establish, and also the survey of possible settlement areas in the colonial Empire.[41] Concluding that 'the voluntary organisations have neither the means nor the competence to undertake the organisation and financing of planned migration on the scale contemplated', the Union called for the governments concerned to cooperate in raising the sum of £75 million, which would finance the migration of some 600,000 individuals, through an international loan guaranteed by the central banks of the Evian governments. In a minute commenting on the League of Nations Union proposal, R. M. Makins argued that the transfer of aliens from one foreign country to another did not involve a direct British interest such as would justify Government participation in financing such transfer. Further, once a departure had been made from the principle of no public funds for refugee relief and settlement, there was the risk that 'colossal sums' might be involved. If governments were to participate in jointly guaranteeing a loan of £75 million to resettle refugees from the Reich, the German Government would have succeeded in despoiling its Jews and having foreign governments foot the bill. Moreover, any exclusion of Poland, Rumania, Hungary and Czechoslovakia from the benefits of such an international resettlement loan would operate as a 'direct incitement to persecution of the Jews in those countries'. The British Government could nevertheless make a contribution, by granting loans for the cost of refugee settlement in such colonies as Northern Rhodesia; such loans would 'increase

[40] See Treasury minute, November 23, 1938, FO 371/22540, W 16543/104/98.

[41] League of Nations Union memorandum, *Action of Governments and of Private Organisations in Regard to Refugees*, December 7, 1938, FO 371/22539, W 16411/104/98.

the prosperity of the Empire' and be justifiable as devoted to the furtherance of a British interest.[42] Lobbying in Parliament and in the press for a Government financial contribution to settlement schemes continued throughout the remaining weeks of 1938 and into the following year, but Government spokesmen remained unwilling to go beyond repeated references to the apparently sacrosanct principle laid down at Evian by the United States Government that no financial assistance by governments for refugee settlement was to be contemplated.[43]

The question of financial assistance continued to bedevil colonial settlement proposals, as the Colonial Office discovered upon moving to implement the suggestions made in the Prime Minister's statement of November 21. After consulting the Foreign Office as to how it should proceed,[44] the Colonial Office contacted the Co-Ordinating Committee for Refugees and invited the Committee to send experts, at the Committee's expense, to survey settlement possibilities in British Guiana and Tanganyika.[45] The Co-Ordinating Committee, however, in a militant mood born of the conviction that the refugee problem was now far beyond its financial resources, rejoined that it could not 'accept the principle that a solution of the Refugee Problem is the responsibility of the private relief organisations'; the most it could undertake was willingness to 'cooperate' in colonial settlement projects if that could be done 'without incurring undue expense'. Colonial Office officials, complaining that 'one might almost suppose that we had devised these Colonial projects for our own benefit, and that the refugee organisations were doing us a great favour by offering to "cooperate" ',[46] ultimately established a reasonable working relationship with Mr Anthony de Rothschild's Emigration Sub-committee. Plans for an investigation of settlement possibilities went forward only slowly, however, and weeks passed without a definite time-table for survey

[42] See Makins, minute, December 8, 1938, FO 371/22539, W 16411/104/98.
[43] See 341 H.C. Deb., November 24, 1938, 1931–1932.
[44] See Parkinson to Cadogan, November 22, 1938, FO 371/22538, W 15495/104/98.
[45] See Calder to Ormerod, November 29, 1938, FO 371/22538, W 15741/104/98.
[46] Shuckburgh to Makins, December 21, 1938, FO 371/22541, W 17051/104/98.

groups to proceed to the territories in question. On December 23, the Colonial Office informed Rothschild that reports were still being awaited from Tanganyika, where in any case the rainy season had just begun; that twenty-five proposed settlers bound for Kenya had reportedly been imprisoned in German concentration camps; and that in Northern Rhodesia the Governor had just set up a committee to look into possible small-scale settlement on the Kenya model.[47]

The Foreign Office, which was bearing the brunt of American and other criticism of delays in the investigation of colonial settlement schemes, was particularly exercised over the case of Northern Rhodesia, where proposals for settlement of Jewish refugees had consistently been blocked by unanimous opposition from the Unofficial (European) Members of the Legislative Council. Northern Rhodesia seemed to the Foreign Office to offer the best prospects for colonial settlement : it had the least population density of any but two or three other territories under British control, an available area of some 165,000 square miles, of which a large part was Crown land, as compared with 10,000 square miles in British Guiana; and the climatic and other conditions were also more favourable than in any of the other colonies suggested as possible settlements. Moreover British Guiana had already been investigated in 1934 by the League of Nations as a possible home for Assyrians forced to flee from Iraq, and had been found unsuitable to support more than a few thousand agriculturalists.

In a strongly-worded minute commenting on a telegram from the Governor of Rhodesia reporting that even a proposal to admit a maximum of 150 refugee settlers was being opposed by his Legislative Council, R. M. Makins reviewed settlement possibilities in the Empire and concluded : 'in all frankness it has to be admitted that the offer of British Guiana and Tanganyika is largely an illusory one, and this must inevitably become apparent in due course'.[48] He went on to explain the direct interest of the Foreign Office in this matter :

From our point of view, it is important that if HM Government are going to do something for the Jews and give a lead to other countries, our offer should be a genuine one.

[47] See Shuckburgh to Rothschild, December 23, 1938, FO 371/22541, W 17173/104/98.
[48] Makins, minute, December 1, 1938, FO 371/22538, W 15621/104/98.

The advantages which we expect to obtain from making territory available in the Colonial Empire for the settlement of refugees from Germany are as follows. We shall take the pressure off Palestine and make the solution of that problem easier, at the same time fulfilling such moral obligations as we may be held to have towards the Jews. We shall be making a constructive contribution to the Central European emigration problem, and to some extent take the pressure off the persecuted minorities. No country can in future reproach us for having made no serious contribution to the emigration problem. Finally, such an offer on our part would have a helpful effect on Anglo-American relations and check the tendency in the United States to blame us for not doing more.

Lastly, though this may be thought to be mainly a Colonial Office point, we shall be increasing the prosperity of the Empire. I have suggested . . . that it might also be open to HM Government to assist in the development of a territory for settlement by making loans from the colonial development fund for road making, railway building, etc.

We appear therefore in a position to make an offer which may turn out to be a major stroke of policy, but we are being held up by the opposition of a handful of settlers.

The Makins view was strongly supported by his colleagues, who saw in the proposals for large-scale refugee settlement the possibility of dramatically transforming the refugee problem, helping solve the intractable Palestine dilemma, and at the same time contributing directly to the enhancement of Great Britain's position in the world. O. E. Sargent wrote on December 2 :

I would like to support Mr Makins most strongly, and very much hope that a further attempt will be made to consider N. Rhodesia as a field for *large scale* Jewish settlement.

I submit that it is a British interest, for the various reasons given by Mr Makins, that HM Government should play a leading and constructive part in dealing with the Jewish problem. In other words, we ought to try by bold and far-sighted action to convert the Jewish population now adrift into an Imperial asset and thus mobilise in our favour the sympathy and gratitude of international Jewry. In present circumstances we cannot hope to do this in Palestine, but in Northern Rhodesia we have a wonderful opportunity for carrying out a far-reaching scheme if we really want to. It is fantastic that we should be held up by a small body of 11,000 Whites, who sit encamped in a corner of this vast uninhabited and undeveloped territory and like dogs in the manger refuse to allow anyone else to enter it.

I hope that it may be found possible for the Secretary of State, on grounds of *foreign* policy, to insist that this question of Northern Rhodesia should be reconsidered with a view to large scale settlement, notwithstanding the opposition of the small White oligarchy now in possession.[49]

Lord Halifax subsequently approved an official letter sent to the Colonial Office[50] urging in strong terms that further consideration be given to large-scale settlement in Northern Rhodesia, particularly in view of the opinion of a former Governor of that colony that settlement of 'thousands or tens of thousands of Jews would be possible' there. The letter reproduced the arguments Makins and Sargent had put forward and repeated that it was a direct interest of British foreign policy for the British Government to take the lead in trying to solve the refugee problem. The Foreign Office concluded:

Lord Halifax would not wish to deny that the offers already made of territory within the Empire may do something to assist in the solution of the problem of emigration from Germany, but in the most favourable circumstances they will be inadequate to meet an exodus caused by fresh waves of persecution, which will lead once again to pressure on His Majesty's Government to take further steps on behalf of the refugees. It is suggested that it would be an advantage from the administrative point of view to anticipate these fresh demands, if it is in any way practicable to do so.

But it is primarily on grounds of foreign policy that I am to urge most strongly that the possibility of large scale settlement in Northern Rhodesia should be reconsidered, and to suggest for Mr. MacDonald's consideration that if the opposition of the small white population in the territory continues it may be found necessary on broad grounds of policy to over-ride their objections.

In a cool reply, the Colonial Office again cited the continuing opposition of the white settlers in Northern Rhodesia and asked what particular number of refugees Lord Halifax might have in mind whose settlement within the Empire 'might be expected to secure those advantages in the field of foreign policy' to which the Foreign Office had referred.[51] The Colonial Office warned more-

---

[49] Sargent, minute, December 2, 1938, FO 371/22538, W 15621/104/98.
[50] See Howard to Under-Secretary of State, December 12, 1938, ibid.
[51] See Colonial Office to Foreign Office, January 2, 1939, FO 371/24073, W 135/45/48.

over that any settlement scheme would have to depend on the good-
will and cooperation of the 'unofficial community' in Northern
Rhodesia. Apparently undaunted, the Foreign Office firmly pointed
out that 'apart from the attitude of the existing settlers' prospects
for large-scale settlement would probably be more favourable in
Northern Rhodesia than in British Guiana, where an adverse report
on settlement possibilities was to be feared, which might in turn

provide plausible grounds, of which advantage would doubtless be
taken in certain quarters, for the suggestion that His Majesty's Government's offer of territory in British Guiana is when put to the test
bound to prove of little or no value.[52]

Taking up the Colonial Office challenge on numbers, the Foreign
Office suggested that a total of 50,000 refugees for the whole
Colonial Empire excluding Palestine, to be settled over five years,
represented 'the minimum that would have the results that . . . can
be attained by bold action in this sphere'. When presented with a
further memorandum on Northern Rhodesia in which the Colonial
Secretary repeated the view of the Governor and his Legislative
Council that large-scale settlement in any part of the territory was
impracticable, the Foreign Office remained highly sceptical and
pressed the Colonial Office to authorise an impartial commission
to proceed to Northern Rhodesia and assess the settlement possibilities there, even if the constitutional issue had to be forced, and
the Legislative Council objections overriden. In internal memoranda
members of the Foreign Office left no doubt that the strong line
they had taken with the Colonial Office was motivated at least in
part by anxiety over Palestine. Sir Alexander Cadogan wrote on
February 21, 1939: 'if we have to limit drastically, or stop altogether, Jewish immigration into Palestine, we shall be on stronger
grounds if we can find a refuge elsewhere'; to which Lord Halifax,
a day later, appended the remark: 'I am quite willing to put all
the pressure we can.'[53]

But despite the energetic intervention of the Foreign Office, a
Northern Rhodesia investigatory commission was constituted only

[52] See Foreign Office to Colonial Office, January 11, 1939, FO 371/24073,
W 135/45/48.
[53] See FO 371/24088, W 3699/1369/48.

after further wearisome arguments with the Governor and the refugee organisations; its discouraging report was issued in late June. All the pressures within and outside Whitehall had resulted by March 1939 in the admission to colonial territories other than Palestine of only about 2,000 refugees from the Reich.[54] The cautious conclusions of the Kenya Settlement Committee, issued after prolonged investigations in January 1939, give some notion as to why so few refugees had been settled in the colonies :

We are of the opinion that the carefully regulated agricultural settle-ment of a comparatively small number of Jews of nordic type on individual holdings—the number to be governed by the absorptive capacity of the Colony—might be an advantage to Kenya. . . . Such settlement should be privately organised and financed, but should, at every stage, be subject to the approval of Government. . . . Jewish immigration should, in our view, be very rigorously supervised and controlled, as . . . it would be impossible for any considerable number of artisans, clerks and professional people to be absorbed in the economic life of the Colony. . . .[55]

The controversy over the merits of a British Guiana settlement continued to be aired in the letter columns of the press and in Par-liament, but even before a commission of experts was chosen and sent out to that territory the ultimate failure of all settlement schemes deprived of government financial support was forecast in a letter to the Prime Minister written by Sir Arthur Salter, MP, in consultation with Sir John Hope Simpson.[56] Salter stated flatly that only government-financed capital expenditure on com-munications could make a large-scale group settlement in British Guiana feasible : private surveys and private efforts were bound to fail because they would necessarily be inadequate in scale. A British Government-financed settlement, on the other hand, might be able to convert undeveloped colonial areas into prosperous communities qualifying for Dominion status, with incalculable advantages to the Empire. In transmitting Salter's letter to the Colonial Office for reply, Lord Halifax noted :

[54] See Hope Simpson, *Refugees. A Review of the Situation Since September 1938* (London, August 1939), p. 109.
[55] See *Settlement Committee Report* (Nairobi, 1939), p. 72, in FO 371/24088.
[56] Salter to Chamberlain, December 15, 1938, FO 371/22540, W 16725/104/98.

it is difficult to avoid Salter's conclusion that Government action is essential if there is to be any really effective investigation of the entire area such as might eventually lead to the settlement of many thousands of refugees.[57]

But Government action of the sort Salter envisaged was not in the event undertaken. In his reply to Salter, the Prime Minister conceded solely that if any large-scale settlement schemes were to succeed, Government 'administrative cooperation' would be necessary; but 'it would be premature to consider any steps of this kind' until settlement possibilities were known.[58]

It was realised by all interested parties that settlement schemes, no matter how conceived and financed, were a long-term measure, and that whatever promise they might contain would be of little use to the masses of refugees who faced immediate danger, sometimes measured in terms of days or even hours. The Intergovernmental Committee on Refugees and the League of Nations High Commission for Refugees were both overwhelmed in the face of the post-*Kristallnacht* emergency, but even before the acute crisis, Lord Winterton complained that the Director of the IGC had fallen into a slough of 'defeatism' in which he had come to concentrate 'far too much on the United Kingdom and British Empire aspect of the refugee problem', and that Rublee had 'almost an *idée fixe* on the subject' of the British Empire's potential contribution toward a solution of the refugee problem.[59] Rublee was in fact totally frustrated by the continuing refusal of the Berlin authorities to receive him, and by the steady contraction of immigration possibilities in Latin America and elsewhere even as the need grew by quantum leaps.

After *Kristallnacht*, as R. M. Makins noted in a pessimistic minute on November 15, the purpose underlying the proposed Rublee visit—to persuade the German authorities to permit some reasonable proportion of emigrants' property to be removed—was probably impossible of fulfilment. The collective fine on the Jewish

---

[57] Halifax to MacDonald, January 4, 1939, FO 371/22540, W 16725/104/98.

[58] See Chamberlain to Salter, February 1, 1939, FO 371/24087, W 2234/1369/48.

[59] See Winterton to Reilly and Makins, November 10, 1938, FO 371/22536, W 14854/104/98

N

community meant a crushing financial burden which would in any event considerably reduce the value of remaining Jewish assets in Germany, and 'the pitiful condition to which German Jews will be reduced will not make them desirable emigrants'. Under these circumstances a visit by Rublee to Berlin would probably be 'both useless and undesirable'. Moreover, Makins continued, in considering the future of the IGC, it should be borne in mind that 'the more emigration is encouraged the greater is the temptation to increase the pressure on Jews in Central Europe'. Makins concluded that the initiative in assessing the future of the IGC be left to Washington, which had after all called the Committee into being.[60]

Rublee's assistant, Pell, was asked to call at the Foreign Office on November 15, and was told that the likelihood of negotiations with Berlin was slender and the future of the IGC itself therefore obscure. Washington, however, when informed of the Foreign Office attitude, refused to discuss the possible winding-up of the IGC in the event of a categorical German refusal to receive Rublee, even though Secretary of State Hull admitted privately that he was not optimistic.[61] Just as the atmosphere of pessimism in London seemed thickest, hints of a sudden thaw in the German attitude began to emanate from Berlin.

Foreign Minister von Ribbentrop advised the American Ambassador on November 15 that 'unofficial persons' might explore refugee questions with Rublee, perhaps in the Netherlands.[62] After a series of Byzantine manœuvres, all cloaked in the secrecy insisted upon by Ribbentrop, a meeting was arranged for December 8 in Brussels where Rublee's assistant Pell and an American colleague were to meet Hans Fischböck, the Austrian Minister of Economics, and Karl-Heinz Abshagen, a German journalist resident in London who had been chosen by Berlin to be the unofficial intermediary in arranging the meeting. After elaborate preparations had been undertaken, the Brussels meeting was abruptly cancelled due to Fischböck's sudden indisposition. The mysterious malady which felled

---

[60] See Makins, minute, November 15, 1938, FO 371/22536, W 15056/104/98.
[61] See Hull to Kennedy, November 16, 1938, *FRUS*, 1938, I, 825.
[62] See Wilson to Hull, November 15, 1938, *FRUS*, 1938, I, 824.

the German emissary appears to have been connected with the desire of Reichsbank President Hjalmar Schacht to take personal charge of the negotiations, which threatened to dissolve in confusion with the number of shadowy third parties already involved. The British authorities were aware that Schacht and Göring had prevailed over Ribbentrop, Goebbels and Himmler in a sharp struggle within the German Government on the question of the transfer of refugees' property, and that Schacht and Göring had been authorised by Hitler himself to effect a settlement of the problem.[63] As if to underscore the new German willingness to discuss the refugee question from the 'technical and economic' points of view, Göring told a meeting on December 9 of all the *Gauleiter* in Germany that they should not be surprised if they were to learn that he was in conference with Jewish groups. This hint was duly leaked to the American Chargé d'Affaires, who in turn reported it to Washington.[64]

Schacht took the opportunity of one of the regular meetings in Basel of the Bank for International Settlements to mention to Montagu Norman, Governor of the Bank of England, his desire to come to London to discuss economic and financial questions including 'the financial aspect of the Jewish problem'.[65] Schacht's proposed visit aroused intense interest in Whitehall, and was discussed at a Cabinet meeting on November 30,[66] when the Prime Minister observed that Schacht's step clearly demonstrated a split between moderates and extremists in Germany; Schacht's visit should be exploited to encourage the moderates and at the same time obtain useful information on the current state of the German economy. The Governor of the Bank of England was thereupon authorised to extend a cordial invitation to Schacht, and it was agreed that the Prime Minister and one or more of his colleagues would see

---

[63] The Foreign Office had this information from S. D. Waley of the Treasury, who had seen the irrepressible Commander Godman on November 28, and learned from Godman of Schacht's intention to come to London 'ostensibly, perhaps, for other reasons but in reality to settle this question'. See Waley to Rublee, November 29, 1938, FO 371/22538, W 15727/104/98.

[64] See Gilbert to Hull, December 9, 1938, *FRUS*, 1938, I, 864.

[65] See Director of the Economic Policy Department to German Embassy, London, December 12, 1938, *DGFP*, V, 911–912.

[66] See Cabinet Conclusions 57(38)8, November 30, 1938, CAB 23/96.

Schacht, without any publicity. It was arranged further that Lord Winterton, accompanied by Sir Frederick Leith-Ross of the Treasury, would meet with Schacht, but without Rublee, whom Winterton considered 'insufficiently experienced in such matters to be safe—either as an adviser or an observer on such an occasion'.[67] To avoid distressing Rublee however a separate meeting between him and Schacht was to be arranged if possible.[68]

As Schacht's arrival in London was being awaited, the refugee question was brought ever more insistently to the attention of the British Government. On December 7, Lord Winterton received a high-ranking deputation from the Council for German Jewry;[69] Viscount Samuel declared bluntly on this occasion that the Council was convinced by recent information it had received that Jews remaining in Germany were in immediate peril of physical destruction. The Council therefore felt it imperative that refugee camps be set up, in Britain and elsewhere, to rescue refugees and then re-train them for ultimate settlement elsewhere. The cost of such camps would be very heavy, and the enormous sums which were being raised by the private organisations were needed for relief and emigration schemes; the deputation therefore asked if any portion of the camp costs could be borne by governments. Winterton told his visitors that Sir Samuel Hoare had authorised him to say that the Home Office had no objection in principle to the notion of establishing transmigrant camps in Britain. Government financial assistance was however another matter; Winterton repeated that any use of public funds on behalf of refugees would not only encourage the Germans to expel their Jews, but would serve as a useful precedent for other governments wishing to banish their own Jewish populations. Sir Robert Cohen countered with the argument that 'if something was not done rapidly, all the potential refugees would be dead'.

Reinforcing fears in Whitehall of a new *Kristallnacht*-style out-

[67] See Winterton to Reilly, December 5, 1938, FO 371/22539, W 16409/104/98.
[68] See Reilly to Brooks, December 14, 1938, ibid.
[69] The deputation consisted of Viscount Samuel, Viscount Bearsted, Sir Robert Cohen, Mr Simon Marks, Mr Neville Laski. Present also were D. P. Reilly of the Foreign Office, and H. E. Brooks, Winterton's assistant. See Record of meeting, December 7, 1938, FO 371/22539, W 16410/104/98.

break was a telegram from Sir George Ogilvie-Forbes reporting a plan proposed out of desperation by Mr Wilfred Israel, envisaging an easing of the world-wide Jewish boycott against German goods in return for an 'armistice' in German measures against Jews. The increase in German exports resulting from the cessation of the boycott could be applied to finance emigration. Summarising the Foreign Office reaction to the Israel plan, R. M. Makins wrote :

Personally I do not think that the proposal for an armistice would have the slightest effect on the German Government. . . . The only possibility of bringing pressure to bear on the German Government is by retaliation, expulsion of German citizens, denunciation of payments agreement, & by a clear indication that until persecution & spoliation of the Jews ceases the policy of appeasement is at an end. Are we prepared to take these strong measures on behalf of the Jews? And if we did take them would they in fact bring the Germans to their senses? Might they not even provoke the massacre which some Jews foresee? The calculation is a difficult one. But I fear it is the case that public measures to help the Jews, such as the provision of financial assistance for refugee camps, will merely encourage the Germans to indulge in further persecution, & secondly that no financial plan, which the German Government are in the least likely to accept, can be produced ready made. It can only emerge from a negotiation.[70]

It was felt impossible, upon reflection, to propose the plan to the German authorities, and a telegram was sent to the British Chargé d'Affaires in Berlin requesting him to tell Israel only that the urgency of the problem was fully recognised by the IGC and the British Government.

Lord Winterton, disturbed by his meeting with the Council for German Jewry, wrote a confidential and personal letter to Lord Halifax on December 9[71] stating that there was every indication that the Germans were about to make another even more drastic and brutal attack on the Jews and that the entire position had now become 'profoundly unsatisfactory' : the time might in fact be approaching when it would be 'necessary to make a formal protest

[70] See Ogilvie-Forbes to Halifax, December 7, 1938, F.O. 371/22539, W 16205/104/98, and Makins, minute, December 8, 1938, ibid.
[71] Winterton to Halifax, December 9, 1938, FO 371/22540, W 16641/104/98.

to the German Government against the treatment of its minorities, if only on the ground of the economic disturbance and embitterment of relationship which it is causing in Europe and the United States'. Winterton also predicted that 'much greater pressure will be put upon His Majesty's Government in the next month or so . . . than has hitherto been the case, to assist migration of refugees by direct or indirect financial assistance'. Winterton reported that he had 'energetically resisted the suggestion on these lines' which had been made by the Council deputation, but that the entire matter had appeared to him so serious that he had seen the Prime Minister and the Chancellor of the Exchequer shortly after his meeting with the Council to put before them 'the views of these very influential Jews, who represent everything that is best in British Jewry'. Winterton conferred with Halifax on December 15, when the danger of an acute flareup in persecution appeared to have passed, and it was agreed that the opportunity afforded by Schacht's visit should be used to try to discuss generally the attitude of the German Government toward the German Jewish community.[72]

When Schacht, who had received Hitler's blessing for his mission,[73] arrived in London, he was received by Lord Winterton, Sir Frederick Leith-Ross, and a colleague of the Treasury. Rublee, who had been advised at the last moment of Schacht's presence in London, was invited after all to participate in the meeting. After an introduction by Governor Norman, who then withdrew, Schacht delivered himself of a few blunt preliminaries. 'It was clear,' he asserted, 'that the Jews would have no future in Germany, that they would be driven out and that in the meantime, unless some change took place, they would be badly treated. On grounds of humanity alone, therefore, it was desirable that something should be done'.[74]

Schacht then unveiled a plan, which he described as acceptable to Field-Marshal Göring, for financing emigration from Germany by means of an international refugee loan. This loan, to be raised

---

[72] See Makins, minute, December 15, 1938, FO 371/22540, W 16641/104/98.

[73] To the intense annoyance of Ribbentrop, Schacht did not trouble to inform the German Foreign Ministry of his intended trip nor of its purpose, which he blandly described as not being 'within the competence of the Foreign Ministry'. See Weizsäcker, memorandum, December 20, 1938, *DGFP*, V, 913.

[74] See Record of Meeting, December 5, 1938, *DBFP*, III, 675–677.

by 'world Jewry', would provide each departing emigrant with a sum deemed sufficient to establish him abroad: the equivalent of 10,000 gold marks in foreign currency. The loan would be guaranteed by a trust fund in Germany of 1·5 billion marks, representing approximately 25 per cent of the remaining Jewish property in Germany. Service of the loan would be made from the proceeds of the export of German goods, whose manufacturers would be paid in marks from the trust fund; thus no foreign exchange would be lost to Germany through Jewish emigration, and the transfer of Jewish assets to other countries would be accomplished through an increase in purchases by foreigners of German goods.[75]

Dr Schacht envisaged the emigration of 400,000 out of the remaining 600,000 Jews and 'non-Aryans' in the Reich; 150,000 wage earners would depart within three years, to be followed by their dependants, up to the number of 400,000. Schacht added that during the operation of his plan the Jews would be allowed to live quietly in Germany, and those 200,000 elderly Jews who could not be emigrated would be permitted to remain in peace until they died out. Winterton and Rublee assured Schacht that in their opinion his plan offered a basis for further discussion. Schacht thereupon stated his willingness to arrange for Rublee's visit to Berlin as soon as Rublee was in a position to give his preliminary view of the plan.

At a subsequent meeting between Winterton and Rublee, it was agreed that Rublee should form a small committee of Treasury experts from several countries represented on the IGC to examine the feasibility of the Schacht scheme; Rublee also undertook to ascertain the views of leading British and American Jews.[76] The committee of financial experts was rapidly formed[77] and met on December 20, concluding after its study that the Schacht plan did

---

[75] This plan, which would have put refugees in a more favourable position than British exporters to Germany, who were paid in blocked marks, bore more than a passing resemblance to the Haavara scheme for transfers to Palestine. See Chapter 2.

[76] See Winterton, memorandum, December 20, 1938, FO 371/22541, W 16931/104/98.

[77] French and Netherlands experts joined Rublee and British Treasury officials in examining the Schacht proposals. See Waley to Strang, December 21, 1938, FO 371/22541, W 16832/104/98.

form a basis for possible discussions, but that negotiations in Berlin were bound to be both arduous and prolonged.

When Lord Winterton reported the results of the Schacht visit to his Cabinet colleagues[78] he had already received some reactions to the Schacht plan from leading British Jews. The reactions were strongly negative: the Jews had 'taken the view that they thought it would be wrong that they should receive concessions at the cost of the British taxpayer'. Both the Prime Minister and the President of the Board of Trade said that 'the scheme was not one which could possibly be accepted'; the President added that it would be tantamount to helping refugees 'at the expense of British traders'. Lord Halifax also expressed reservations about any plan which would help the Nazi regime overcome its serious economic difficulties. The Home Secretary, although agreeing that the Schacht plan was difficult to justify, said that the refugee problem would be impossible to solve unless the Jews could somehow take part of their capital out of Germany; he felt therefore that it was vitally important that contact be maintained with Berlin on the plan.

When details of the Schacht proposal became more widely known, it was bitterly denounced within the Jewish community, especially in the United States, where there was indignation over Schacht's assumption that the mythically infinite financial resources of 'international Jewry' could be tapped by crudely extortionate measures designed to remedy Germany's chronic shortage of foreign exchange. It was moreover realised that if Schacht's scheme succeeded it might well serve as a model for action by the Polish and Rumanian Governments. President Roosevelt, sensitively attuned to American press criticism, promptly characterised the plan as 'asking the world to pay a ransom for the release of hostages in Germany and barter human misery for increased exports'.[79]

But despite the considerable misgivings of Washington and London, the Schacht plan was not rejected out of hand: in the absence of any other alternative, it was extensively discussed in Berlin by Rublee and his American colleagues Pell and Cotton. In talks between January 11 and February 2, 1939, the plan was modi-

[78] See Cabinet Conclusions 60(38)6, CAB 23/96, December 21, 1938.

[79] See Feingold, *Rescue*, p. 52.

field in several respects;[80] although the German Government took care not to recognise the existence of the IGC as such, an agreed formulation of the modified plan was ultimately embodied in an exchange of letters between Rublee and Ministerialdirektor Wohlthat on February 1 and 2, 1939.[81]

The Rublee-Wohlthat arrangement envisaged the emigration over a five-year period of 150,000 wage-earners and their 250,000 dependants, and retained from the Schacht plan the feature of a trust fund consisting of at least 25 per cent of existing Jewish property in Germany. The trust property in the fund was to provide the costs of emigration, including travel on German carriers, and the purchase of equipment for individual wage-earning emigrants and capital goods for refugee settlement. A private international corporation established by 'world Jewry' would make arrangements for any transfers from the trust fund, and maintain the necessary contact with the German authorities; the Haavara scheme for transfers to Palestine would as a special case continue in operation. Emigrants would be permitted to take with them certain personal effects, including professional equipment and household goods, but excluding jewellery, art objects or any precious metals.

The German Government for its part refused to enter into any concrete undertaking as to how Jews would be treated in the Reich while awaiting emigration.[82] Moreover, the Wohlthat-Rublee plan provided only for the minimal German-currency costs of emigration; foreign exchange requirements for settlement projects would still have somehow to be financed outside the arrangement. Finally, the German negotiators made it clear that the plan would be put into effect only when Berlin was satisfied that 'the countries of immigration are disposed to receive currently Jews from Germany in conformity with the program'.[83] Not one of the countries of immigration proved willing however to commit itself in an unambiguous

[80] See Rublee memorandum of these discussions, *FRUS*, 1939, II, 82–84. Discussions began with Dr Schacht, and were continued with Ministerialdirektor Helmut Wohlthat of Göring's Economics Ministry after Schacht's abrupt resignation from the Presidency of the Reichsbank on January 20.

[81] Reproduced in Gilbert to Hull, February 3, 1939, *FRUS*, 1939, II, 77–81.

[82] See Weizsäcker, memorandum, January 18, 1939, *DGFP*, V, 926.

[83] See Rublee to Hull, February 6, 1939, *FRUS*, 1939, II, 83.

fashion to receive refugees from the Reich on the terms dictated by Berlin.

The cynicism of the Wohlthat-Rublee plan was well recognised in Whitehall, where it was summarised by S. D. Waley of the Treasury as a scheme in which

if the Governments concerned satisfy Germany that they are disposed to receive at least 30,000 wage earners a year for 5 years and their dependants later, Germany will grant Poor Law Relief to Jews in Germany and 'conditions which have led' to putting entirely innocent peoples into concentration camps and subjecting them to every form of physical torture 'should automatically disappear'. The Germans reserve the right to steal all Jewish property, except the Trust Fund amounting to 25 per cent of the total (as assessed by the Germans), and some very restricted possibilities for transferring the Trust Fund into foreign exchange would be granted, but these will amount to very little if the Germans apply the system with goodwill and to nothing at all if (as is only too probable) they do not. . . .[84]

The Foreign Office understood that the scheme would enable the German Government to pass on to other countries 'the essential problem of transfer of population', and that if it were accepted it might encourage the Poles, Rumanians and Hungarians to do likewise. Despite grave reservations however the Foreign Office conceded that the plan might offer some slender hope of substituting 'orderly emigration for the present haphazard *sauve qui peut* exodus' and of somewhat mitigating the persecution of Jews and 'non-Aryans' within the Reich.[85] The plan was therefore reluctantly accepted, at least as a basis for further contacts with the German authorities.

At a full meeting of the IGC in London on February 13, Lord Winterton formally declared that the British Government had noted the results of the Rublee talks in Berlin, and was prepared to participate 'in facilitating the orderly execution of a programme of emigration'.[86] The Wohlthat-Rublee scheme was nonetheless to prove fruitful only of memoranda, Anglo-American acrimony, and

[84] See Waley to Randall, February 7, 1939, FO 371/24080, W 2244/520/48.
[85] See Randall, minute, February 8, 1939, FO 371/24080, W 2146/520/48.
[86] See Montagu-Pollock to Henderson, February 16, 1939, FO 371/24080, W 2700/520/48.

sporadic meetings with German emissaries until finally interred by the outbreak of the war in September 1939.

Despite elaborate finance and settlement schemes, the crux of the refugee problem—the need for visas and time—remained untouched. Visas were forthcoming, if at all, in a slow trickle; time had nearly run out; and on January 24, 1939, Göring, in his capacity as Commissioner of the Four-Year Plan, announced the formation of the Central Reich Office for Jewish Emigration, under the direction of SS Gruppenführer Reinhard Heydrich. This Office, which united representatives of all German Government agencies concerned with Jewish emigration, was designed to 'streamline the entire present procedure . . . and make it as simple as possible for the Jews'; agencies of the Gestapo were now officially to take charge of the emigration, on the model of the Central Office for Jewish Emigration in Vienna, which had since August 1938 accumulated a fund of valuable expertise in all the complex aspects of the expulsion process.[87] At the first session of the Reich Central Office, on February 11, Heydrich stressed that the Rublee-Wohlthat plan should not be relied on as a basis for organised emigration; all agencies concerned should therefore endeavour to promote emigration 'by all other means available' regardless of the Rublee-Wohlthat arrangement.[88]

What Gestapo 'promotion' of emigration meant in practice was connivance with German, Italian and other shipping lines and travel agencies in their carrying of refugees without papers or financial resources, to be dumped at ports all over the world. It meant in addition the organisation of illegal immigration on a large scale: refugees were rounded up, frequently after harrowing ordeals in concentration camps or Gestapo prisons, and flung into the woods bordering the German frontiers, or aboard obsolete vessels which crept down the Danube and into the Mediterranean en route to Palestine. Pell of the IGC complained bitterly to Wohlthat that his

[87] Branches of the Central Reich Office were subsequently established in Berlin, Breslau, Frankfurt, Hamburg and Prague. These and other offices ultimately organised, with largely the same personnel, the deportations to the East which began shortly after the conquest of Poland.

[88] See minutes of the first working session of the Committee of the Central Reich Office for Jewish Emigration, February 11, 1939, *DGFP*, V, 933–936. Wohlthat was present at this meeting.

Committee must be given a 'breathing spell in which to organise settlement projects', and that it was difficult to reconcile this necessity with orders the Berlin police had given the Jewish community there to prepare 100 Jews each day for emigration. Wohlthat agreed that these police measures should be discouraged, but he 'did not know what the authorities could do to put a stop to the activity'.[89] The maze of restrictive and discriminatory legislation in which Jews and 'non-Aryans' were enmeshed, and the police and other measures taken against them, had their desired effect: it was estimated by June 1939 that 120,000 refugees had left the Reich in 1938–1939, of whom the largest number fled in the winter months spanning the two years.[90]

In December 1938, as if to mock the efforts of governments and private agencies to find havens for refugees, the entire problem was yet further complicated by the desperate situation of the Jewish community in Danzig. Local Nazi leaders in the Free City rapidly promulgated decrees on the German model to eliminate Jews from Danzig, and representatives of the 3,000 remaining members of the Jewish community approached the British Consul-General on December 2 with an urgent appeal for asylum in some part of the British Empire.[91] This request put the British Government in an embarrassing position: it was felt that the Danzig refugees had a special claim on members of the League Council, and because of the unique status of the Free City they could not without conceding German claims to the City be assimilated to refugees from the Reich so as to come within the jurisdiction of the IGC or the League High Commissioner for Refugees. Despite urgent representations by the British Consul-General that only a speedy and comprehensive emigration scheme could help the Danzig Jews, London considered it impossible even in this case to depart from the existing policy of extending no Government financial help to refugees.[92] The Foreign

---

[89] See Pell to Hull, March 4, 1939, *FRUS*, 1939, II, 95–97.

[90] See Hope Simpson, *Review Since September 1938*, p. 24. This number should be compared with the estimated 150,000 refugees who left the Reich in the five preceding years.

[91] See Shepherd to Halifax, December 2, 1938, FO 371/22539, W 16012/104/98.

[92] See Shepherd to Halifax, and Reilly, minute, December 22, 1938, FO 371/22541, W 17163/104/98.

Office pressed the Home Office to enlist the voluntary organisations in an effort to accelerate the migration of Danzig refugees, and arrangements were subsequently made to rescue most of the children, about fifty of whom came to Britain under the auspices of the British Movement for Care of Children from Germany.[93] The adults among the Danzig Jews fared less happily : their position became increasingly precarious until the local branch of the Zionist Revisionist Party conceived a desperate scheme for mass immigration to Palestine, without visas or other previous arrangements. Despite strong British warnings to shipping companies and to the Rumanian and Italian authorities against granting transit facilities, a party of some 450 Jews left Danzig on March 4 by special train to Constanza, and there embarked by Greek steamer ostensibly for Haiti but actually for Palestine. Only some of these managed to enter Palestine; the remainder scattered throughout the world.[94]

Throughout the winter of 1938–1939, and into the spring months, the search for places of asylum became obsessive : no corner of the globe was too outlandish for consideration. It was even judged appropriate to make soundings in Moscow, despite the hysterical xenophobia revealed by the purge trials, as to whether the Soviet Government would admit refugees from the Reich.[95] The British Embassy in Moscow put paid to any such notion, however, writing that 'despite the absence of any anti-Semitic policy on the part of the Soviet Government, an infinitely larger number of Jews have in all probability been executed in the Soviet Union during the last

[93] See minutes on FO 371/24085, W 5586/551/48. On April 12, 1939, the Council for German Jewry formally agreed to consider refugees from Danzig entitled to the same relief and settlement facilities as those from the Reich itself. See Council to Home Office, April 12, 1939, FO 371/24085, W 6550/551/48.

[94] See Shepherd to Halifax, April 6, 1939, FO 371/24085, W 4190/451/48. This large-scale illegal immigration attempt appears to have aroused the interest of the King, who requested an explanation of the situation. His Private Secretary wrote to Lord Halifax on February 28: 'The King had heard from Gort on his return from Palestine that a number of Jewish refugees from different countries were surreptitiously getting into Palestine, and he is glad to think that steps have been taken to prevent these people leaving their country of origin. . . .' See Hardinge to Halifax, February 28, 1939, FO 371/24085, W 3567/551/48.

[95] This suggestion was made by Sir Samuel Hoare, who felt it advisable to canvass possibilities in the Soviet Union 'as a matter of tactics'. See Roberts to Vereker, December 29, 1938, FO 371/22540, W 16557/104/98.

two years than in Germany under the National Socialist régime, while an equal if not larger number have been placed in concentration camps'.[96]

For a time in November and early December of 1938, the French colony of Madagascar was mooted as a possible settlement for not only German refugees but Polish Jews as well. The French Government was however wary of sending German refugees in any numbers to French colonies, either in Madagascar or in New Caledonia, and made any offer to settle refugees in French territories conditional on other governments making similar offers for their own possessions.[97] Another project, to install German Jewish refugees in Haiti, was abandoned after the American State Department expressed its objections from 'racial, economic, and strategic points of view'.[98]

Haunted by the dilemma of finding suitable territories not only for the German refugees, but for the vast Jewish populations of Eastern Europe, the United States Department of State, with the active encouragement of President Roosevelt, seized on the notion of the Portuguese colony of Angola as a most promising region. Under-Secretary of State Welles considered the possibilities of Angola 'of such importance as to warrant heroic efforts to overcome the political obstacles';[99] among the alternatives canvassed was a leasehold or indeed purchase of large blocks of land in Angola from the Portuguese Government. Myron C. Taylor took the occasion of a visit to London in late January 1939 to bring Roosevelt's interest in Angola directly to the attention of the Prime Minister, who cautiously undertook merely to explore through Lord Winterton the feasibility of an approach to Portugal through diplomatic channels.[100] Lord Halifax refused however to take up the matter with Lisbon, pointing to Portugal's extreme sensitivity on all colonial questions and to the possibility of causing serious offence. Sir Alexander Cadogan wrote on February 1 :

[96] See Vereker to Halifax, January 21, 1939, FO 371/24097, W 1541/1541/48.
[97] See record of IGC meeting, December 2, 1938, FO 371/22539, W 16140/104/98.
[98] See Welles to Mayer, *FRUS*, 1939, II, 62.
[99] See Welles to Roosevelt, January 12, 1939, ibid., 65. Angola had been considered as the site of a possible Jewish settlement in 1912, but negotiations for the purchase of land there were interrupted by World War I and never resumed.
[100] See Taylor to Hull, January 25, 1939, ibid., 74.

'I really wouldn't touch this. We have large tracts in the world which have not been populated, and I do not think it is for us to ask our very susceptible ally to find room in her colonies for the Jews . . . if we can't or won't find room in our Empire, I do at least hope we shall not ask the Portuguese to do more than we are prepared to do.' [Halifax commented :] 'I quite agree. Let the Americans do it.'[101]

The Americans for their part doggedly refused to be discouraged and the Foreign Office subsequently conceded that 'soundings of a most informal character' might be made, preferably through private channels. Despite the Portuguese Minister's declaration in Washington on April 15[102] that Lisbon did not wish to contemplate cession of any part of Angola for Jewish colonisation, the State Department remained preoccupied with the question and even after the outbreak of war pressed the Foreign Office to support an approach to the Portuguese Government, something which the Foreign Office with equal consistency declined to do.[103]

Other large-scale settlements were envisaged in such places as the Philippines, where an agricultural settlement for about 10,000 refugees was projected on Mindanao, but abandoned after the Commission which explored that project reported pessimistically.[104] British Guiana, although never conceived of in other than long-range terms, seemed initially to offer a more promising prospect for a settlement of a size commensurate with the growing need.[105]

The British Guiana settlement proposal, it had always been made clear, was not to receive any financial support from the British Government; that did not however preclude Lord Winterton from expressing the 'hope', even before public announcement was made of the British Guiana plan, that the United States Government 'would be in a position to make a substantial contribution, and announce this contribution very shortly'.[106] Washington stolidly refused to take

[101] FO 371/24097, W 1645/1645/48.
[102] See Moffatt, memorandum, April 15, 1939, *FRUS*, 1939, II, 101–102.
[103] See Makins, minute, September 22, 1939, FO 371/24097, W 14069/1645/48.
[104] See Hull to Kennedy, July 15, 1939, *FRUS*, 1939, II, 137.
[105] Prime Minister Chamberlain, in talks with the French Government which touched, *inter alia*, on the Jewish refugee question, described British Guiana as 'the most hopeful territory . . . suitable for settlement by white people, unlike many other British and French colonies'. See Record of Anglo-French Conversations held at the Quai d'Orsay, November 24, 1938, *DBFP*, III, 295–6.
[106] See Rublee to Hull, November 17, 1938, *FRUS*, 1938, I, 827.

this hint and betrayed no willingness to make any financial contribution, preferring to adhere strictly to the Evian doctrine that the private organisations alone must find the funds necessary for refugee settlement.[107]

The British Jewish organisations concerned with the Guiana scheme recognised that in the absence of any government aid the major source of the enormous sums required to develop the territory must be the American Jewish organisations,[108] they therefore made strenuous efforts to enlist the aid of President Roosevelt's private Advisory Committee on Refugees in financing and mounting the preliminary survey of British Guiana. The American Jewish bodies represented on the President's Committee were however suspicious of the entire Guiana scheme, feeling that British policy on immigration to Palestine gave rise to legitimate doubts as to whether immigration to British Guiana might also be cut off at a later date for political reasons.[109] Rublee was therefore instructed to obtain confirmation from the Foreign Office of Washington's assumption that the British Government did not contemplate any limitation on the settlement of refugees in British Guiana 'in substantial numbers, as rapidly as the physical and financial difficulties can be overcome'.[110]

The misgivings of the American Jewish organisations were ultimately overcome, and a mixed Anglo-American Commission departed for British Guiana early in February 1939, with a mandate to report to President Roosevelt's Advisory Committee on Political Refugees on all aspects of the feasibility of large-scale colonisation

---

[107] See telegram from Hull to Pell, instructing him to 'discourage in every possible way the introduction of any official plan which makes the financing of the emigration of refugees dependent upon governmental participation', and reminding him that the United States Government had 'made it clear from the first time it issued the invitation to the Evian Conference that . . . the responsibility for financing rests with the private groups'. June 12, 1939, *FRUS*, 1939, II, 124.

[108] See Rublee to Hull, December 9, 1938, reporting a conversation with Anthony de Rothschild. *FRUS*, 1938, I, 865.

[109] See Welles to Taylor and Rublee, December 5, 1938, ibid., 855.

[110] See Welles to Rublee, December 14, 1938, *FRUS*, 1938, I, 870. There is no record in the available British or American documents that the British Government gave the assurances sought by the State Department. See, however, Chapter 8 for Lord Winterton's statement on July 13, 1939, that the British Government had no intention of permitting ' "mass settlement" in Guiana or anything resembling the situation in Palestine'.

in the territory. Pending the Commission's report, however, the weary search for places of asylum continued. The world map was scoured repeatedly for settlement possibilities; the correspondence columns of the British press resounded with the polite controversies of ex-colonial administrators and others debating the climatic and other merits of obscure islands and jungle-covered valleys whose salubrious delights had previously gone unremarked.[111] The sole port in the world where no visas or other papers were required of those wishing to land remained Shanghai, a city whose International Settlements constituted an enclave where foreigners were entirely free of Chinese jurisdiction. Nominally ruled by a Muncipal Council elected by non-Chinese residents, policed by a Volunteer Corps including units of the British Indian Army, the Shanghai International Settlements were in fact administered by the Consuls of the major powers in China, who were baffled and alarmed by the thousands of refugees from the Reich who suddenly streamed into their city in late 1938 and into 1939.[112]

As the refugees poured into Shanghai, destitute after having parted with their last savings to secure sea passages, the Foreign Office was implored by the British Consul-General there to find funds and territories for the repatriation of these paupers, whose mass influx threatened the entire European position in the city. The refugees were concentrated in the poorer suburbs of Shanghai, where most led a precarious existence, unable to compete for scarce work with the native Chinese, and supported on thin rations by charitable organisations. Beyond informing the IGC of the position, and officially deprecating the travel of Jews to Shanghai in British ships, there was nothing the British Government felt it could do to remove the pressure of refugees from the settlement. In a harshly-worded report on the situation, the British Passport Control Officer in Berlin wrote:

[111] See, e.g. Sir Ernest Bennett, MP to Halifax, December 7, 1938, on Sokotra Island in the Persian Gulf, FO 371/22538, W 15784/104/98; *Manchester Guardian*, January 10, 1939, on Trinidad; New Guinea proposal in *The Times*, February 16, 1939.

[112] By April 1939, there were between 6,500 and 8,000 Jewish refugees from the Reich in Shanghai. See Hope Simpson, *Refugees*, p. 47. This community had increased to approximately 20,000 by the outbreak of war. See A. Tartakower and K. R. Grossman, *The Jewish Refugee* (New York, 1944), p. 322.

We in this office have warned Jews and Jewish organisations here of the danger of proceeding to Shanghai. They refuse to listen to us and say that Shanghai under any conditions is infinitely better than a Concentration Camp in Germany. One can perhaps understand their point of view. . . . It is useless to talk to the German Government whose declared object is to destroy these people body and soul; it makes no difference to them whether destruction takes place in Germany or in Shanghai. I rather think preference would be given to the Far East as their shipping companies are paid for the freight . . . it might be considered humane on our part not to interfere officially to prevent the Jews from choosing their own graveyards. They would rather die as free men in Shanghai than as slaves in Dachau. . . . It is not possible for me to report the number of refugees proceeding from German and Italian ports, but I am of opinion that the movement will continue to the utmost capacity of ships sailing east.[113]

In February and March 1939, however, the British and American Embassies in Berlin made representations to the German Government requesting the official discouragement of the lucrative traffic in refugees by German shipping lines proceeding direct from German ports to Shanghai. The Wilhelmstrasse's reaction to both the British and American démarches was predictable : Jews were not wanted in Germany, and the German Government 'would not hinder their going anywhere, Shanghai included'.[114]

The most important of the 'anywheres' to which German policy was driving refugees remained Palestine. After the British Government's rejection in November 1938 of the Woodhead Report recommending partition of Palestine into Arab and Jewish states, preparations went forward for a conference to be held in London in February and March 1939, at which the Jewish Agency, the Palestine Arabs, and neighbouring Arab states were invited to state their respective views on possible solutions to the Palestine problem. The opening session of the conference took place on February 7, 1939, against a background of continuing violence in Palestine itself, where a prolonged and strenuous military campaign by large British forces had not succeeded in putting down the Arab rebellion which had

---

[113] Foley to Ogilvie-Forbes, January 17, 1939, FO 371/24079, W 1017/519/48. See also Foreign Office to Consul-General, Shanghai, January 3, 1939, FO 371/ 22541, W 1700/104/98.

[114] See Geist to Hull, March 3, 1939, *FRUS*, 1939, II, 94.

flared up again in late 1937.[115] Despite the disturbances in Palestine, a large proportion of whose Arab population was in open revolt at the time, total Jewish immigration into the country in 1938 was 11,222, of which some 55 per cent represented immigrants from Germany.[116] Painfully aware of the increasingly desperate situation in the Reich, the Palestine Jewish community offered in November 1938 to receive for adoption 10,000 Jewish children from Germany. This proposal, and a larger offer made later in November to absorb 100,000 young Jews, practically the whole of the younger generation left in Germany, were both rejected by the Government in London which felt itself unable to take a step which would further inflame the Arabs—who had demanded a complete halt to Jewish immigration—and thus perhaps prejudice the outcome of the Round Table Conference. In his statement to the House of Commons conveying the Government's decision not to permit the entry of 10,000 children to Palestine, the Colonial Secretary said that the request was not being 'permanently refused'; immigration to Palestine would be one of the subjects to be considered at the Conference. If it were meanwhile considered necessary to evacuate the children from Germany, they could be received in Britain if the refugee organisations would guarantee their maintenance. The issue of the admission of 10,000 children to Palestine was thus firmly linked with British domestic refugee policy.[117]

Confronted with the rejection of their requests for an increase in legal Jewish immigration, and an ever-worsening situation in Europe, the Jewish community in Palestine proceeded to organise illegal immigration on an increasing scale. Although illegal immigration into Palestine, both Jewish and Arab, had existed for many years, the pressure in Central and Eastern Europe now transformed it into a large-scale enterprise.[118] Despite the strengthening of the

[115] See Royal Institute of International Affairs, *Great Britain and Palestine, 1915–1945* (London, 1946), pp. 109–123. The guerilla warfare subsided only in May, 1939.

[116] Figures quoted in Hope Simpson, *Refugees*, p. 83.

[117] See 342 H.C. Deb., 1975–6, December 14, 1938, and J. C. Hurewitz, *The Struggle for Palestine* (New York, 1950), p. 96.

[118] Hope Simpson, *Refugees*, estimates that some 7,000 Jewish immigrants entered Palestine illegally in 1938; this figure is almost certainly understated. Op. cit., p. 86. See Jon and David Kimche, *The Secret Roads* (London, 1954), pp. 15–44.

Palestine police and coastal patrols, Jewish immigrants were landed at night along the coast, often after long voyages in ill-equipped and sometimes dangerously unseaworthy vessels. Once scattered among the Jewish population, the refugees were virtually impossible to find and deport. Moreover, in the organisation of illegal immigration the Palestinian Jews had an ally in the German authorities, who were pleased to embarrass the British administration and to take advantage of any possibility 'for getting a Jew out of Germany'. The Gestapo and other agencies concerned with Jewish emigration were also determined that the large-scale illegal traffic to Palestine now increasingly being organised by Poland and Rumania should not block the channels for removing 'their' Jews from the Reich.[119]

In London, the Round Table Conference met throughout February and March, with the presentation of diametrically opposed Arab and Jewish cases, revealing little if any scope for a possible compromise. Further discussions between the delegations and the British Government resulted in deadlock; British Government proposals were then made, and duly rejected by both Arabs and Jews. The Conference came to an end on March 17, in an atmosphere of unrelieved bitterness on both sides and in the knowledge that the British Government would now prepare and impose its own solution. That solution, which embodied a dramatic reversal of the entire British policy on immigration to Palestine, was to be announced in an official White Paper on May 17, 1939.

The exigencies of the international situation perforce demanded the lion's share of attention in British Government consideration of refugee policy during the early months of 1939, but the refugees had also begun to impose severe strains on the domestic scene, with consequent political repercussions. As the backlog of visa applications relentlessly mounted, and the administrative delays appeared to lengthen in inverse proportion to the amount of time the Gestapo

---

[119] Ministerialdirektor Wohlthat told the first working session of the Committee of the Central Reich Office for Jewish Emigration that Palestine could absorb 800,000 to 1,000,000 Jews; this number would be supplied from other countries in case no Jews from Germany reached Palestine. The meeting agreed that Germany should exploit the opportunity afforded by illegal immigration to Palestine, but without any 'official participation'. See Minutes, February 11, 1939, *DGFP*, V, 933–936.

permitted refugees to make their exit arrangements, Ministers were bombarded with hostile queries in Parliament and in the press concerning alleged inefficiencies, overlapping, waste and sheer confusion in the Home Office, Foreign Office and Ministry of Labour departments concerned with refugees.

Suggestions made by Members of Parliament and others for a unified Government department to deal with refugee matters were firmly resisted, however.[120] Even Lord Cecil's magisterial blast in the form of a question in the Lords as to whether the Government was aware that its arrangements for dealing with refugees were 'scandalously insufficient', and that delays which might mean life or death were constantly occurring, was turned aside on the grounds that all cases continued to require the most careful, and therefore time-consuming, consideration.[121] Some months later Cecil wrote privately to R. A. Butler at the Foreign Office :

I knew that Winterton (alas!) has been put in charge of the German-Jewish Refugees. But that does not, apparently, extend to Hungarian Refugees; nor does it extend to Spanish Refugees; nor, I imagine, to Polish Refugees. He therefore has a very fragmentary authority to deal with the matter, and there is really a lot to be done, as you know. Moreover, there are a number of voluntary aid societies, some of whom no doubt are competent, but those I have come across are mainly incompetent. . . . In my view, if there were a properly organised Refugee Department, they would have some official dealing with the aid committees and seeing that they really did carry out their duties, at any rate so far as it is a national duty. At present I am convinced that there is an immense amount of energy, and therefore probably of money, being wasted. . . .[122]

In an internal memorandum prepared for a House of Commons debate on refugee questions,[123] the Aliens Department of the Home Office emphasised that the careful investigation of a refugee's circumstances before issuing him a visa was undertaken at the request of the refugee organisations themselves, who in the absence of such investigation found themselves saddled with unassimilable refugees

[120] See Chamberlain statement, December 13, 1938, 342 H.C. Deb., 1793–4.
[121] See 111 H.L. Deb., 673–4, December 22, 1938.
[122] Cecil to Butler, March 6, 1939, FO 371/24076, W 4242/45/48.
[123] Home Office memorandum, undated but probably written on November 19 or 20, 1938.

whose maintenance was a heavy burden on funds which had been raised for the purposes of training and emigration. Since 1933, despite steady increases in personnel, the ever-growing volume of refugee work had consistently outstripped the staff available to deal with it. After the Anschluss, when the Home Office had also been required to cope with the demands of air-raid precaution work, arrears had accumulated until there were toward the end of November some 10,000 files awaiting disposition. *Kristallnacht* had made an already bad position 'infinitely worse' : in the week following November 9–10, the entire administrative staff and most of the senior clerical staff of the Aliens Department had been forced to attend 'incessantly to telephone enquirers and callers, pleading for immediate action to rescue some unhappy friend or relative in Germany'. There were also 'innumerable letters from MPs' to be dealt with, and no work on arrears had been possible. The refugee organisations were in a similar position; the congestion in the German Jewish Aid Committee alone had 'become practically unmanageable'.

The crux of the problem was numbers, the memorandum made plain : the Aliens Department had been established on the assumption that immigration to the United Kingdom would be negligible; but with pressures mounting to admit ever-larger numbers of immigrants and transmigrants, the entire Department would have to be reorganised on a larger scale. The memorandum concluded that as long as the general policy approved by the refugee organisations were continued, no mere modifications of procedures could produce a saving of manpower sufficient to enable the arrears to be speedily cleared and 'the future faced with equanimity'.

By the beginning of 1939, certain steps were nevertheless taken by the Home Office to streamline and accelerate its procedures. A simplified card system for the admission of transmigrants, trainees and elderly refugees over the age of 60 was agreed with the refugee organisations, and enabled visas to be granted immediately for refugees in these categories.[124] Substantial staff increases were made, and the Aliens Department removed to new and larger offices on

[124] See Jagelman to Secretary, Co-Ordinating Committee for Refugees, December 20, 1938, FO 371/24074, W 443/45/48.

January 21. In addition, at the end of January, a disused Army camp at Richborough in Kent, the Kitchener Camp, was re-opened under the auspices of the Council for German Jewry and used to house and train up to 3,500 male refugees between the ages of 18 and 35 pending their re-migration elsewhere.[125] The desirability of setting up a standing interdepartmental committee to deal with all aspects of the refugee problem also became apparent to the Home Secretary and his colleagues and on January 18, a Cabinet Committee on Refugees was appointed to keep the entire question under review and to report when necessary to the Cabinet.[126]

Within the private organisations themselves, however, chaos often continued to reign, and for the same reasons as in the case of Government departments : too few case workers, despite a near trebling of staff between April and November 1938, too little experience, a plethora of committees, and the sudden, overwhelming rush of refugee clients. By February 1939, the leading refugee organisations, which had been scattered at over twenty addresses in London alone, joined to purchase a former hotel in Bloomsbury which as Bloomsbury House became for several years the headquarters for most refugee work. Physical centralisation of refugee efforts was helpful, but the basic cause of confusion and delay remained : the sheer numbers of refugee organisations, and their frequently overlapping appeals and functions.[127] Some progress was made in coordinating case work by the reorganisation in January 1939 of the Co-

[125] See Home Office memorandum, January 26, 1939, FO 371/24074, W 1368/45/48.

[126] Members of the Committee were the Home Secretary, Secretary for the Dominions and Colonies, the President of the Board of Trade, the Chancellor of the Duchy of Lancaster; and Parliamentary Under-Secretaries to the Ministry of Labour and the Foreign Office, in addition to the Financial Secretary to the Treasury. See Cabinet Conclusions 1(39)5, CAB 23/99. The initiative for the establishment of this Committee appears to have come from Lord Winterton, who expressed apprehension over continuing criticism of Government refugee policy after Parliament reassembled following the 1938 Christmas recess. See Reilly, minute, January 11, 1939, FO 371/24087, W 1089/1089/48. On January 15, Lord Halifax wrote on the same file : 'PM told me in Rome that he had it in mind to set up a Cabinet Committee to deal with all these Refugee questions.'

[127] A pamphlet published in *The Jewish Chronicle* in February 1939 lists nineteen different fund-raising organisations, three major and numerous minor case-work committees; and seven sub-committees of the Co-Ordinating Committee for Refugees itself. See Joseph L. Cohen, *Salvaging German Jewry, A Guide to Those Who Wish to Help* (London, 1939).

Ordinating Committee for Refugees, under the chairmanship of Lord Hailey, a former Governor of the Punjab and United Provinces. He in turn recruited Sir Henry Bunbury, a former Permanent Under-Secretary at the General Post Office, as Director of the largest case-work committee, the German Jewish Aid Committee, of which Mr Otto M. Schiff remained the Chairman.[128] But all these efforts at 'coordination' and reorganisation were merely palliative : the 'creaking machinery of guarantees and permits, visas and transports' was crushed by numbers; successive administrative improvisations, however ingenious, could not elude that fact.[129]

More serious than administrative muddle in its potential effect on British refugee policy was the groundswell of anti-refugee feeling to which Sir Samuel Hoare referred in his Parliamentary statement of November 21, 1938. The Aliens Department of the Home Office observed with disquiet that the admission of refugees 'whether as workers, merchants, manufacturers or professional men, excites the anxiety of sections of the community, which look to the Government for protection'.[130] As refugees were assisted by the private organisations to find jobs or emigration opportunities often not available to British subjects, resentments inevitably grew.

Moreover, opposition of certain Fascist and other extreme right-wing political groups to aliens, particularly Jewish aliens, had been consistent since 1933, and was expressed in such organs as *The Fascist*, the *Fascist Week*, and a spate of pamphlets arguing that aliens competed for British jobs and were threatening to take over the country.[131] As the numbers of refugees increased following the Anschluss and the worsening situation in Germany, anti-refugee attacks became more frequent, and the argument that all refugees were somehow tainted—an argument sedulously propagated by the German press—commended itself to a wider audience. The sheer ubiquity of refugees proved an irritant, and it was difficult for many

---

[128] See Bentwich, *Refuge*, pp. 38–40.

[129] Professor Norman Bentwich, intimately connected with the refugee work, later confessed : 'the altogetherness of everything overwhelmed us, and the forced march of time overtook our puny efforts.' See his *Wanderer Between Two Worlds* (London, 1941), p. 283.

[130] See Home Office memorandum, GEN 29/3/254, November 19–20, 1938.

[131] See Robert Benewick, *Political Violence and Public Order* (London, 1969), pp. 46–154.

observers to grasp that refugees had been expelled from their home-lands not for what they had done, nor even for their beliefs, but because of what they helplessly and unavoidably were: the descendants of unsuitable ancestors.

Propagandists of the extreme right, such as Lord Londonderry, Admiral Sir Barry Domvile, or Sir Arnold Wilson, contributed in letters to the editor and other publications to the notion that Jewish refugees were carriers of Marxism and other forms of decadence, and were an unsound element in British society.[132] Other sources of anti-refugee agitation were openly pro-German groups such as the Anglo-German Fellowship—which in December 1937 had some 700 members, including financial and industrial figures of eminence and many Members of Parliament—and The Link, sponsored by Admiral Sir Barry Domvile. Newspapers which took a strong pro-appeasement line, notably the *Daily Express* and the *Daily Mail*, regarded the influx of refugees to Britain as a needless irritant in Anglo-German relations as well as a source of potential damage to the British working class.[133] The sturdy xenophobia of these news-papers, expressed in constant references to the 'arrogance' and other shortcomings of the refugees, had a far wider appeal however than merely to working-class readers.

The conspicuousness of the refugees; their unfamiliar clothes, accents and behaviour; their often highly-strung condition and their desperate search for jobs; their propensity, common to all émigrés everywhere, to congregate for mutual support in certain areas and certain occupations, led to the widespread assumption that they numbered in many scores if not hundreds of thousands, and that they posed serious social and economic dangers to Britain. Although Parliamentary questions revealed repeatedly that the number of German and Austrian aliens actually permitted to remain in Britain —and those under stringent conditions as to employment—was in fact severely limited,[134] the myth that hordes of penniless and aggres-

---

[132] See Margaret George, *The Hollow Men* (London, 1967), pp. 142, 149–151.

[133] See D. C. Watt, *Britain Looks to Germany* (London, 1965), p. 23.

[134] By April 1939, 20,299 German, Austrian and Czech refugee adults had been admitted to Britain, and 4,837 children. See Hope Simpson, *Refugees*, p. 69 and James Parkes, *The Emergence of the Jewish Problem, 1878–1939* (London, 1946), p. 227.

sive Herr Doktors had descended on British shores proved peculiarly persistent, and fed the anti-refugee campaign. 'Innumerable refugees to add to the tangle', wrote Virginia Woolf in her diary for February 28, 1939, adding 'there—I've recorded them when I said I wouldn't.'[135]

Contemporary observers agreed :

'Jews are news.' It is not an enviable kind of limelight that beats upon the Chosen People. Everybody in England is talking pogroms instead of football-pools.[136]

Malcolm Muggeridge noted that

Sir John Simon found it necessary to issue a statement that, despite a biblical name, he was of Welsh extraction; Lord Camrose, proprietor of the *Daily Telegraph*, brought a successful libel action against an organ of the British Union of Fascists for having falsely implied that he was a Jew; in one of his articles, Dean Inge suggested that Jews were using 'their not inconsiderable influence in the Press and in Parliament to embroil us with Germany' . . . Anti-Semitism was in the air, an unmistakable tang.[137]

The refugee organisations themselves, concerned over the growing feeling against their clients, departed in late 1938 and early 1939 from the policy they had pursued since 1933 of responding only occasionally to anti-refugee statements, and sponsored letters to the editor, and several pamphlets pointing out that refugees were in no sense competing unfairly with British labour, and that they did not represent an undesirable element in British life.[138] The Jewish organisations also distributed to the refugees in their care a pamphlet, in German and English, which reveals in its list of instructions the sensitivity of the Anglo-Jewish community to the growth of anti-Semitic feeling which accompanied the influx of refugees.

---

[135] Virginia Woolf, *A Writer's Diary* (London, 1953), p. 311.
[136] Wyndham Lewis, *The Jews, Are They Human?* (London, 1939), p. 7.
[137] Muggeridge, *The Thirties*, p. 263.
[138] A report of the Jewish Defence Committee to its parent body, the Board of Deputies of British Jews, stated in February 1939 that there had been evidence in the previous month or two of a concerted anti-refugee campaign; the Committee had responded by sponsoring a pamphlet titled *The Refugees: The Plain Facts*, which it hoped would dispel allegations unfavourable to the refugees. See Jewish Defence Committee, Report, February 19, 1939, WH.

The pamphlet[139] adjured each refugee to regard himself as 'in honour bound' to start immediately to learn English and its correct pronunciation; and to refrain from speaking German or reading German newspapers in public, or indeed from speaking in a loud voice altogether. The refugee was also urged not to criticise Government regulations, nor the way things were done in Britain, and not to make himself conspicuous by his manner or dress. 'The Englishman', refugees were informed, 'attaches very great importance to modesty, under-statement in speech rather than over-statement, and quietness of dress and manner. He values good manners far more than he values the evidence of wealth.' Other instructions to the refugee were not to take part in any political activities, and especially not to 'spread the poison of "It's bound to come in your country" '— a notion to which British Jews particularly objected. In conclusion, the pamphlet requested each refugee to 'spread courage by word and deed' and to 'be loyal to England, your host'.

In the struggle for public sympathy on the refugee problem, the Jewish organisations and other pro-refugee groups had one consistent ally in the *Manchester Guardian*, whose efforts to enlighten both public and Government on the dimensions and urgency of the post-*Kristallnacht* crisis were reflected in leaders and special articles urging Government financial aid and a more flexible and sympathetic administration of the regulations governing the entry of aliens to Britain. Such traditional Parliamentary liberals as Josiah C. Wedgwood and Eleanor F. Rathbone were also insistent in pressing questions exposing cases of slowness and unnecessary rigidity on the part of Government officials.[140] Those members of the Labour left who were in close touch with Social Democrat and other opponents of the Nazi regime had no need to be reminded of the refugee problem; nor did certain members of the press corps such as G. E. R. Gedye, who had observed at first hand the brutalities

---

[139] *Helpful Information and Guidance for Every Refugee*, published in January 1939, by the German Jewish Aid Committee in conjunction with the Jewish Board of Deputies.

[140] See Josiah C. Wedgwood, *Memoirs of a Fighting Life* (London, 1941), p. 266, for a description of his pro-refugee efforts, which were accomplished 'in the teeth of every obstruction from Government, from anti-Semites, and from many English Jews who feared for themselves lest anti-Semitism should increase here'.

of Nazi rule in Austria. Their efforts on behalf of refugees comple-
mented those of the anti-German right wing, whose members in
Parliament included Harold Macmillan, Viscount Cecil and Leo
Amery, and whose exemplar within the Civil Service was Sir Robert
Vansittart. The more conservative critics of Government policy
saw the refugees as living proof of the folly of appeasement, and
attacked vigorously the Government's reluctance to maintain with
sufficient generosity an older tradition of British hospitality for
political refugees.[141]

That the refugee problem, critical as it was at the beginning of
1939, was bound to become worse, was clear to British and other
observers of Hitler's post-Munich menaces to the rump Czech state,
and further East. Negotiations on the British Government loan to
the Czechs were deliberately delayed by London

as a means of making the new Czechoslovak Government realize that
we still count, and that in particular attention should continue to be
paid to our views in regard to the Jewish and refugee questions.

But the days in which Britain could exercise effective influence in
Prague were over; the British Minister there reported frankly that
no Czech Government had 'any option but to submit to German
dictation whether in the political or economic field'.[142]

Despite the frantic attempts of the Czech Government to placate
Hitler, the German campaign of threats and subversion continued to
gain momentum, culminating in the brutal presentation of an ulti-
matum to the aged President Hacha in the early hours of March 15,
and the formal dissolution of the Czech state at dawn as German
troops occupied Bohemia and Moravia. On the same date the Hun-

---

[141] See Watt, *Britain*, p. 21.

[142] See Newton to Halifax, December 5, 1938, FO 371/21577, C 15244/
2320/12. The Czech loan agreement ultimately signed on January 27, 1939
provided for an Anglo-French advance to Czechoslovakia of £16,000,000, of
which half was to be an outright gift and half a loan. £6,000,000 of the
£8,000,000 loan was to be used to refund part of the original £10,000,000
advanced to the Czech Government after Munich; the balance of £4,000,000
remaining from that advance also represented a gift, to be used for the relief
and settlement of refugees. These arrangements were overtaken by the German
invasion, however, and most of the British gift remained at the Bank of England.
On March 22, it was announced that £3,250,000 remaining from the gift would
be utilised to make grants for refugee emigration. See Hope Simpson, *Refugees*,
p. 40.

garians helped themselves with German consent to Ruthenia, and the puppet who reigned over Slovakia put his state too under the protection of the Reich.[143] With the first German troops came the Gestapo, and the emissaries of the Reich Central Office for Jewish Emigration, who established a Prague bureau on the lines of those existing in Vienna and Berlin. The noose had tightened round an indeterminate but undoubtedly very large number of new refugees, whose fate was beyond the British Government's capacity to affect by any diplomatic action.[144] Those refugees who could make their way across the heavily guarded frontier into Poland represented a mere fraction of those trapped by the occupation.[145]

The international bodies charged with responsibility for refugees faced the challenges of 1939 after yet another change of administration. George Rublee, who had always stated his intention to return to private law practice after a limited period, resigned as Director of the IGC as of the end of 1938 and was succeeded by Sir Herbert Emerson, who also became the High Commissioner of the reorganised League High Commission for Refugees in January 1939. Emerson's appointment to these two posts was meant to assure greater efficiency in coordinating the work of the IGC and the High Commission; the two bodies, in accordance with American wishes and German sensitivities, were nevertheless to remain distinct.[146] The State Department, which gave its blessing to Emerson's dual appointment,[147] also attached importance to a continuation of discussions on the Wohlthat-Rublee plan, despite the extinction of Czecho-

---

[143] See Thorne, *Approach of War*, pp. 100–105.

[144] The British special representative in Prague, R. J. Stopford, had estimated on December 7 that there were at that time some 127,000 refugees in Czechoslovakia, of whom 96,000 were Czechs, 8,000 Germans, 400 Poles, 21,000 Jews, and 1,600 others. Stopford surmised that the number of Jewish refugees was probably in fact larger by some 7,000 to 10,000, since a great many Jews had been afraid to register with the police. His figures also failed to include any refugees from Slovakia or from Ruthenia. See Stopford to Central Department, December 7, 1938, FO 371/21588, C 15388/11896/12.

[145] See Hope Simpson, *Refugees*, pp. 38–41.

[146] On January 17, 1939, the mandate of the High Commission for Refugees was extended to protect former Czechoslovak nationals. See Hope Simpson, *Refugees*, p. 18.

[147] See Welles to Taylor, December 30, 1938, *FRUS*, 1938, I, 885. Emerson continued to be assisted by Pell as Vice-Director of the IGC; Lord Winterton stayed on as Chairman, with Myron C. Taylor as Vice-Chairman.

slovakia.[148] But these discussions and other international efforts to soften German intransigence on the refugee question became increasingly irrelevant after the fall of Prague.[149]

For the refugees from the Reich, the crucial events marking the end of the first quarter of 1939 were the invasion of Czechoslovakia and the failure in London of the Round Table Conference on Palestine. The first event swelled the number of refugees;[150] the second foreshadowed the virtual closing of one of the last avenues of escape.

The German occupation of Bohemia and Moravia and the flood of rumours, threats and pleas for assistance which followed in Eastern Europe, were to give rise to radical departures in British foreign policy in belated efforts to contain the menace of German expansionism. But as of April 1939 Whitehall's refugee policy remained fixed on two seemingly immutable principles : first, no Government financial assistance for the emigration and settlement of refugees; second, immigration into Great Britain itself must be strictly limited in view of the numbers of British still unemployed and the risk of fanning anti-alien and anti-Semitic feelings among the population.

These twin pillars of policy were nevertheless to be substantially modified by September 1939, under the pressures of enormous growth in the numbers of refugees, the moral dilemma posed by the virtual closing of Jewish immigration to Palestine, and the change in the political climate as war with Nazi Germany rapidly approached.

[148] See Welles to Pell, March 23, 1939, *FRUS*, 1939, II, 98.

[149] Lord Halifax and Prime Minister Chamberlain raised the refugee question with Mussolini on the occasion of their visit to Rome in January 1939; the Duce felt his intervention with Hitler would not be of much use, however. See Record of Conversations between British and Italian Ministers, Rome, January 11–14, 1939, *DBFP*, III, 519.

[150] Perhaps several thousand refugees, of whom half were Jews, were also added to the pool of those fleeing from the Reich when Memel and its hinterland were ceded under duress by Lithuania to Germany on March 23, 1939. See Thorne, *Approach of War*, pp. 106–109.

8

Last Moments

March — September 1939

A man falls into a river. He is about to drown. From both banks, heedless of their own danger, people jump into the water to save him. A man is grabbed from behind and thrown into the river. He is about to drown. People on both banks of the river look on with growing alarm at the desperate attempts of the drowning man to swim, and think 'if only he doesn't save himself on *our* shore'.[1]

WITH the march of German troops into Prague on March 15, and the establishment of the Gestapo throughout what had been Bohemia and Moravia, refugees of all categories found themselves in the gravest and most immediate danger. The members of local refugee committees in Prague were arrested and their papers confiscated; the frontiers sealed and emigration temporarily brought to a complete halt.[2] Certain prominent political refugees were granted asylum in several foreign legations,[3] but their number was minute in comparison with the thousands of refugees who now went underground, or streamed toward the Polish frontier individually and in ragged groups, in the slender hope of evading German, Czech and Polish border patrols.[4] These refugees included Sudeten Jews and politicals,

---

[1] Alfred Polgar, *Prager Tagblatt*, September 18, 1938, quoted in Kurt R. Grossmann, *Emigration* (Frankfurt, 1969), p. 6.

[2] See Randall, minute, March 18, 1939, FO 371/24081, W 4700/520/48.

[3] Some eight refugees, including Wenzel Jaksch of the Sudeten Social Democrat Party, found shelter in the British Legation, and were ultimately given safe conduct on March 24 to leave Czechoslovakia. See minutes on FO 371/24082, W 5589/520/48.

[4] By March 31, about thirty refugees per day were illegally crossing into Poland. See Hope Simpson, *Refugees*, p. 39.

Czech politicals, Jews from the new Protectorate, and former Reich Jews and politicals. The Poles, anxious as ever to insulate themselves from a further influx of Jews, took ever more stringent measures, including summary expulsion of those illegal entrants who could be found in border areas; but the refugees, with the Gestapo at their heels, kept arriving despite all obstacles.

Although Prime Minister Chamberlain could not initially bring himself to condemn Germany for the destruction of Czechoslovakia, the utter failure of his appeasement policy was plain to others; and following a stormy Commons debate and two days' reflection, Chamberlain warned Hitler in a historic *volte-face* on March 17 that Britain would resist his further territorial ambitions in Europe. By the end of March the Government had guaranteed the independence of Poland, and consultations were proceeding on a possible joint Anglo-French-Russian guarantee for Rumania.

The Foreign Office and other Government departments were meanwhile deluged with letters, telegrams and calls from deputations, all pleading in the most urgent terms for diplomatic intervention to prevent refugees from being arrested or turned back at the Polish frontiers, and for energetic efforts by the British Government to provide transport and other means of rescuing those in greatest danger.[5] The British Minister in Prague was immediately instructed to facilitate in every possible way the departure of all refugees who had visas for the United Kingdom; and representations were made by the Ambassador in Berlin to try to remove German obstacles to emigration.[6] But the odds against successful escape steadily mounted: Gestapo arrests continued, the German authorities imposed an exit visa requirement which made it impossible for political refugees to leave the new Protectorate legally, and those few refugees who were permitted from early April to depart on special trains were often shunted back and forth on German railways, and in many cases re-arrested or merely robbed

---

[5] See appeals from National Council for Civil Liberties, Artists Refugee Committee, P.E.N. Club, Society for Protection of Science and Learning, the Archbishop of York, Eleanor F. Rathbone and other MPs, and numerous other groups and individuals in FO 371/24081.

[6] See Halifax to Lindsay and Phipps, March 16, 1939, FO 371/24081, W 4548/520/48.

before being allowed out of Reich territory. While the Swiss Government unhelpfully closed its frontiers entirely to refugees from Czechoslovakia,[7] and the Dutch authorities threatened to act likewise, the Polish border guards continued to expel all Jews among the refugees coming into Poland. And the delays at the British Passport Control Office in Prague mounted alarmingly.

Prominent among those who had consistently warned of the impending fate of Czechoslovakia, and whose anxious appeals to the Government now had an added note of bitterness, was Eleanor F. Rathbone, MP, who in a series of letters and telephone calls implored the Foreign Office to instruct the Passport Control Office in Prague to issue British visas without waiting for German permits, and to relocate the Prague Legation's Visa Department where callers could not so easily be kept under Gestapo surveillance. She also urged that the diplomatic bag be used to transmit small sums of money to refugees who could thus be enabled to escape through Germany. 'But I recognise', she wrote of this last request, 'that this would be "irregular" and your Legation at Prague may be trusted to countenance no irregularities for an object towards which they have always shown complete indifference.'[8] Stung by this accusation, A. W. G. Randall of the Foreign Office minuted resignedly :

Having consulted Treaty & Passport Control Depts. I am going to try to soothe Miss Rathbone's injured feelings by conversation. She is particularly indignant because I refused to transmit English currency to Prague by the FO bag, ostensibly for British subjects, but really for refugees in hiding. It is difficult to persuade people like Miss Rathbone that the consciousness of the necessity for an all-round view, and for maintaining good faith or at least good relations between us and the Germans is not cynical, inhuman indifference.[9]

Not content with letters to the Foreign Office or with a drumfire of Parliamentary questions, Miss Rathbone wrote to the *Manchester Guardian* early in April[10] castigating the Government in strongest terms for its unchanged policy of 'selfish isolationism' vis-à-vis refugees, and pointing out that the effect of the Government's

---

[7]See Swiss Minister's note, March 17, 1939, FO 371/24081, W 4639/520/48.
[8]See Rathbone to Randall, March 23, 1939, FO 371/24081, W 4984/520/48.
[9] Randall, minute, March 28, 1939, ibid.
[10] See *Manchester Guardian*, April 6, 1939.

P

'rigid, perpetually changing regulations' was to admit to Britain precisely those refugees who were most difficult to absorb or to re-emigrate : elderly professional or commercial people possessing capital or well-off English friends. Rejecting the argument that greater generosity toward refugees might harm British workers or increase anti-Semitism, Miss Rathbone demanded 'a clear break with the fatal policy of Evian' on no Governmental financial aid to refugees; the establishment of temporary reception camps for up to 50,000 transmigrants; streamlining of the conditions of admission, preferably by putting the whole refugee problem in the hands of a single Minister; and finally the allocation of the unexpended portion of the £4 million grant and £6 million loan to Czechoslovakia for the benefit of refugees from that country. Absolving civil servants and Ministers of 'intentional inhumanity', Miss Rathbone called nonetheless for public opinion to demand these reforms in Government refugee policy 'loudly, insistently and persistently'.

From other quarters too voices were raised expressing grave disquiet over the refugee situation. Colin R. Coote, a leader writer on *The Times*, wrote privately to Lord Winterton on March 24[11] to report that every member of his staff 'down to the office boy' was being bombarded with desperate appeals on behalf of refugees, and that allegations of British red-tape, particularly in the Home Office, were too numerous to overlook. Moreover, 'wherever one touches the voluntary refugee organisations one finds unrelieved chaos'. Asserting that 'the record of HMG in this matter is not glorious', Coote requested an early interview with Winterton. At that meeting, he was told that the Home Office rejected criticisms of its claimed rigidity and inefficiency; the chief delay in extricating refugees from the Reich arose from the official difficulties made by German tax, police, municipal and other authorities; and further delays were caused by the extreme financial stringency of the voluntary organisations, all of whom were now very near the end of their resources.[12]

Another fact to which the Home Office might legitimately have made reference was that many thousands of British visas had been granted to refugees who had not yet made use of them to enter the

[11] See Coote to Winterton, March 24, 1939, FO 371/24081, W 5248/45/48.
[12] See Brooks to Randall, March 29, 1939, FO 371/24081, W 5248/45/48.

United Kingdom. On May 8, 1939, the Passport Control Department of the Foreign Office reported with some alarm that a total of 79,271 visas had been granted since May 1 in the previous year, and that some 50,000 of these had not been used. It was apparent to Passport Control Officers that many refugees had obtained British visas as a hallmark of respectability and a form of insurance, without any present intention of using them. The Foreign Office thereupon wrote to the Home Office, pointing out that if any large proportion of the 50,000 refugees holding British visas were to decide suddenly to use them, the resulting influx might have 'serious consequences', particularly in the event of war. The Foreign Office also queried whether some use could not be made of the high number of visas actually granted in order to rebut criticisms of allegedly ungenerous Government refugee policies. The Home Office did not apparently reply officially, and after further inquiries A. W. G. Randall of the Foreign Office wrote on July 17 : 'I have spoken to Mr Cooper H.O. two or three times about this. He does not take a serious view of the situation, as he thinks many of the people who do not use the visas will never do so.'[13]

In the course of a Commons debate on the adjournment,[14] speaker after speaker castigated the Government for insufficient awareness of the time factor in the refugee equation : while settlement possibilities were laboriously being investigated, many thousands of refugees were in imminent peril. Colonel Wedgwood, in a characteristically blunt speech, decried all 'dreams of colonisation' elsewhere than in Palestine, and urged in strongest terms that the only way to prevent the threatened expulsion of Jews from Eastern Europe was to put pressure on the Polish and Rumanian governments in return for British guarantees and military assistance. He suggested moreover that the Government took its views on refugee matters from Lord Winterton, who had not in the past 'been celebrated for his affection for Jews'.[15] Other Members stressed that the burden on the voluntary organisations had now become intolerable, and that only prompt Government financial and administrative help could

[13] See memoranda and correspondence on FO 371/24100, W 7740/323/48 and W 8127/232/48.
[14] See 345 H.C. Deb., 3043–3087, April 6, 1939.
[15] Ibid., at 3065.

solve the problem. In his reply for the Government, Lord Winterton repeated that not one of the thirty-two IGC governments was prepared to admit either any moral obligation to solve the refugee question or 'financial liability for the transfer and upkeep . . . or for the permanent settlement of refugees'; the 'unhappily pervasive . . . sub-current of anti-Semitism or anti-alienism' which existed in many countries made it impossible for governments to do more for refugees than for their own people. The British Government would nevertheless, Winterton concluded, 'be prepared to consider . . . sympathetically' the possibility, in certain specific cases, of furnishing personnel and services to accelerate overseas settlement schemes.

Winterton's stock response to his Parliamentary critics was made with knowledge of an increasingly strident diplomatic campaign being waged by the Polish and Rumanian governments to engage the IGC in a solution of what they regarded as their respective acute 'Jewish problems'. Beginning shortly after *Kristallnacht*, the Polish Government, which had perennially raised the issue of Jewish emigration to Palestine, sharply stepped up its pressure, calling on the British Government to propose that the IGC deal with all Polish Jewish emigration; or at least do its utmost to ensure inclusion of the 10,000 or more Polish Jews expelled from Germany within the purview of the IGC. The first proposal was firmly and consistently rejected, and even the more modest claim was set aside initially, on narrowly legalistic grounds.[16]

The British Ambassador in Warsaw warned that if no assistance was granted to Polish Jews to emigrate their position would almost certainly deteriorate, writing:

There is no decrease in public interest in the Jewish question and most Poles generally regard it as inevitable that in order to induce a state of mind favourable to emigration amongst the Jews, their position here must be made less comfortable. Local excesses—not organised, as recently in Germany, but more or less spontaneous—are of not infrequent occurrence. . . .[17]

Count Raczynski, Polish Ambassador in London, called at the Foreign Office to complain of Lord Winterton's 'bureaucratic and

[16] See Winterton to Raczynski, November 22, 1938, FO 371/22537, W 15316/104/98.
[17] Kennard to Halifax, November 20, 1938, FO 371/21638, C 14496/1667/72.

unsympathetic view' of Poland's Jewish problem, and to threaten that 'if nothing was done for the Polish Jews, the Polish Government would inevitably be forced to adopt the same kind of policy as the German Government, and indeed to draw closer to that Government in its general policy'.[18] In Warsaw itself, ominously, a committee representing all sections of the Jewish community had meanwhile been formed under Polish Government pressure to study the 'possibility of encouraging Jewish emigration'.[19]

On February 13, the IGC formally considered the Polish Government's request to extend its mandate to cover Jews of Polish nationality who had recently been expelled from the Reich. Several representatives were without instructions however, and to the intense irritation of the Polish authorities no decision was taken at this meeting.[20] On the occasion of Colonel Beck's visit to London between April 4 and 6 for a discussion of the British guarantee of Poland's frontiers, Halifax assured Beck that the British Government would be willing to 'consider sympathetically the position of Polish emigrants, once the immediate refugee problem' was on its way to a solution. British sympathy was conditional : it depended on Poland's observing 'due tact' and maintaining 'her present reputation for tolerance in regard to her Jewish minority.'[21] Despite continuing vigorous efforts on the part of the Polish Ambassador in London, the British Government refused to go beyond this point, and limited itself to supporting Polish claims for an extension of the IGC's mandate solely to those 10,000 Jewish refugees of Polish nationality who had been expelled from Germany, an extension which was reluctantly admitted by the other IGC members only on July 19, 1939.[22]

The Rumanian Government too pressed insistently for British

[18] See record of Winterton-Raczynski conversation, December 7, 1938, FO 371/22539, W 16393/104/98 and Strang, minute, December 9, 1938, FO 371/22540, W 16615/104/98.

[19] See Kennard to Halifax, December 9, 1938, FO 371/21638, C 15379/1667/62.

[20] See Halifax to Kennard, February 22, 1939, FO 371/24075, W 2824/45/48.

[21] See brief for Halifax-Beck talks, April 1, 1939, FO 371/24084, W 5796/520/48.

[22] See Roberts to Raczynski, May 4, 1939, FO 371/24082, W 6251/520/48 and August 2, 1939, FO 371/24084, W 9133/520/48.

Government assistance in emigrating its Jews through the IGC, calling formally in December 1938 for 'a radical and early solution of the Jewish question' in Rumania by means of internationally assisted migration.[23] King Carol himself told the British Minister that it should not be 'insuperably difficult for the Evian powers to find a small territory in which the Jews could exercise sovereign rights' and which could absorb some 200,000 Rumanian Jews.[24] The British Minister in Bucharest cautioned that the Rumanians should not tempted 'above what they are able to bear' and suggested that 'even a token emigration of an organised party of Jews to some destination in the British Empire' could enable the Rumanian Government to inform its people that success had been achieved 'by an appeal to reason and not by the application of brutality'.[25] When the Rumanian Foreign Minister in his turn visited London in late April, he repeated that for his Government the Jewish question was a 'capital question': something had to be done 'to fit the problem into a wider international frame'.[26] Lord Halifax told the Foreign Minister that he had not forgotten what Colonel Beck had said on the same subject; the situation in Palestine had confronted the British Government also with the problem. Halifax confined himself none-theless to declaring only that the British Government was 'not without hope that it might be possible to make a rather large contribution to the problem by utilising the resources of British Guiana'; in that event, the Government 'hoped to be able to give to the questions of Polish and Roumanian Jews the place due to them within the framework of the larger problem'.

British Guiana was in the event to prove a slender reed indeed on which governments anxious for large-scale solutions to the refugee dilemma could rest their hopes. The Anglo-American commission which had landed in the colony in mid-February made extensive

[23] See Rumanian aide-mémoire, December 5, 1938, FO 371/22539, W 16119/104/98.

[24] See Hoare to Halifax, December 30, 1938, FO 371/24073, W 274/45/48. R. M. Makins minuted on Hoare's despatch on January 5, 1939: 'It is a matter of sheer practical necessity which drives the Intergovernmental Committee to confine itself to refugees from Germany. The existing problem is unmanageable. It is quite out of the question to tackle anything more.'

[25] See Hoare to Ingram, February 4, 1939, FO 371/24080, W 2938/520/48.

[26] See record of conversation, April 23–26, 1939, *DBFP*, V, No. 295.

aerial and ground surveys of some 41,900 square miles, and concluded in its report that European settlement would be feasible in the area surveyed and that the basis for agricultural and some industrial development existed.[27] The Commission had certain reservations, however, and recommended cautiously that an initial trial settlement of some 3,000 to 5,000 young persons be established in order to test whether Europeans could adjust to the difficult climatic and other conditions of settlement in the interior of British Guiana; the approximate cost of establishing such a settlement for a period of two years was very tentatively estimated at $3 million.

The Foreign Office greeted the British Guiana Refugee Commission's report with undisguised relief; it was seen as affording, contrary to all initial expectations, an opportunity for the British Government to take the lead in attempting a large-scale constructive solution to the refugee problem.[28] Refugee settlement in British Guiana, it was also emphasised, now offered 'a very useful opening for an enterprise in imperial development, in a much neglected colony', an enterprise of which the Americans should not be permitted to 'take charge'.[29] Of equal importance was the chance that the British Guiana proposals might take some of the heat out of the extreme adverse reactions which were nervously anticipated, particularly from the American Jewish community, to the new Palestine policy which was about to be announced in a White Paper. At an interdepartmental meeting held on May 4 to consider the Guiana report, the Colonial Secretary referred to this aspect of the proposed settlement scheme, stressing 'in particular the importance of energetic action in British Guiana to offer some consolation to the Jews, who would be bitterly disappointed by the decision of HM Government about Palestine. He was therefore very anxious that the statement of the attitude of HM Government to the British Guiana report should be issued as soon as possible'.[30] The meeting agreed

[27] The Foreign Office received an advance copy of the Report on April 29; the final version was published as *Report of the British Guiana Refugee Commission to the Advisory Committee on Political Refugees appointed by the President of the United States of America* (London, 1939), Cmd. 6014.

[28] See minutes on FO 371/24089, W 6980/1369/48.

[29] See Reilly, minute, May 1, and Randall, minute, May 2, ibid.

[30] See Reilly, memorandum, May 4, 1939, FO 371/24089, W 7499/1369/48.

that all measures should be taken to press on rapidly with the adoption of the Commission's proposals—but the possibility of using any British Government funds for settlement in the colony was 'completely ruled out, except perhaps for certain administrative and other services'.[31] The voluntary organisations were therefore intended to bear virtually the entire cost of refugee settlement in a colony where sole access to the region proposed for such settlement was by river canoe or launch, cattle trails or light aircraft—and where road construction and forest clearing alone were optimistically estimated to require several years.

The Cabinet, acutely aware that the Palestine draft White Paper contained a drastic reversal of policy on Jewish immigration[32] which was bound to arouse bitter opposition in Palestine itself, in Parliament and in the United States, anxiously debated at several of its meetings the relation between possible reactions to the White Paper and to the report on British Guiana. The Colonial Secretary, who had originally urged the desirability of the earliest possible issue of the Palestine White Paper,[33] later favoured waiting until the British Guiana report could be made available, emphasising 'the importance of taking some action to ease matters for the Jews'. He stated that 'drastic action . . . against the Mufti [of Jerusalem, Haj Amin Effendi al Husseini] would, of course, help in this direction' but that the British Government ought also 'to go further and to offer to make available for Jewish immigration some British territory in another part of the world. . . . British Guiana . . . was by far the most hopeful possibility.'[34]

---

[31] Ibid. Apart from Treasury objections, the Colonial Office view, strongly seconded by Lord Moyne, Chairman of the Royal Commission on the West Indies, who was present at the meeting, was that any use of Government funds for refugee settlement in British Guiana 'would cause such an outcry in the West Indies in general' as to be 'quite out of the question'.

[32] The White Paper provided that a total of 75,000 Jewish immigrants of whom 25,000 were to represent 'a contribution towards the solution of the Jewish refugee problem' were to be admitted to Palestine over the next five years, after which time no further Jewish immigration would be permitted without Arab consent. The numbers of illegal immigrants entering Palestine would be deducted from the yearly quotas making up the 75,000 overall total. See *Statement of Policy*, May 1939, Cmd. 6019.

[33] See Cabinet Conclusions 24(39)6, CAB 23/99, April 26, 1939.

[34] See also Cabinet Conclusions 26(39)5, CAB 23/99, May 3, 1939.

At the Cabinet meeting of May 10,[35] the Colonial Secretary marshalled once more the considerations which dictated early publication of the White Paper, including the growing unrest among the Arabs, who knew that the Paper was ready and tended to assume in the absence of publication that 'Jewish influences were at work to secure modifications in their favour'. On the other hand, the Labour Opposition had urged postponement in view of the 'strong and protracted opposition' the White Paper would doubtless provoke among the Jews in Palestine and elsewhere. The United States Ambassador, when consulted as to the possible impact of the White Paper in his country, had said that its publication 'would not make much difference to a situation which was already difficult'. The Jews, according to Mr Kennedy, 'were unpopular in America' but they might nevertheless manage 'to work up a certain amount of anti-British agitation' over Palestine which would not probably affect the projected visit of the King and Queen to the United States. The Home Secretary, echoed by the Prime Minister, held that the Government's statement on the British Guiana Commission's report should be issued well in advance of the publication of the White Paper, and after further discussion it was agreed that this statement should appear as soon as possible and should 'emphasise the large possibilities of the scheme'; the Palestine White Paper was to be published approximately one week thereafter.

The British Guiana Refugee Commission's report was thereupon published simultaneously in Britain and the United States on May 10, but initial reactions to it on the part of both refugee organisations and the press were at best tepid. The Zionists in particular assailed the report for excessive optimism, and for its potential diversion of material and human resources from Palestine. A day later, in response to a Parliamentary question, the Prime Minister issued a statement of Government policy[36] welcoming the British Guiana report and offering to lease lands in the interior which might be found suitable for refugee settlement 'on generous terms'. The Government would 'assume that this experimental settlement will be financed from private sources' although 'if the prospects

---

[35] See Cabinet Conclusions 27(39)7, CAB 23/99, May 10, 1939.
[36] 347 H.C. Deb., 862–864, May 12, 1939.

of development are good and the capital forthcoming is adequate
for the purpose of large scale settlement', the Government would be
prepared to meet the cost of arterial communications from the coast
to the interior settlement areas; a large measure of autonomy could
ultimately be granted to a substantial community, and it was hoped
that arrangements could be made to begin settlement in the autumn
of 1939. A much less sanguine view of British Guiana settlement
prospects was published in *The Times* of May 20, in the form of a
lengthy letter from A. J. Schwelm, an expert on colonisation whose
authority to speak on the subject was termed 'unquestionable' in a
Times leader of the same date. Schwelm stated that European settlement in British Guiana was impracticable and 'doomed to failure'.
His letter evoked a typically protracted *Times* correspondence :
rejoinders and counter-rejoinders from other experts and ex-colonial
residents, most directed to the climatic rather than financial aspects
of the problem.[37]

Long before concrete steps were taken to give substance to the
British Guiana Refugee Commission's recommendations, the
Colonial Office was conscious that within British Guiana itself and
in the Royal Commission on the West Indies there was much less
optimism on the possibilities of economic development in the colony
than had been evidenced by the Refugee Commission. Moreover,
preliminary soundings which had been taken with the Co-Ordinating
Committee for Refugees had revealed that the British Jewish community was unable to finance the scheme outlined in the Guiana
report, or even the experimental proposal for an advance party of
3,000 to 5,000 settlers. The main financial burden of settlement
would therefore fall on the American Jewish community; the British
Jewish groups were in any case convinced that the settlement of some
500 persons in all was as much as should initially be undertaken.
The Colonial Secretary told a meeting of the Cabinet's Committee on the Refugee Problem that he and the West Indies Commission too agreed with the Co-Ordinating Committee in favouring
a much smaller scale experimental settlement than had been advocated in the Guiana report, but that he hoped the Government
'would carefully refrain from making this suggestion and should

[37] See *The Times*, May 24, May 27, 1939.

leave it to other interested parties to propose it'.[38] Discussions on the physical and especially financial difficulties of the proposed experimental settlement were to drag on between London, New York and Georgetown until overtaken by the war, which put an effective end to speculations on British Guiana as a refugee haven.[39]

As the Cabinet had surmised, the Palestine White Paper was acceptable to neither Arabs nor Jews: the Arabs condemned the new policy for its only partial acceptance of their demands, while the Jews rejected it *in toto* as a breach of faith and an abject capitulation to Arab terrorism.[40] The intensity of the emotions aroused by the White Paper may partially be gauged by a harsh private exchange between Dr Chaim Weizmann and the Colonial Secretary on May 13. As reported by Dr Weizmann in a confidential memorandum:

The conversation reached its crisis when Dr Weizmann, in analysing the Government's new policy, said that at least in Hitler one found the virtue of an absolutely frank brutality, whereas Mr MacDonald was covering up his betrayal of the Jews under a semblance of legality. He added that Mr MacDonald was handing over the Jews to their assassins. Mr MacDonald showed great indignation and said it was of no use to talk to him like that. He said he knew that the Jews had been calling him a hypocrite and a coward. Dr Weizmann replied: I have never called you a coward.[41]

The bitterness of the anti-British reaction was strongest within the Palestine Jewish community, which saw the White Paper as a rejection of their hopes for a National Home and a callous slamming of the door in the face of thousands of refugees and potential refugees whose only hope of asylum now lay in Palestine.[41] The Palestine Jews were united in considering the furtherance of Jewish immigration into Palestine by any means, legal or illegal, as a moral imperative. In efforts to increase the flow of this immigration, the Jews had the cynical and self-serving assistance of the Gestapo, the Polish,

[38] See Conclusions, Fourth Meeting of the Cabinet Committee on the Refugee Problem, May 9, 1939, CRP (39), 4th Mtg., FO 371/24090.

[39] For a discussion of abortive refugee colonisation schemes, see Tartakower and Grossmann, *Jewish Refugee*, pp. 510–515, and Feingold, *Rescue*, pp. 90–125.

[40] See J. C. Hurewitz, *The Struggle for Palestine* (New York, 1950), pp. 102–106.

[41] Weizmann, memorandum, May 14, 1939, S 25/7563, ZA.

Rumanian and other governments, and a host of middlemen: smugglers, ship brokers, agents of all sorts who battened on the misery of thousands of would-be immigrants whose desperation drove them into attempting the hazards of the clandestine passage to Palestine.

The British authorities in London and Jerusalem observed with growing alarm that the advantages sought in issuing the White Paper—rallying Arab and Moslem support to Britain's side in the event of war—were rapidly being eroded, as illegal Jewish immigration increased despite the imposition of steadily harsher measures to combat it at every point along the route to Palestine. The Palestine CID noted pessimistically in a report dated May 1[42] that illegal immigration was being organised on a large and increasing scale by certain Jewish political groups, particularly the Revisionists, for their political ends;[43] and by private groups and individuals for profit. Refugees who had 'literally "nothing to lose" . . . put their entire resources at the disposal of persons in a position to assist them to get to Palestine'. With these funds transit visas, passports and other travel documents were obtained from the consuls in Vienna, Berlin or elsewhere of such countries as Liberia and the Dominican Republic. France, Italy, Switzerland and to a lesser degree Belgium actively connived at the illegal traffic by issuing *saufs-conduit* to groups of refugees whose stated destinations—China, Haiti or other —were patently bogus. Switzerland in fact went further and 'openly encouraged organisers of illegal transports to Palestine to come to Switzerland to organise transports'. The Polish Government abetted the traffic by turning a blind eye to the large-scale arrangement of travel to Palestine under the guise of 'tourism' by Polish Jews to such unlikely countries as Chile or Bolivia. In their turn, Rumanian Government officials, most often for a cash consideration, watched unconcernedly as packed special trains arrived from Poland at Rumanian ports and Jews were herded aboard small, unseaworthy vessels for the attempted run to the Palestine coast. Typical of indignant British consular reports was one by the Consul-General

[42] See CID Jerusalem, A Report on the Organization of Illegal Immigration to Palestine, May 17, 1939, FO 371/24092, W 10171/1369/48.

[43] For a discussion of illegal immigration and Zionist policy, see Yehuda Bauer, *From Diplomacy to Resistance* (trans. ed., Philadelphia, 1970), pp. 60–64.

at Galatz who wrote that the Rumanian local authorities, 'generally most punctilious in demanding that safety and decency rules shall be fulfilled to the letter', had 'openly connived at the flagrant breach' of these rules as some 900 emigrants were packed into one small Greek vessel 'with a total disregard of all regulations and precautions'.[44] The Greek Government's contribution was in the form of bland official ignorance that most of the wretched hulks engaged in the refugee movement were of Greek registry, and frequently manned by Greek crews as well.

British representatives in Rumania, Greece, and other countries along the immigration route made repeated efforts to secure the cooperation of governments in suppressing the traffic, but in vain : the most urgent representations were turned aside with mendacious assurances, vessels of one registry switched with impunity on the high seas to flags of other nations, and only occasional derisory sentences were meted out to those agents or ship captains who had not adequately bribed officials. The Palestine Government itself now resorted to wholesale detentions of those ships which could be intercepted, and to increasingly desperate attempts to return illegal immigrants to their ports of embarkation.

The leitmotif of reports streaming into London was the sense of horror felt by diplomatic observers at the conditions prevailing in the illegal traffic. The British Consul-General at Galatz declared roundly:

This trade is, in fact, one of the most brutal that has been devised since the abolition of slave trading. . . . The unfortunate victims, fleeced already of a large part of their fortunes, are herded on board of old condemned ships and finally brought to the shores of Palestine in such a state of distress that it is believed that the humanity of the British authorities will not be able to refuse to accept them.[45]

Of a group of 1,500 would-be immigrants confined on ships lying off Beirut, the British Minister in Athens wrote :

. . . shocking conditions reminiscent of slave trade and I cannot believe that public opinion in England would tolerate their being left to their fate.[46]

[44] See Macrae to LeRougetel, March 10, 1939, FO 371/24088, W 5960/1369/48.

[45] Consul-General to Minister in Bucharest, June 17, 1939, FO 371/24091, W 9953/1369/48.

[46] Waterlow to Halifax, May 23, 1939, FO 371/24090, W 8689/1369/48.

News of ships boarded, immigrants arrested, and others turned back to Europe aroused passionate protest in Palestine itself and in Parliament, where Colonel Wedgwood and others harried the Colonial Secretary with slashing attacks on a policy which they asserted was having the effect of sending refugees back to the concentration camps. In a debate on the adjournment on June 5, Wedgwood condemned in strongest terms the use of the Royal Navy to intercept and turn back vessels, some of which had been at sea for up to three months, protesting that 'conduct worthy of Hitler, conduct worthy of the Middle Ages, cannot be carried on by the British Government in 1939'. The Colonial Secretary denied 'inhuman indifference to the lot of the refugees' and explained that the Government was confronted with a problem of 'scores of thousands, which would become hundreds of thousands of Jews from countries in Europe where there is persecution and where there is no persecution, seeking to overcome the law in Palestine and land and settle there'.[47]

Both the Colonial Office and the Foreign Office continued to deny charges of inhumanity, pointing out that most of the illegal immigrants were Jews from Poland and Rumania who were not technically refugees.

Despite continuing diplomatic pressures on Rumania and Mediterranean countries, and greatly reinforced police measures, the movement of transports to Palestine increased inexorably. The situation had become so serious by July 7 that the Foreign Office expressed its grave concern at 'the disastrous effect of the continuance of illegal immigration into Palestine' on the entire British position in the Middle East and in all Moslem countries. German and Italian propaganda ceaselessly hammered at the theme that Britain was in fact conniving at the immigration, and Moslem opinion was becoming convinced by the continuing British failure to stop the influx that the accusation was true.[48] Estimating that despite all precautions 5,300 illegal immigrants had landed in Palestine since the beginning of May, and that other thousands had doubtless landed undetected—and with reports of several thousands more *en route*—

---

[47] See 348 H.C. Deb., 171–178, June 5, 1939.
[48] See Reilly, note, July 10, 1939, of interdepartmental meeting held on July 7, FO 371/24092, W 10846/1369/48.

the Foreign Office embarked on a strenuous diplomatic campaign
to put maximum pressure on governments involved in all phases of
the traffic: Brazil, China, Liberia, Panama and others which
granted visas or flags of convenience; Poland, Hungary, Yugoslavia
and Rumania which pushed out immigrants and organised over-
land transports; and Rumania, Greece and other countries whose
ports were used by vessels making for Palestine. The Foreign Office
urged the Colonial Office in its turn to adopt more stringent measures
in Palestine, including the confinement of illegal immigrants pending their deportation, suggesting that 'any criticism of confinement
might be met by reference to the fact that illegal immigration into
Palestine is now ceasing altogether to be a refugee movement and
is taking the form of an organised political invasion'.[49] Other courses
of action urgently considered by the Foreign Office were the negotiation of agreements with such countries as Greece, Panama and
Rumania authorising the boarding of their ships outside Palestine
territorial waters, and even the extension of the doctrine of 'hot pursuit' to enable the Royal Navy to stop the practice of vessels transferring their passengers to small boats outside the Palestine maritime
boundary.[50]

On July 12, in an answer to an arranged Parliamentary question,
the Colonial Secretary announced to the House that the numbers
of illegal immigrants landing in Palestine had been so great of recent
months that no immigration quota whatsoever would be issued for
the next quota period, from October 1, 1939 to March 31, 1940.[51]
This action evoked a deeply-felt exchange of letters between Josiah
Wedgwood, MP and Lord Halifax. Wedgwood wrote by hand to
Halifax on July 13, 1939:[52]

You—alone of all the Govt.—should know as well as I do that there
are occasions when the laws of God (or conscience) conflict with the

---

[49] See Randall to Under-Secretary of State, July 21, 1939, FO 371/24092,
W 10846/1369/48.

[50] See minutes and correspondence, August 1939, on FO 371/24092, W 10468/
1369/48, and FO 371/24094, W 12663/1369/48. Proposals to extend Palestine
territorial waters for police purposes were opposed on principle by the Admiralty
and the Board of Trade, and were not carried out. See Dunn to Randall, September 30, 1939, FO 371/24095, W 14272/1369/48.

[51] See MacDonald, statement, 349 H.C. Deb., 2275–2276, July 12, 1939.

[52] See FO 371/24092, W 10676/1369/48.

laws of man and should be obeyed at the cost of any self-sacrifice. All our progress here and in USA (perhaps some in India) has depended on such conduct. Hugh Cecil once said 'Acts of Parliament don't make things right or wrong'; still less does expediency. The two Palestine orders—forbidding immigration of Jews and forbidding Jews to acquire land wherefrom to live,—have no moral justification, no Parliamentary justification either, for they are contrary to humanity and justice. There was a time when you had to stop natives acquiring the right to use land in the Highlands of Kenya. You did not like it, but you understood my point of view. Don't try to pull wool over my eyes about this worse thing. Do your duty, of course, but let me do mine, with a little understanding. Yours, Josiah C. Wedgwood. P.S. All Jews are refugees!

Halifax replied on July 18 :

My dear Joss, I am afraid I cannot follow you into the details of your last three letters about Polish and Czech refugees; these are primarily questions for the Treasury and the Home and Colonial Offices. . . . Nor can I altogether follow you in the philosophy of your last letter, for surely there must be cases where absolute justice is impossible to achieve, and we—not being omnipotent—have to choose. No one can feel more intensely than I the hardships and injustices of the refugees which move you so deeply, but as a responsible Minister I am compelled to realise that there are limitations to what can be done. The illegal immigration of Jews (many of them not refugees) into Palestine may, for example, have done an injustice to thousands of more deserving people. . . . I must ask you to accept my assurance that all the Ministers and Departments concerned are as alive to the seriousness of the refugee situation as you are yourself, and are working as hard as they can to find a practicable solution which will not make the general problem more complicated and distracting than it is already.

Wedgwood's outcry was echoed by the Jewish community in Palestine and elsewhere, but the immigration ban was not withdrawn. The response of Jewish organisations and individuals was inevitably a continuation of efforts to land as many Jews as possible in Palestine, at whatever cost.

Attempts by the British authorities to send back to their ports of embarkation shiploads of immigrants apprehended off Palestine failed repeatedly however when the Rumanian and other governments refused to accept them. The Rumanian Government's sole contribution to the British dilemma, after months of fruitless pressure by the British Minister in Bucharest, was to impose on August 2 a ban on the transit of all Jewish emigrants through Rumania. This prohibition, whose harshness far exceeded British requests, proved in the event incapable of full enforcement.[53] Some 800 Polish Jews were caught at the port of Constanza by the Rumanian ban, and the Rumanian Government thereupon urgently requested their admission to some British territory. This request was strongly supported by the British Minister in Bucharest, who wrote that the condition of these immigrants who had been 'locked up in trains for over four days' was worse than anything the British Consul at Constanza had seen in all his experience of the illicit traffic to Palestine. The Minister was nonetheless informed that these Jews could not be admitted to Palestine or elsewhere in the colonial Empire; if the Rumanian Government refused to allow them to remain, they would have to go back to Poland.[54] The Palestine Government meanwhile became increasingly apprehensive over Jewish demonstrations and riots which might accompany the forcible embarkation of immigrants, many of whom were women.[55] Moreover, such attempts were highly embarrassing at Geneva, where the Permanent Mandates Commission of the League of Nations had condemned the White Paper policy as in violation of the Palestine mandate, and the Council of the League had under consideration the British Government's reply to the Mandates Commission's findings.[56] In London, press and Parliamentary criticism of the refugee aspect of the Government's Palestine policy had also been growing, and was inclined to take Colonel Wedgwood's view that it was difficult in practice to distinguish refugees from the Reich from the impoverished and discriminated-against masses of Polish and Rumanian Jews who also sought refuge in Palestine. Finally, the military and financial

---

[53] See Rumanian Government Note, August 2, 1939, FO 371/24093, W 11798/1369/48.

[54] See Halifax to LeRougetel, August 2, 1939, FO 371/24093, W 11476/1369/48.

[55] See Reilly, minutes of meeting at Colonial Office concerning case of the SS *Colorado*, with 363 illegal immigrants aboard, August 21, 1939, FO 371/24093, W 11580/1369/48.

[56] See Royal Institute of International Affairs, *Great Britain and Palestine*, pp. 126–8.

costs of enforcing the White Paper policy mounted in steady and alarming proportion to the growth of illegal immigration.[57]

Until and well beyond the outbreak of war, the formidable dilemma of illegal immigration into Palestine continued to plague the authorities in London and in Jerusalem; the supply of refugees was inexhaustible, the routes of the migration impossible to seal except after Nazi occupation of Eastern Europe had so narrowed the possibilities of escape that only a few hundreds rather than thousands could struggle through.[58]

The prolonged effort to prevent illegal immigration to Palestine had serious repercussions on British domestic policy toward refugees as well as on foreign relations : as the numbers of refugees entering the United Kingdom mounted throughout the late spring and early summer months,[59] the Home Office turned anxiously to the Colonial Office in the hope that as many as possible of these could be received in Palestine.[60] With Richborough Camp at or near capacity, and settlement possibilities in the Western Hemisphere steadily dwindling, the Home Office faced the probability that many refugees who had been admitted as transmigrants would have to stay on in Britain indefinitely. When the decision was taken to suspend all Jewish immigration into Palestine, the Home Office urgently inquired of

[57] The Palestine Government estimated on August 19 that it might cost as much as £690,000 for capital expenditure and £700,000 annually in running costs—exclusive of costs to be incurred 'ultimately in dispersion and distribution' of immigrants—in order to provide the ten or so camps deemed necessary to intern the 10,000 to 20,000 illegal immigrants whose arrival was anticipated in Palestine. See Officer Administering Government to Colonial Secretary, August 19, 1939, FO 371/24093, W 11949/1369/48. The total revenue of the Palestine Government in the fiscal year ended March 31, 1940 amounted to £6·8 million. See Royal Institute of International Affairs, *Great Britain and Palestine*, p. 80.

[58] On the very eve of war, the possibility of persuading the Turkish Government to close the Bosphorus to ships carrying illegal immigrants was canvassed, but legal advisers at the Foreign Office indicated that the Straits Convention precluded Turkey from doing so. The British Ambassador was nonetheless instructed to 'suggest to Turkish Government unofficially that they should do what they can to delay ships carrying illegal immigrants'. See Halifax to Knatchbull-Hugessen, September 1, 1939, FO 371/24094, W 12071/1369/48.

[59] By May 20, 1939, nearly 35,000 refugees from the Reich had been admitted to the United Kingdom. See brief for House of Lords debate, June 10, 1939, FO 371/24076, W 9048/145/48.

[60] See Conclusions, Fifth Meeting of the Cabinet Committee on the Refugee Problem, July 3, 1939, CRP (39), 5th Mtg., FO 371/24077, W 10239/45/48.

the Colonial Office whether this ban was meant to cover refugees as well, and represented that it would face 'political difficulties' if it 'became generally known that an important avenue of settlement had been closed for an indefinite period'.[61] Despite the Home Office plea that this was 'a matter of paramount importance', the Colonial Office confirmed that the Palestine Government meant its ban on immigration to cover both ordinary and refugee immigration, and the Foreign Office refused to intervene in the matter.[62]

By the summer of 1939, all aspects of the refugee problem had become inextricably tangled : the common root of the dilemma remained however the lack of finance. The private refugee organisations, facing extreme financial shortages, imposed strict requirements on all those who applied to them on behalf of refugees : any person willing to sponsor a child refugee was required to deposit £50 to cover the costs of re-emigration; refugees admitted as trainees had to be paid standard wages; and sponsors of refugees over 60 had to guarantee maintenance for the life of these refugees. These and other rules, as Colonel Wedgwood pointed out in a strongly-worded open letter to the Home Secretary,[63] effectively excluded 'the poor, the friendless and the male Jews' from Britain. Wedgwood pleaded that the Home Secretary should not insist on the re-emigration of children and trainees, and that he release the Jewish community from its 1933 pledge of maintenance so that the refugee organisations in turn could relax their demands for guarantees. Sir Samuel Hoare agreed to permit young refugees between the ages of sixteen and eighteen to be admitted as domestic servants and to give 'favourable consideration' to the admission of skilled manual workers, but Colonel Wedgwood in a further letter nevertheless urged that the Home Secretary 'hint' to the German Jewish Aid Committee 'that

---

[61] See Cooper to Hibbert, July 27, 1939, FO 371/24093, W 11321/1369/48.

[62] D. P. Reilly of the Foreign Office commented on July 28: 'In view of the paramount importance, both in Palestine & in Moslem countries, of stopping the illegal immigration, I think this is justified—& in spite of the disadvantages here from a Home Office point of view, I don't think we ought to put any pressure on the CO to modify their decision. It may help to bring home to the Jews that they must stop the illegal immigration. If the Home Office have to restrict admission here while the suspension of immigration into Palestine continues, it is unfortunate, but can't be helped—& the Home Office must act accordingly.' FO 371/24093, W 11321/1369/48.

[63] See Wedgwood to Hoare, *Manchester Guardian*, May 26, 1939.

they might accept less stringent guarantees'.[64] Such a 'hint' was not given to the German Jewish Aid Committee or to any other refugee relief organisation, but it had become obvious to all concerned with the refugees, both in and outside Whitehall, that some measure of British Government financial assistance had now become indispensable if even the limited schemes being proposed for refugee settlement were to have any chance of success.

In early June, Sir Herbert Emerson, in his capacity as Director of the IGC, submitted a confidential memorandum to the Foreign Office suggesting that the Evian governments join in subscribing to an international fund, in proportion to private contributions; the proceeds would be used for both settlement and maintenance of refugees.[65] At about the same time, a similar scheme occurred to Mr Lionel de Rothschild, who was convinced that no American funds would be forthcoming for the British Guiana or other colonial settlement plans unless British Jewish financiers and the British Government gave a lead. Rothschild's proposal contemplated the raising of an international loan to finance refugee settlement, half of which would be subscribed by governments and half from private sources; a £5 million tranche of an initial issue of £20 million would be raised in London. The Rothschild plan and the variant Emerson plan both met with Home Office and Foreign Office approval, on the condition that any British Government effort to extend a measure of financial assistance to refugees should 'not be an isolated one, but should be proposed for the very purpose of inducing the indispensable cooperation of the United States and other governments'.[66]

The July 3 meeting of the Cabinet Committee on Refugees discussed the issue, and agreed that the Government could no longer defer a fundamental decision on financial assistance to refugees. Parliament was expecting a statement of refugee policy before the recess, and the IGC was to meet in London on July 19 and 20.[67] The Home Secretary noted that the Rothschild plan, which had

[64] See *Manchester Guardian*, June 14, 1939.
[65] See Emerson, memorandum, June 10, 1939, FO 371/24076, W 9339/45/48.
[66] See Randall, minute, June 30, 1939, FO 371/24077, W 10160/45/48.
[67] See Conclusions of the Fifth Meeting, Cabinet Committee on Refugees, July 3, 1939, CRP (39) 5th Mtg., FO 371/24077, W 10239/45/48.

the support of the Co-Ordinating Committee for Refugees, was relatively limited in scope and that money raised in Britain would not be spent outside the Empire. After reviewing the evidence, the Cabinet Committee concluded that further progress in refugee settlement could not be achieved without financial assistance from governments, and recommended that the British Government participate jointly with other governments in a pound-for-pound matching scheme to provide that assistance.

Although this decision on a fundamental reversal of Government policy had been taken in principle on July 3, there had been no opportunity to obtain the full Cabinet's approval before the Government had to face an onslaught in the House of Lords on precisely the issue of financial assistance for refugees. Upon Lord Lyttelton's motion calling attention to the magnitude and nature of the refugee problem,[68] speaker after speaker, including the Bishop of Chichester, Lord Cecil, Lord Reading and Lord Noel-Buxton, rose to declare that refugees could no longer be rescued and settled out of private funds, and appealing with great emphasis to the Government for a change in its policy of financial aloofness. The unenviable task of replying to this heavy barrage fell on a junior Minister, the Marquess of Dufferin and Ava, Parliamentary Under-Secretary at the Colonial Office, who had attended the Cabinet Refugee Committee meeting. Lord Dufferin repeated the standard arguments against a change in Government policy either on the admission of more refugees to Britain, or on the provision of financial help, a prospect for which he held out no hope.

In advance of the Cabinet's discussion, Sir Samuel Hoare, as Chairman of the Cabinet Committee on the Refugee Problem, summarised for his colleagues the reasons now requiring a reversal of the policy maintained firmly since Evian of no government financial assistance for refugee settlement.[69] Some 40,000 refugees in Britain, the majority of whom were transmigrants, were being supported by organisations whose funds had been 'strained to the utmost' : the Society of Friends and the German Jewish Aid Com-

---

[68] See 113 H.L. Deb., 1011–1068, July 6, 1939.
[69] Cabinet Committee on the Refugee Problem, Interim Report, July 7, 1939, C.P. 151(39), CAB 24/288.

mittee were now unable to provide for the emigration of all refugees for whom they had given guarantees, mainly because such emigration had been delayed through no fault of the organisations. The refugees could not be repatriated to their countries of origin, and if a large number were not emigrated within a few months, their maintenance could no longer be assured and they might have to be supported from public funds, thus facing the British Government with an acute domestic crisis and a possible threat to the Rublee-Wohlthat plan which alone offered some hope of rescuing a fraction of the refugees' property from the Reich. Hoare pointed out moreover that the British Government might at any time be confronted with proposals by Poland and Rumania for Jewish emigration from those countries, proposals to which the Government had pledged its 'sympathetic consideration' at the time of Colonel Beck's visit in April. Finally, both the British and American Jewish communities were of the opinion that no private money would be forthcoming for settlement in British Guiana without Government participation; it was desirable 'even on grounds of prestige alone' that the Guiana experiment should not fail.

Hoare stated that the main objections to Government financial help for refugees were the general financial stringency in Britain, the reluctance of other governments to participate, and the probable objection of public opinion to the provision of more favourable terms for refugee migrants than for British nationals, Ultimately, however, the case for Government financial assistance rested on the stark fact of the 'probable breakdown which would result without it'.

When the Cabinet met on July 12[70] the Home Secretary led the discussion, emphasising that unless Lord Winterton were authorised to announce to the IGC the possibility of British Government assistance toward refugee settlement 'there was a danger that the other parties concerned would throw in their hands'. The Chancellor of the Exchequer supported this view, arguing that if the refugees admitted as transmigrants were to remain in Britain indefinitely there was in any event a 'strong possibility that they would become dependent on public funds'. He felt nevertheless that the British Government's offer of assistance should be made on two conditions :

[70] See Cabinet Conclusions 37(39)11, CAB 23/100.

financial contributions should be 'in respect of emigration overseas' and the British Government should not give a lead, but should merely indicate willingness to contribute if other governments did likewise.

The Minister of Labour was the sole Cabinet member to oppose the Home Secretary's view, on the grounds that it would be 'very difficult to justify giving better facilities to foreign refugees than to our own people to settle in the Empire', or to prefer the claims of refugees to assistance over those of British subjects in such distressed areas of the Empire as Newfoundland or the West Indies. He predicted moreover that 'in a few months' time' the refugees could be absorbed in the British labour market.

The Colonial Secretary confessed that he was most anxious about finding places where refugees could be settled; the survey he subsequently gave of possibilities in the Empire demonstrated that the colonies 'could only contribute very little, unless development proved possible in British Guiana on a large scale'. He nevertheless supported the recommendations in the Home Secretary's report, but warned that if refugees were thus assisted financially 'there would be an irresistible demand for taking similar action in regard to certain British subjects'. After other Ministers had expressed cautious assent to the new policy, the Prime Minister said that he felt the Home Secretary's conclusion should be adopted 'provided it was clearly understood that it was *essential* that the cooperation of the United States of America should be secured'. Such American cooperation would help the Government to meet any criticism of the new policy, Mr Chamberlain added. The Cabinet formally decided to authorise Lord Winterton to make a statement to the IGC offering financial assistance, but to take preliminary soundings of Myron C. Taylor before doing so. In a private comment to Lord Winterton, Sir Samuel Hoare revealed that the new policy had only been approved after long discussion :

It was clear that, whilst nobody liked the idea, it was a choice of evils and the greater evil would be a collapse of the relief organisations next year. A very definite view was expressed that similar contribution by the USA must be a pre-requisite of our contribution and that British money ought to be spent primarily upon settling the refugees

that are now in the United Kingdom. It was also the general view
that it would be a mistake to make such a statement at the Evian
Committee meeting unless you were satisfied, after talks with Mr
Myron Taylor, that the Americans were likely to take similar action. . . .
My inclination would be to keep the statement up your sleeve and
only produce it if the USA were prepared to cooperate.[71]

Winterton met with the American Ambassador on July 13, and
told him of the policy agreed the day previous by the Cabinet,[72]
requesting Kennedy to inform Washington and invite the United
States Government to associate itself with the British Government
statement he proposed to make at the July 19 meeting of the IGC.
The Ambassador reacted to Winterton's statement noncommittally,
confining himself merely to pointing out that the private foundation
envisaged as a prerequisite of the Rublee-Wohlthat plan was on the
point of being incorporated, and that its formation was the 'essential first step in the financing of the refugee work'. Winterton and
his colleagues consistently derided the view that the foundation
would prove of any value; Washington, on the other hand, envisaged
the Co-ordinating Foundation as an independent, self-financing
entity which would deal with Berlin and act as agent for a number
of mass resettlement schemes providing homes for millions. Berlin
too urged speed in organising the foundation, claiming in the person
of Ministerialdirektor Wohlthat that only such a body offered hope
of a successful refugee migration from Germany. Wohlthat visited
London in May and June, when his insistence on speed aroused
grave suspicion among leading British Jews, who were in any case
far from eager to make massive investments in what was regarded
as essentially a blackmail scheme on the part of the Nazi authorities.[73]
The Co-ordinating Foundation was eventually incorporated in
London on August 1;[74] Paul Van Zeeland, a former Belgian Prime
Minister, was appointed Exective President of the Foundation late

---

[71] Hoare to Winterton, July 12, 1939, FO 371/24077, W 11149/45/48.
[72] See Kennedy to Hull, July 13, 1939, *FRUS*, 1939, II, 131–134.
[73] See report of Wohlthat's visit in Randall to Holman, June 7, 1939, FO 371/
24084, W 9383/520/48, and Feingold, *Rescue*, pp. 69–89.
[74] Subscribers were: John W. Davis, Paul Baerwald, Nathan L. Miller and
Lewis L. Strauss of the United States; Lionel de Rothschild, Lionel N. Cohen,
KC, Lord Bessborough and Harold B. Butler of Great Britain. See Memorandum
and Articles of Association, FO 371/24085, W 11909/520/48.

that month, but his grandiose schemes for large-scale settlements and huge refugee loans were overtaken by war.[75]

Assured in advance that the Washington authorities would not oppose his statement,[76] Winterton told the IGC meeting on July 19 that the British Government now felt it necessary to depart from the principle agreed at Evian, and was

examining the manner and extent to which private subscription to an international fund to assist in defraying the expenses of overseas emigration of refugees might be encouraged by Government participation, possibly on a basis proportionate to the amount of private subscription.

He added that if other governments were prepared to cooperate, the British Government would take the initiative in proposing a scheme for the purpose.[77]

The United States delegate, Myron C. Taylor, responded by merely undertaking to consult Washington, cautioning the IGC that of course any contribution of funds would have to be authorised by Congress.[78] Other delegates were equally circumspect, and the sole concrete result of the IGC meeting was the acceptance by the Chairman and Director of the Committee of an invitation by President Roosevelt to discuss the entire refugee problem at yet another conference, this one to be held at the White House in the autumn.

Prime Minister Chamberlain announced in the Commons on July 19 that the Government was 'examining the question of Government participation in defraying the cost of emigration of refugees',[79] and the alignment of press comment on this long hoped-for move was predictable: *The Times* and the *Daily Telegraph* approving;[80] the *Daily Mail* concerned that Britain had assumed an enormous liability, which was in any case Germany's responsibility;[81] the

[75] See Welles to Van Zeeland, December 6, 1939, *FRUS*, 1939, II, 156.
[76] See Hull to Kennedy, July 15, 1939, *FRUS*, 1939, II, 136.
[77] See Winterton, statement, July 19, 1939, FO 371/24077, W 10942/45/48.
[78] See Taylor, statement, *FRUS*, 1939, II, 139–140.
[79] See 350 H.C. Deb., 406–407, July 19, 1939.
[80] See *The Times*, July 22, 1939, *Daily Telegraph*, July 20, 1939.
[81] See *Daily Mail* leader, 'Paying Germany's Debt', July 20, 1939.

Daily Express frank in opposition.[82] The *Manchester Guardian*, while welcoming the 'important change' in Government policy, called for Britain to give an example of generosity that would cause the other Evian governments to share the cost of large-scale settlement.[83]

Another aspect of Government financial assistance to refugees which continued to agitate pro-refugee groups was the Chancellor of the Exchequer's consistent refusal to augment the £4,000,000 which had been made available as a gift to assist the migration of refugees from Czechoslovakia. A campaign was launched by Eleanor Rathbone to press the Government for further assistance, primarily on the grounds that the German invasion of Prague had enabled the Government to escape a commitment to lend up to £4,000,000 more for refugee needs; it was contended that only a further gift to pay for the transport and ultimate settlement of refugees from Czechoslovakia stranded in Poland could adequately meet the British Government's moral responsibility for the part it had played 'in the disappearance of the Czech State'.[84] A deputation of MPs from all parties called on the Chancellor of the Exchequer on August 2 to urge that up to £2,000,000 beyond the original gift should be made available in lieu of the originally projected £4,000,000 loan.[85] This proposal was rejected, as were further pleas in the course of a Parliamentary debate on August 4, when Lord Winterton, in a sharp rejoinder to charges by Miss Rathbone and Colonel Wedgwood that British responsibility for Czech refugees was 'undeniable', observed that they and other critics of Government policy 'think that everything that has happened in Europe is due to some original sin of the British Government . . . the Government have done the best they could for these unfortunate refugees'.[86]

As the inevitability of war became increasingly apparent, the

[82] See *Daily Express*, July 21, 1939: 'Jews all over the world should be willing to help the persecuted and homeless of their own race. Our own Exchequer cannot bear the burden.'

[83] See *Manchester Guardian*, July 22, 1939.

[84] See Rathbone letter, *Manchester Guardian*, July 22, 1939, and leaders of July 24 and August 3, 1939.

[85] See Rathbone, memorandum, August 2, 1939, FO 371/24100, W 11538/1873/48.

[86] See 350 H.C. Deb., 2906, August 4, 1939.

efforts of the refugees to escape the threatened Continent were more than matched by the steady increase in restrictions on immigration in country after country, all over the world. The countries of temporary refuge—France, Belgium and particularly Switzerland—strengthened their frontier controls, and even the hitherto hospitable Netherlands was forced to exclude all but the most urgent cases after November 1938, and to set up special camps for refugees beginning in December. With countries of ultimate settlement such as Palestine virtually closed to legal immigration, refugees turning to Latin America found that the most promising asylums—Argentina, Brazil, Colombia, Nicaragua—were officially closed, and that even those countries which were willing in principle to admit immigrants frequently imposed severe restrictions on non-agriculturalists or on Jews. The United States quota for refugees from Germany and Austria was filled up to three years in advance by the spring of 1939, and many refugees found themselves unable to run the gauntlet of guarantees, affidavits and other obstacles set up by United States immigration law and often unsympathetic American consular authorities.[87]

Within the British Empire, Australia was willing to admit up to 5,000 refugees a year for three years; New Zealand had admitted a few families; Canada, after prolonged negotiations, accepted some hundreds of refugee farmers from the former Sudetenland and a number of refugees with capital; South Africa had admitted only a few individuals since October 1938, and had firmly rejected any notion of large-scale refugee immigration. In the colonies, the over-populated West Indian islands were virtually closed after January 1939, and subsequently arriving refugee vessels were refused permission to land.[88] This refusal failed to stop the traffic, however,

---

[87] See Hope Simpson, *Refugees*, Chapters VI–X, and Wyman, *Paper Walls*, pp. 68–71.

[88] With the active pressure of the Gestapo, ships were chartered in Hamburg to land refugees wherever the authorities might permit. See, e.g., correspondence concerning the attempted landing of SS *Caribia* at Trinidad, February 1939, FO 371/24074, W 1165/45/48; and minutes on SS *Königstein*'s trip to Barbados in late February, on which A. W. G. Randall wrote: 'We are now seeing a development which was anticipated—that the creation of facilities merely stimulates the refugees to desperation and the German Govt. to further blackmail, against our humanitarian feelings.' FO 371/24087, W 3069/1369/48.

and the wanderings of ships laden with refugees continued throughout the world.

The most dramatic among many cruises of errant refugee vessels was that of the SS *St Louis*, which sailed from Hamburg on May 15, 1939 with 907 German refugees, who found on reaching Cuba that their expensively purchased landing permits issued by the Cuban Commissioner of Immigration had meanwhile been cancelled. Despite offers of financial guarantees, the refugees were not permitted to land, either in Cuba or in any other Latin American country; nor were they allowed to enter the United States, although more than 700 of them had already obtained United States visas, and were only awaiting their quota numbers.[89]

As the *St Louis* was returning to Germany after fruitless attempts to land its passengers at a Caribbean port or in the United States, Otto M. Schiff of the German Jewish Aid Committee called at the Home Office to ask whether it might be possible to admit some of the passengers to Great Britain. Schiff was told that such an acceptance of refugees, none of whom had been vetted in any way, might operate as a precedent which could lead to repetition of a Gestapo-inspired 'ruse' *ad infinitum*.[90] On June 11, the Passenger Committee of the *St Louis* sent a despairing cable to the Prime Minister begging for asylum before the vessel reached Hamburg. A conference was held the next day at the Home Office between representatives of refugee organisations and Government officials,[91] at which, despite the clear dangers of giving way, it was nonetheless agreed that since the Belgian, Dutch and French governments had jointly offered to receive two-thirds of the *St Louis* passengers, the British Government could admit the remainder, for whose maintenance the American Jewish refugee committee agreed to undertake responsibility. Replying to a Parliamentary question, the Parliamentary Under-Secretary at the Home Office announced this decision on June 13, emphasising that the

[89] See Gustav Schröder, *Heimatlos auf hoher See* (Berlin, 1949), for the former captain's account of the *St Louis* voyage.

[90] See Cooper, minute, June 10, 1939, FO 371/24101, W 9189/9189/48.

[91] Present were Lord Winterton, Sir A. Maxwell and E. N. Cooper of the Home Office; Sir Herbert Emerson and Pell of the IGC; A. W. G. Randall of the Foreign Office; Mr Schiff; and Messrs Linder and Baerwald of the American Joint Distribution Committee.

special arrangements made in this case cannot be regarded as a precedent for the reception in future of refugees who may leave Germany
before definite arrangements have been made for their admission elsewhere.[92]

Elsewhere in the British Empire, severe restrictions on immigration were imposed in Kenya on April 20;[93] but small-scale settlement schemes continued to be laboriously investigated in other
colonial territories. The Northern Rhodesia Commission reported
its discouraging findings in late June,[94] and when its report and a
similar one on Nyasaland were laid before Mr Anthony de Rothschild's Emigration Sub-Committee on June 27, the Committee
concluded that the capital cost of the Northern Rhodesia and Nyasaland settlement schemes would be so prohibitive as to preclude the
refugee organisations from considering the schemes at all : it would
have cost an estimated £500,000 to settle only 400 to 500 refugee
families. The Committee and the Colonial Office agreed accordingly
to suspend publication of the Rhodesia and Nyasaland reports.[95]

The British Guiana scheme, that other hoped-for large contribution to a solution of the refugee problem, proved a source of contention among the refugee groups, the Colonial Office, and the
Americans : the very scale of the proposed settlement remained in
dispute. Pell of the IGC duly reported to Washington that in the
course of a meeting on July 13 with Winterton and other British
officials, Winterton had lost his temper when Sir Herbert Emerson
had suggested the term 'mass settlement' for the proposed Guiana
scheme. Winterton reportedly declared

that it was not the intention of the British Government to permit 'mass
settlement' in Guiana or anything resembling the situation in Palestine.
He said at most it would agree to the establishment of a group of 50
here and 50 there interspersed throughout the territory and not forming a homogeneous mass of Jews. He said that the idea which seemed
to be held in American circles that something akin to a Jewish state
could be set up anywhere in the world was Utopian in the extreme,

[92] See 348 H.C. Deb., 1111–1112, June 13, 1939.
[93] See *The Times*, April 20, 1939, reporting a bill passed by the Kenya Legis-
lature empowering immigration authorities to demand of would-be immigrants
a bond of £500 instead of the former £50.
[94] See Hibbert to Reilly, June 21, 1939, FO 371/24091, W 9662/1369/48.
[95] See Hibbert to Reilly, June 30, 1939, FO 371/24092, W 10132/1369/48.

impossible of fulfilment, and would be opposed by the British Government.

At this same meeting, according to Pell, Sir Herbert Emerson observed that 'the trouble in this whole refugee affair was the trouble of the Jews and most eastern people. There was always some other scheme in the background for which they were prepared to sacrifice schemes which were already in hand'.[96]

But the Guiana project could not realistically have been described as 'in hand'. The Colonial Secretary complained on July 14 to members of Rothschild's Committee that there had been little reaction in the United States to the offer of territory in British Guiana, an offer which it had been hoped 'would have an electrifying effect on American opinion', with the consequent raising of large funds for experimental settlement. In the absence of such funds, Mr MacDonald warned, the British Government might have to reconsider its offer of territory.[97] The stumbling-block remained finance : Rothschild indicated that his Committee could not possibly proceed unless the British Government could relieve it of the 'starting-up' expenses of establishing an experimental farm, of import duties on materials required by the settlers, and of the costs of medical and veterinary services. Rothschild suggested these costs should be met out of the international fund the Prime Minister had mentioned on July 19, or by the British Government directly.[98] The Treasury was reluctantly considering these requests when war came and Rothschild had to inform the Colonial Office that he could no longer count on previously-obtained promises of financial support from private sources.[99] The British Guiana scheme was definitely abandoned when the Government itself felt it necessary to withdraw the tentative offer of a matching grant for refugee settlement in general;[100] and the minor dimensions of the Empire's

[96] See Kennedy to Hull, *FRUS*, 1939, II, 134.
[97] See Colonial Office memorandum, July 14, 1939, FO 371/24093, W 11225/1369/48.
[98] See Hibbert to Hale, August 15, 1939, FO 371/24094, W 12099/1369/48.
[99] See Hibbert, minute, September 20, 1939, FO 371/24095, W 14694/1369/48.
[100] See minutes, Colonial Office meeting on refugees, September 14, 1939, FO 371/24078, W 13868/45/48.

contribution to the refugee problem were harshly illuminated when the Colonial Office later revealed that the total number of refugees from the Reich who entered British colonial dependencies other than Palestine from 1933 to the end of September 1939 was 'in the neighbourhood of 3,000'.[101]

As the war clouds gathered throughout the summer of 1939, the refugee problem had clearly outstripped any private, national or international efforts to reach a solution. When a report reached the Foreign Office in late August that the German authorities were now proposing to expel all Jews from Bohemia and Moravia, the response was an effort to obtain confirmation from the Berlin Embassy, and a grim prediction that the results of the reported German move would be 'disastrous'; it had simply become impossible for any of the countries of refuge to absorb refugees at a greater rate than they were now doing.[102]

In Great Britain, the refugee organisations, whose resources had dwindled to near the vanishing point, decided in the late summer to limit all further applications for admission, fearing that in the event of war they would be financially responsible in any case for a large number of unemployable aliens, and unable to contemplate providing for more. At the outbreak of war, on September 3, all visas granted to Reich nationals automatically ceased to be valid, and after consultation within Government departments and with the refugee organisations, the Government decided, chiefly for security reasons, to admit to Britain only refugees who had already succeeded in reaching neutral or allied countries. Such refugees were nonetheless required to re-submit their visa applications to be specially investigated in the light of wartime conditions.[103]

When the war began, there were nearly 50,000 refugees from Germany and Austria, and about 6,000 from Czechoslovakia in the

[101] See Hibbert to Carvell, December 22, 1939, FO 371/24097, W 19149/1369/48.
[102] See Farquhar to Holman, August 22, 1939, FO 371/24085, W 12070/520/48. The Berlin Embassy judged the time 'not suitable' to obtain confirmation of the expulsion policy from the German authorities. See Holman to Farquhar, August 25, 1939, on W 12633/520/48.
[103] See Ronald to Kennedy, October 16, 1939, FO 371/24101, W 14595/3231/48.

United Kingdom.[104] On September 4, Sir John Anderson, the newly-appointed Home Secretary, announced in the House of Commons the imposition of a standstill order on all aliens from Reich territories, including refugees. All such aliens over sixteen were required to register with the police, and not to move more than five miles from their registered addresses.[105] Local tribunals were set up to examine each alien and decide his status; and after a good deal of confusion, the vast majority of alien refugees were released from security restrictions and many of them absorbed in war industry.[106]

The position of the Intergovernmental Committee in wartime was also a preoccupation of the British Government. Clearly, the main object of the IGC—to negotiate with the German Government to improve the conditions for the refugee exodus—was impossible of achievement once war came, and negotiations between belligerents were out of the question.[107] President Roosevelt clung nevertheless to the notion of an IGC, and the proposed White House conference on refugees remained on the agenda. After an interdepartmental meeting had arrived at recommendations for British Government policy,[108] the American Ambassador was informed by Lord Winterton and Sir Herbert Emerson that Britain could not undertake to assist the emigration in wartime of Reich nationals;[109]

[104] See Sir John Anderson's reply to a Parliamentary question in 352 H.C. Deb., 538, October 12, 1939. A Home Office memorandum prepared for the Washington refugee conference stated that the Reich refugees then in the United Kingdom could be divided into the following categories: children under 18, 9,028; young persons for agricultural and technical training, 2,493; persons awaiting emigration, 1,707; elderly persons for permanent residence, 877; domestic servants, 4,461; Richborough Camp, 1,700; refugees for settlement in Britain, 28,685. See Home Office memorandum, September 20, 1939, FO 371/24078, W 14035/45/48.

[105] See 351 H.C. Deb., 366–370.

[106] This policy was later reversed again, when a German invasion seemed imminent: a large number of male refugees were interned and some deported to the Isle of Man, Canada or Australia. Sir Samuel Hoare later declared roundly that 'never was there a more obscurantist act'. See Templewood, *Nine Troubled Years*, p. 241. Eleanor Rathbone and other MPs led a vigorous campaign which resulted ultimately in the abolition of the new restrictions, and almost all the internees who had not been deported overseas were thereupon permitted to return to their homes and places of work.

[107] See Halifax to Lothian, September 2, 1939, FO 371/24078, W 13064/45/48.

[108] See Conclusions of War Cabinet Committee on the Refugee Problem, September 25, 1939, FO 371/24078, W 14062/45/48.

[109] See Kennedy to Hull, *FRUS*, 1939, II, 145–146.

the IGC could as far as Britain was concerned continue in existence, but should confine its activities to settling refugees who had already left Reich territory and were principally resident in such neutral countries as Switzerland, the Netherlands, or Shanghai; schemes for large-scale settlement in British colonial territories were to be suspended for the duration of the war.[110]

Although the German authorities let it be known through the ever-resourceful Dr Wohlthat that the German Government still desired to emigrate Jews, and that it was essential in its view that the work of the IGC be continued,[111] the British Government's position that the IGC could no longer as a body negotiate with Berlin meant in effect that the Committee was to continue in being in name only.[112] The fourth plenary meeting of the IGC at Washington on October 26, 1939 contented itself with the *pro forma* recognition of the painfully obvious : that 'there was an urgent need for further openings for the permanent settlement of refugees' and that 'the problem of involuntary migration might be greatly increased'. The by now traditional response of the IGC to this urgent need was to consider it necessary that 'surveys should continue of all possible openings for the permanent settlement of involuntary migrants in various parts of the world'.[113] No mention was made of easing restrictions on immigration in the likeliest country of refuge not yet involved in war : the United States of America.

It was also plain that in war conditions the British Government could contemplate no new financial commitments, and the scheme announced on July 19 for possible governmental support of refugee settlement was therefore not raised at the Washington conference.[114] It was felt in Whitehall that the end of restrictions on alien employment would in any case reduce the need for such

---

[110] It was however found necessary to concede to the Jewish Agency for Palestine the right of entry to that country for those Jews who had already received immigration certificates before the outbreak of war. See Randall, minute, October 4, 1939, FO 371/24085, W 14428/520/48.

[111] See Kennedy to Hull, September 29, 1939, *FRUS*, 1939, II, 149.

[112] See Randall, minute on talks with Achilles of American Embassy, October 4, 1939, FO 371/24085, W 14428/520/48.

[113] See Department of State statement, October 26, 1939, *FRUS*, 1939, II, 152.

[114] See Hale to Randall, September 16, 1939, FO 371/24078, W 13740/45/48.

R

government aid.[115] But by December the War Cabinet's Committee on the Refugee Problem was required to reverse its policy of no assistance : the private organisations which had been maintaining some 13,000 refugees were by then totally without funds and insisted that more could not be raised privately in wartime. Appalled at the prospect of 13,000 aliens coming on the rates, the War Cabinet authorised a payment from Exchequer funds at the rate of 8s. per refugee weekly, to be matched by the refugee committees.[116]

With the virtual end of international action on behalf of refugees, the hermetic sealing of borders throughout Europe, and the shutting also of Palestine, the trap had definitely closed on an estimated 400,000 Jews still remaining within the expanded Reich, and on approximately 2 million more in the German-occupied portions of Poland.[117] For these unfortunates time had at last run out. In December, somewhat later than planned, the first transports of Jews rolled eastward from the Reich into the *Generalgouvernement* of Poland, a mass deportation which represented the first stage on the road to the Final Solution.[118]

[115] See Kennedy to Hull, September 29, 1939, *FRUS*, 1939, II, 146.
[116] See War Cabinet Conclusions 112(39)5, December 12, 1939, CAB 65/2. At this Cabinet meeting, Sir Samuel Hoare, by then Lord Privy Seal, declared that 'he was satisfied that the voluntary organisations had done their best to fulfil the undertakings which they had made when the refugees concerned were admitted to this country, but that the war and the consequent increases in taxation had entirely changed the position for them'. Hoare's magnanimous view contrasts sharply with the pique displayed by Lord Winterton, who told the War Cabinet Committee on the Refugee Problem that he and Sir Herbert Emerson 'felt very annoyed that the Jewish Organisation [sic!] had failed to give them an earlier warning of the position'. Winterton's reaction seems somewhat disingenuous in view of repeated warnings, by the Jewish and other refugee bodies, that their funds were running short, warnings which had begun as early as April 1938. See Draft Conclusions, Seventh Meeting, War Cabinet Committee on the Refugee Problem, CRP (39) 7th Mtg., December 8, 1939, FO 371/24101, W 18484/323/48.
[117] Some 1,250,000 refugees succeeded in fleeing to those portions of Poland occupied by the Soviet Union. See Feingold, *Rescue*, p. 321.
[118] See Raoul Hilberg, *The Destruction of the European Jews* (Chicago, 1961), p. 138.

9

A Balance Sheet

The one form of international action which would have provided
the most substantial relief for the refugees would have been a
widespread lowering of immigration barriers. Most nations, however, were prepared to do no more than suggest this course of
action for their neighbours.[1]

LOOKING back from September 1939 to the beginnings of the German
refugee problem, the development undergone by British Government refugee policy may be observed with some clarity. The guide-
lines laid down in response to the very first influx of refugees—that
Great Britain was not a country of immigration and that its large
population and substantial unemployment precluded any but a
carefully restrictive policy of granting asylum—remained fixed
throughout the period 1933–1939, but they did undergo modifications in response to political pressures as well as the ineluctable fact
of rising numbers.

From January 1933 to September 1935, those numbers were consistently small, and enabled the Government to offer asylum with
some liberality to the comparatively few, often well-off and well-
connected refugees who presented themselves at the ports. Although
certain interests within the country, notably the medical and dental
professions, registered immediate alarm at the prospect of any refugee immigration, their concern and the anti-alien sentiment of portions of the press found little echo among the wider public. Even
in Palestine, where refugees from Germany had enormously swelled
the figures of Jewish immigration in this period, there were only
comparatively minor disturbances. In the international sphere, the

[1] Malcolm J. Proudfoot, *European Refugees: 1939–52* (London, 1957), p. 31.

futility of representations to Berlin over anti-Jewish persecution of German citizens was early recognised, and the desire to avoid giving offence to Germany consistently coloured League of Nations efforts to deal with the problem. The British Government cautiously supported the High Commissioner for Refugees in his diplomatic efforts, but carefully avoided any Government expenditure or greater involvement in the refugee question than was absolutely necessary, despite the prodding of Viscount Cecil and groups such as the League of Nations Union.

The phase of persecution ushered in by the promulgation of the Nuremberg Laws in September 1935 and the subsequent increase in emigration with a view to permanent settlement failed to alter the Home Office policy of 'rigid but sympathetic control'. The numbers of refugees continued to be manageable and a careful immigration policy resulted by 1937 in the admission to Great Britain of several thousand 'desirable, industrious, intelligent and acceptable persons' whose entry into the country aroused comparatively little interest in Parliament or in the press. But if the infiltration of refugees into the home islands had gone relatively smoothly, such was not the case in Palestine, where growing Arab alarm over Jewish immigration culminated by April 1936 in a general strike which led in turn to widespread guerilla warfare. The subsequent recommendation of the Peel Commission in June 1937 that immigration to Palestine should henceforth have a maximum political level foreshadowed the eventual closing of Palestine to substantial Jewish immigration and was a particularly bitter blow to German refugees, for whom Palestine remained the sole country to which a reasonable proportion of their assets could still be transferred. Elsewhere on the international scene, British Government efforts were directed largely toward supporting measures to define the legal status of refugees, and to encouraging the ineffectual attempts of the League High Commissioner for Refugees to make headway in negotiations with Berlin and with countries of potential settlement.

The Anschluss in March 1938 and the panicky mass flight from Austria which followed ended all hope that League refugee work could be wound up by the end of 1938, and roused both the British Government and wide segments of the public to the grim realisation that the refugee exodus now represented a most serious and large-scale domestic as well as international problem. The German Jewish Aid Committee's letter to the Home Office warning of its inability to accept financial responsibility for any refugees from Austria except those selected after consultation with it served to strengthen the Government's determination to impose a visa requirement on Reich nationals, thus establishing a control on the possible influx at a point far removed from British ports. Under the impact of the Anschluss, public awareness and concern over the refugees spread far beyond the comparatively limited circles originally concerned with the problem, and were reflected in a chorus of press and Parliamentary criticism of Government policy. The Home Office, highly sensitive to the possible growth of anti-alien and anti-Jewish sentiment, and to charges of red tape and inefficiency, struggled to deal with thousands of urgent applications in the full glare of unwelcome publicity.

After the Evian conference of July 1938 the international aspect of British Government refugee policy was marked by continuing efforts to find places of mass settlement within the British Empire, thus not merely deflecting criticism over the newly-imposed restrictions on immigration to Palestine, but also preparing for a possible future exodus of Jews from Eastern Europe. The continuing disturbances in Palestine and the realisation that the refugee issue could become a significant irritant in Anglo-American relations lent urgency to the compulsive search for places of settlement.

As conditions within the Reich steadily worsened and refugees were permitted to take with them ever-dwindling fractions of their property, the financial aspect of the problem came to dominate all others. The British Government, in common with all the other governments represented on the Evian-born Intergovernmental Committee, stood adamant in refusing governmental financial assistance and steadfastly insisted that it was up to Germany, 'the country of origin', to establish the pre-condition for an orderly migration by permitting the refugees to take some of their property with them. It was felt, not without reason, that any governmental assistance would merely act as an incentive to the German authorities to despoil their nationals more thoroughly before pushing them out of the Reich. But the growing strength of rearming Germany enabled her to defy all the Evian governments on this as on other issues; the Intergovernmental Committee's feebleness was mirrored in the protracted and one-sided negotiations between its Director and the authorities in Berlin on conditions of exit. In its efforts to support these negotiations, the Foreign Office was haunted by knowledge that the Polish and Rumanian Governments were also interested onlookers, whose diplomatic pressures conveyed a clear warning of their readiness to adopt increasingly harsh measures in order to force the international community to absorb some of their unwanted Jewish citizens as well.

With the cession of the Sudetenland to Germany the question of Czech refugees became acute. The moral ambiguities of the British position at Munich made the pressures on the Government to intervene more actively on behalf of these refugees well-nigh irresistible. The admission *en bloc* of Sudeten Social Democrats to the United Kingdom, the despatch of a British Government representative to Prague, and the use of the Czech Government loan proceeds to aid refugees were all significant departures from past policy; and although the Czech case was consistently held by Government spokesmen to be unique, it became increasingly difficult, as the Foreign Office had predicted, to maintain a distinction in practice between refugees from Czechoslovakia and refugees from the Reich itself.

After *Kristallnacht* and its drastic consequences for the remaining Jews and 'non-Aryans' within the Reich, countries all over the world adopted more restrictive immigration regulations. Great Britain however responded to the growing dimensions of the emergency by adopting progressively more flexible policies, and this despite the unmistakable evidence that rapid immigration of refugees was increasing the reservoir of anti-alien and anti-Semitic feeling in the country. Despite severe strains on its staff, the Home Office eased entry to the United Kingdom for children, domestics, trainees and transmigrants, for whom a special camp was established. These and other administrative innovations went some way toward meeting the pleas of pro-refugee groups, and represented an important change from the previous assumption that little more could be done for the refugees than was already being done, and that nothing could in any case be done too rapidly.

The several strands of British refugee policy in the international sphere now converged on Palestine, where the irreconcilable obligations of the Mandate and the growing danger of war eventually led to the adoption of the White Paper policy, a 'convulsive gesture of self-preservation'[2] designed to secure Britain's strategic position in the Middle East. Acutely aware that Palestine was one of the prime neuralgic points in Anglo-American relations, and that the White Paper policy would inevitably lead to increased tension with Washington; and sensitive as well to the world-wide human and moral dilemma posed by this barring of their promised National Home to thousands of Jews fleeing persecution, the Foreign Office now harried the Colonial Office with increased determination over settlement schemes elsewhere in the Empire. But all notions of large-scale settlement foundered on obstructionism within the Colonial Office and in the colonies themselves, and on the demonstrable inability of the private organisations to raise the enormous sums required to finance settlement in remote, undeveloped tropical areas.

Finance thus remained the crux of the problem, and paradoxically it was the increased generosity of the British Government in admissions policy that at last forced a reversal of policy in this area; for the influx of refugees from the Reich and from Czechoslovakia had become so large by the summer of 1939 that the refugee organisations themselves had to request a slow-down in admissions, and the whole notion of admitting refugees as transmigrants threatened to disintegrate. In this acute emergency the Government reluctantly jettisoned its long-standing refusal to help defray the costs of emigrating refugees—a refusal which had virtually hardened into constitutional principle—and undertook to do so if other governments would join in the effort.

The significant modifications of British Government refugee policy in the period after the Anschluss demonstrated the Government's responsiveness to the energetic lobbying of pro-refugee groups and individuals; but the strongest influences on Government policy were the sheer size of the problem, and the British responsibility for the Jewish National Home in Palestine. The numbers of refugees eventually forced the easing of admissions to Great Britain, the streamlining of administrative procedures, and ultimately the offer of Government financial assistance. In the absence of the burden of the Palestine Mandate, however, Great Britain in its geographical isolation from the refugee flood might well have been able to withstand political pressures for greater generosity. But the adoption of the White Paper policy in Palestine and the resultant acutely uncomfortable barrage of criticism compelled greater liberality elsewhere in the Empire, including at home.

The standard charges, based on a narrow view of the Palestine problem, of British Government lack of generosity or indeed of indifference to the fate of refugees from the Nazi regime must receive the verdict 'not proven'. The initial Government response to the refugee problem was to be sure sluggish and even niggardly compared with those of several countries bordering Germany : caution remained the watchword until the incorporation of Austria in the Reich literally brought the problem home to British shores. Administrative muddle there also most certainly was, particularly when the machinery of both the Home Office and the voluntary organisations was swamped in the crowded months following the Anschluss. Lack of imagination, and a dogged refusal to depart rapidly enough from rigidly legalistic procedures—those damning accusations so often hurled by Eleanor Rathbone and Josiah Wedgwood—can fairly be imputed to certain Ministers and civil servants responsible for the formulation and execution of refugee policy. But despite confusion, hesitations, and often a lack of appreciation that time could literally mean life or death, a relatively large number of refugees did manage to find sanctuary within Great Britain and her dependencies, and a comparison with other countries yields a not unimpressive record, most particularly when Palestine is taken into account.

Approximately 50,000 refugees from the Reich and 6,000 from Czechoslovakia entered Great Britain between 1933 and October 1939. In the same period, 136,000 refugees from the Reich and from Spain found refuge in the United States.[3] Also in the pre-war period, 40,000 refugees from the Reich were admitted to France; 23,000 to the Netherlands; 25,000 to Belgium and 10,000 to Switzerland.[4]

Although the United States admitted more refugees from the Reich than any other single country, its record in relation to capacity was far less generous than that of many, including Great Britain. The American national origins quota system was consistently and rigidly adhered to, and despite a good deal of humanitarian rhetoric from the White House, no attempts were made to widen the quotas. The annual quotas for German and Austrian immigrants were in fact under-issued in every year except 1939 : even after *Kristall-nacht* the Administration refused to alter the sacrosanct quota system or its extremely time-consuming administration. One reason for this state of affairs, often obscured by the continuing uproar over immigration to Palestine, was the curiously negative attitude of the American Jewish community to the prospect of any large influx of refugees into the United States, and the resultant refusal of the community's leaders to urge more than token changes in immigration law or procedures.[5]

A particularly striking example of the gap between American rhetoric and practice is afforded by the fate of a proposal made early in 1939 to admit up to 20,000 refugee children to the United States. After a bitter debate the Wagner-Rogers bill authorising admission failed to reach the floor of Congress. At precisely the same time hospitality was being mobilised on a large scale to bring 10,000 child refugees rapidly into Britain.[6]

France and other countries bordering on Germany were required to deal with refugees from the Reich who simply appeared within their territory in large numbers, especially after *Kristallnacht*. This phenomenon forced such countries as Belgium and the Netherlands to set up refugee camps, and to recognise earlier though no less reluctantly than Great Britain that the reception of refugees would ultimately involve some charge on public funds. The British Govern-

[3] See Proudfoot, *European Refugees*, p. 27.
[4] See Hope Simpson, *Refugees*, p. 52.
[5] See Feingold, *Rescue*, p. 42; and his immigration figures, p. 313.
[6] See Wyman, *Paper Walls*, Chapter 4.

ment, which never had more than a handful of illegal entrants, established the Richborough Camp primarily for humanitarian reasons and admitted unaccompanied child refugees from the same impulse.[7]

What the critics of Whitehall's policy often failed to comprehend, in their understandable anguish over the plight of refugees, were the tragic limitations on any Government action, and the extent to which responsible Ministers had to bear in mind often conflicting considerations when formulating policy on the refugee question. The humanitarian issue, to which such Ministers as Lord Halifax and Sir Samuel Hoare were notably responsive, and the older British tradition of asylum for the political refugee, were only two of the elements which had to be weighed. Against these, on the domestic scene, there were the dilemmas posed by still-large unemployment, the anti-refugee representations of certain organised professions and associations, and a pervasive reluctance to accept any sizeable numbers of foreigners, whoever they might be, into Britain. There were too the resentments engendered by proposals to assist non-British migrants with Government funds, and the possible precedents such assistance might establish for as yet unknown groups. Moreover, the fateful pledge given by the Jewish community in 1933 that no Jewish refugee admitted to the United Kingdom would become a public charge operated in the last year before the war in an entirely unforeseen way to tie the hands of the Home Office in issuing visas, and thus to exclude those refugees for whom private guarantees of maintenance could not be found. The Home Office consistently took its lead on admissions policy from the private organisations, a logical consequence of their assumption of the ultimate financial responsibility for refugees admitted to Britain: a blank cheque issued at a time when no one foresaw the dimensions of the burden which had been freely undertaken. If therefore more refugees could not be admitted, as Colonel Wedgwood frequently pointed out, the fault lay perforce quite as much with the refugee organisations as

---

[7] See Tartakower and Grossmann, *Jewish Refugee*, p. 221, reporting that the inmates of the Richborough Camp were 'treated with cordial hospitality both by the authorities and the local population', and commenting further that 'quietly, without display or publicity, the British authorities admitted thousands of refugees year after year, relatively more than the United States'.

with the Government. Despite these obstacles, however, the 50,000 were admitted—and very many more visas were issued but not taken up by would-be immigrants.

Internationally, the Government faced not only the desperate dilemma of Palestine, but also the wretched probability that any greater generosity to refugees from the Reich might well stimulate the impatience and rapacity of the Polish and Rumanian Governments, each hovering on the point of following the German example. The confiscation and expulsion techniques refined in Berlin were eminently exportable; and it could legitimately be feared that suggestions of government financial support for migration or settlement schemes might simply play into the hands of the Nazi persecutors and their imitators further to the East, already adept in the cruder methods of human dumping.

The refugee problem thus represented a tangle of complicated deteriorating issues which compelled harassed British Ministers, only too well aware of Britain's severely strained resources, to assume grave responsibilities of unknown but threatening dimensions: for by the summer months of 1939 it had become clear that whatever the larger political situation in Europe, entire populations were now in actual or potential danger of summary expulsion from their native lands.

When a balance sheet is nevertheless drawn and Great Britain's refugee policy compared with that of other countries it emerges, in the context of the pre-war period, as comparatively compassionate, even generous. There were no simple answers, no obvious or rapid solutions. But the problem was at least in part comprehended; needs were to some extent met; the drawbridge to safety within British territory was in fact only partially raised. It must not, finally, be overlooked that despite all the evidence of brutal persecution few if any in responsible Government positions could have predicted that would-be emigrants left behind in the Greater Reich faced not merely privation, but an organised and ultimately largely successful attempt at physical annihilation.

Appendix I

Migration Statistics

Statistics on refugee migration in the period 1933–1939 are notoriously unreliable, for several reasons. First, the countries of origin seldom recorded all cases of emigration, even when the departing national was forced to sign an undertaking not to return. Second, there was no single organisation, either international, governmental or private recording actual numbers of refugees. The Jewish organisations maintained the most accurate statistics, but then only for individuals who came officially to their attention when applying for assistance : many refugees thus escaped notice altogether. Moreover, the countries of reception often found it impossible to distinguish in practice between ordinary travellers and refugees. Such statistics as were kept were often deliberately understated by governments or by the refugee organisations, desirous of minimising anti-alien and anti-Semitic feeling. Sometimes, on the other hand, statistics were inflated to demonstrate that a country had received more refugees than it in fact had. To these several factors must also be added the natural distortions arising from births and deaths, as well as from re-migration from one country of transit to another, or from these to countries of ultimate settlement.[1]

Sir Herbert Emerson, League High Commissioner for Refugees, estimated that 215,000 Jews left Germany between April 1933 and July 1, 1939. About 11,000 more left in July and August. Approximately 134,000–144,000 Jews left Austria and Bohemia-Moravia up to the outbreak of the war. Thus a total figure for Jewish refugees from the Reich up to September 1939 would amount to 360,000–

---

[1] See Hope Simpson, *Refugee Problem*, pp. 139–142 and Appendix VI; and Werner Rosenstock, 'Exodus 1933–1939. A Survey of Jewish Emigration from Germany', Leo Baeck Institute, *Year Book*, 1956, Vol. I, 373–390.

370,000.[2] To these figures must be added 'non-Aryans', political refugees, Catholics and others. Sir Herbert Emerson estimated in his final report to the League Assembly in October 1939 that a total of 400,000 refugees had left Greater Germany since 1933.[3]

Year	Nationality	Landed	Embarked	Refused Leave to Land
1932	Austrian	4,878	4,734	54
	German	41,065	39,803	243
1933	Austrian	5,657	5,120	49
	German	51,712	48,449	435
1934	Austrian	7,161	6,313	46
	German	55,877	54,922	332
1935	Austrian	9,706	8,315	58
	German	59,026	57,150	307
1936	Austrian	13,391	10,040	74
	German	74,870	71,734	338
1937	Austrian	18,722	13,610	93
	German	80,236	78,261	345
1938	Austrian	14,499	11,968	215
	German	79,652	72,358	274
3 months ended March 31 1939	Austrian	426	353	1
	German	29,429	14,858	67
3 months ended June 30 1939*	Austrian	677	657	4
	German	61,248	32,234	119

Source: Home Office, Reports under the Aliens Order, 1920, Statistics in Regard to Alien Passengers who Entered and Left the United Kingdom, 1932–1939, in *House of Commons Papers*.

*Note: The figures for the three months ended June 30 are distorted by holiday visitors, most of whom would have left the United Kingdom within the following months, for which statistics are unavailable.

[2] See Eugene M. Kulischer, *Europe on the Move* (New York, 1948), p. 191. The German census of 1933 showed a total of 499,700 Jews (*Glaubensjuden*) in the Reich; to these must be added 3,100 Jews from the Saar (according to the census of July 1933), yielding a total of 502,800 for Germany. There were approximately 180,000 Jews in Austria in 1938. Ibid.

[3] Kulischer, *Europe*, p. 191. Kulischer notes that the Reich Statistical Office gave a figure of 400,000 as a rough estimate of the number of refugees from the Reich up to May 1939. See also discussions of migration statistics in Genschel, *Verdrängung*, p. 291, and Werner Röder, *Die deutschen sozialistischen Exilgruppen in Grossbritannien 1940–1945* (Hannover, 1968), pp. 15–19.

The number of refugees from Germany and Austria admitted to Great Britain up to October 1939 was given by the Home Secretary as 49,500, including 9,000 children. Some 6,000 refugees from Czechoslovakia found asylum in Great Britain during the same period.[4]

The table on page 270 shows the number of aliens from Germany and Austria who entered and left the United Kingdom in the years 1932–39.

The following tables show the number of British persons employed and unemployed, and the number of aliens employed, in the United Kingdom between 1932 and 1939 :

Year	Estimated number of insured persons in employment at yr.-end (Thousands)	Numbers registered unemployed at yr.-end (Thousands)	Average %–age of unemployment among insured workers for yr.	Employment of Aliens		
				Permits applied for	Permits granted [a]	Permits refused
1932	9,440	2,723	22·0	10,112	8,957	1,155
1933	10,008	2,224	19·8	9,628	8,584	1,044
1934	10,259	2,086	16·6	11,396	10,286	1,110
1935	10,629	1,869	15·3	12,934	11,344	1,590
1936	11,182	1,629	12·9	18,072	16,390	1,682
1937	11,444	1,665	10·6	24,431	21,319	3,112
1938	12,263	1,804	12·6	25,923	22,347	3,576
1939 [b]	18,480	1,270	[d]	[c]	[c]	[c]

Source : Ministry of Labour, *Annual Report*, 1933–1939.

[a] In each of these years, at least 50 per cent of all permits issued were in respect of employment in private domestic service, and 20 per cent or more for engagements as concert and stage artists and musicians.

[b] At June 12, 1939.

[c] After the outbreak of war, the Ministry of Labour ceased to issue permits for the admission of aliens to employment; such permission was granted by the Home Office.

[d] Annual percentage not meaningful after the outbreak of war.

The following table shows the number of labour permits granted, according to nationality, in the period 1932 to 1939 :[5]

[4] See 352 H.C. Deb., 538, October 12, 1939. Malcolm J. Proudfoot, *European Refugees: 1939–52* (London, 1957), estimates the total number of refugees from Greater Germany and from Spain who entered Great Britain between 1933 and 1939 at 80,000; his figures must be assumed to include transmigrants.

[5] These figures include labour permit renewals.

Year	Number of Permits Granted	
	Austrians	Germans
1932	435	2,954
1933	599	2,481
1934	1,170	2,495
1935	2,094	2,236
1936	4,575	3,206
1937	7,208	2,942
1938	1,957 [a]	7,440
1939	[b]	[b]

Source: Ministry of Labour, *Annual Report*, 1933–1939.

[a] Figures quoted for Austria relate to the period January 1–April 31; thereafter, nationals of Austrian origin were included in the statistics for Germany.

[b] After the outbreak of war, the Ministry of Labour ceased to issue permits for the admission of aliens to employment; such permission was granted by the Home Office.

The following table shows total recorded legal Jewish immigration to Palestine in the years 1932 to 1939 :

Year	Recorded Immigration into Palestine
1932	9,553
1933	30,327
1934	42,359
1935	61,854
1936	29,727
1937	10,536
1938	12,868
1939	16,405

Source: Royal Institute of International Affairs, *Great Britain and Palestine 1915–1945* (London, 1946), p. 63.

The Jewish Agency for Palestine reported total Jewish immigration into Palestine from Greater Germany in the period 1933–1938 was 45,100—but this figure is almost certainly understated.[6]

[6] See Hope Simpson, *Refugees*, p. 83. Simpson's figures show the following percentages of total Jewish immigration to Palestine accounted for by immigration from Greater Germany: 1933, 25 per cent; 1934, 23 per cent; 1935, 13 per cent; 1936, 29 per cent; 1937, 35 per cent; 1938, 55 per cent. Ibid. Illegal Jewish immigration to Palestine was estimated at 12,442 for the year 1939, according to the Royal Institute of International Affairs report, cited *supra*.

Appendix II

Immigration Regulations

United Kingdom
Under the provisions of the Aliens Restriction Act of 1914, as amended most importantly by the Aliens Order of 1920, an alien was given leave to land only if he could demonstrate that he was able to support himself and his dependants. If he intended to take up employment he was required to have a permit issued to the prospective employer by the Ministry of Labour; such permits were in practice issued sparingly, and only after satisfying the Ministry that no British labour was available to take up the position requested by an alien. Until 1938, no distinction was made in either law or practice between aliens as a class and alien refugees; Reich Germans, Austrians and Czechoslovak nationals possessing a valid passport were not required to have visas, and permission to land was generally given to persons coming to the United Kingdom on business, for visits to friends, or for purposes of study. Aside from the prohibition against taking up unauthorised employment, conditions other than a time limitation were seldom attached to their stay. When a visa system for holders of German and Austrian passports was introduced in 1938, refugees seeking to enter British territory had to apply for visas to Passport Control Officers attached to British Embassies and Consulates : these officers vetted each application from both financial and security points of view, a frequently time-consuming procedure which often required reference to London for decision. More stringent regulations accompanied the visa requirement, and required the intending migrant to demonstrate either possession of financial resources or definite guarantees of maintenance until such time as he might leave the United Kingdom for permanent settlement elsewhere.[1]

[1] See C. F. Fraser, *Control of Aliens in the British Commonwealth of Nations*, (London, 1940).

s

Palestine and the Empire

The Palestine Immigration Ordinance of 1933 stipulated that immigrants of the following categories could be admitted : A. Persons of independent means, defined as : (i) persons possessing a capital of not less than £1,000; (ii) members of liberal professions with a capital of not less than £500; (iii) craftsmen with capital of not less than £250; (iv) persons with a secured income of at least £4 per month; (v) those with capital of at least £500 able to 'give certain assurances as to their prospects in Palestine'. B. An eleemosynary class including students, orphans, or those of religious occupation. C. Persons having definite prospects of employment. D. Dependants of permanent residents or of immigrants in categories A through C. Admission of immigrants in category C (the 'labour' category) was controlled by a Labour Schedule prepared once every six months by the High Commissioner for Palestine after considering the labour requests of the Jewish Agency for Palestine, a report by his own Department of Migration, and a survey of Arab and Jewish unemployment. Once each Labour Schedule was approved, the Palestine Government distributed immigration certificates to the Jewish Agency, which in turn allocated them to selected immigrants who then had to be vetted by a British Passport Control Officer before proceeding to Palestine. Virtually all the immigrants in the labour category were required to undergo agricultural or industrial training under Zionist auspices to adapt them for settlement in Palestine.[2]

Immigration policy in colonial dependencies other than Palestine varied according to the stage of constitutional development each territory had attained : generally, however, European immigration was restricted as a matter of policy in most African and Asian colonies, whether or not the Governor legislated solely or with the concurrence of a Legislative Council.

[2] See Palestine Royal Commission (Peel Commission), *Report*, Cmd. 5479 (London, 1937).

Bibliography

MANUSCRIPT SOURCES

1. RECORDS OF GOVERNMENT DEPARTMENTS AND INTERNATIONAL AGENCIES
High Commission for Refugees (Jewish and Other) coming from Germany. United Nations Library, Geneva
    Files and reports, 1933–1936
The Central Zionist Archives. Jerusalem, Israel
Jewish Agency for Palestine : Political Department and Central Bureau for the Settlement of German Jews in Palestine, 1933–1939
Great Britain. Public Record Office, London
Cabinet Papers Colonial Office : Palestine
    Foreign Office : General Correspondence, Political (FO 371)
    Home Office : Aliens Department

II. PRIVATE PAPERS

American Jewish Archives. Cincinnati, Ohio : Felix M. Warburg Papers
Cambridge University : Templewood Papers
University of Liverpool Library : Eleanor F. Rathbone Papers
Royal Institute of International Affairs, London : Refugee Survey, 1937–1938 : Special Reports, German Refugees
Weizmann Archives. Rehovoth, Israel : Chaim Weizmann Papers
Woburn House. London : Board of Deputies of British Jews : Annual Reports; Aliens Committee : Reports and Minutes; Joint Foreign Committee : Reports and Minutes

PRINTED SOURCES

I. PRIMARY SOURCES

Published Governmental and International Documents
E. L. Woodward and R. Butler, eds., *Documents on British Foreign Policy, 1918–1939*, 3rd Series (London, 1949)
Documents on German Foreign Policy, 1918–1945, Series D, 1937–1945 (London, 1949–1957)

s*

The Dominions Office and Colonial Office List, 1933–1939

The Foreign Office List and Diplomatic and Consular Year Book, 1933–1939

Department of State, Washington, *Foreign Relations of the United States*, 1933–1939

High Commissioner for Refugees, *Reports to the Assembly of the League of Nations*, 1937–1939

Proceedings of the Intergovernmental Committee, Evian, July 6–15, 1938

Reichsgesetzblatt, Teil I, Berlin, 1931–1939

Parliamentary and Command Papers

Hansard, 5th Series. *Parliamentary Debates*, House of Lords, House of Commons

Home Office, *Aliens Immigration Returns*. 1932–1939

Ministry of Labour, *Annual Reports*. 1932–1939

Palestine Royal Commission, *Report* (Peel Commission Report), Cmd. 5479, 1937

Palestine Partition Commission, *Report*, Cmd. 5854, 1938

Foreign Office, *Convention Concerning the Status of Refugees coming from Germany* (with Final Act). Cmd. 5780, 1938

Dominions Office, *Report of the Overseas Settlement Board*, Cmd. 5766, 1938

Palestine: A Statement of Policy, May 1939, Cmd. 6019, 1939

Colony and Protectorate of Kenya, *Settlement Committee Report*, Nairobi, The Government Printer, 1939

British Guiana Refugee Commission to the Advisory Committee on Political Refugees appointed by the President of the United States of America, *Report*, Cmd. 6014, 1939

Home Office, *Czech Refugee Trust Fund and Directions to the Trustees*, Cmd. 6076, 1939

Foreign Office, *Papers Concerning Treatment of German Nationals in Germany, 1938–1939*, Cmd. 6120, 1939

Home Office, *German and Austrian Civilian Internees*, Cmd. 6217, 1940

Reports of Refugee Organisations

Academic Assistance Council (Society for the Protection of Science and Learning), *Annual Reports*, 1934–1939

Association of Jewish Refugees in Great Britain, *Bulletin*, 1941–1951

The Central British Fund for German Jewry, *Reports*, 1935–1937

Christian Council for Refugees from Germany and Central Europe, *Reports*, 1938, 1943

Comité voor Bijzondere Joodsche Belangen, *De Arbeid van het Comité 1933–1938*, Amsterdam, 1938

The Co-Ordinating Committee for Refugees, *Bulletin*, 1939

The Council for German Jewry, *Reports*, 1936–1938

Demokratische Flüchtlingsfürsorge, *Fünf Jahre Flucht, Not und Rettung*, 1938

Jewish Refugees' Committee, *Reports*, 1933–1935

Reichsvertretung der Juden in Deutschland, *Arbeitsberichte*, 1933–1938; *Informationsblätter*, 1937–1938

Reichsvereinigung der Juden in Deutschland, *Jüdische Auswanderung nach Australien und anderen Gebieten des englishchen Imperiums*, 1939

World Jewish Congress, *Protocoles des séances*, 1933, 1934, 1936

Contemporary Newspapers

The Times, Manchester Guardian, Daily Telegraph, Daily Express, Daily Mail

Selected provincial newspapers, *The Jewish Chronicle*, selected German newspapers including *Völkischer Beobachter*

Memoirs, Diaries and Contemporary Publications

Adams, Walter, 'Refugees in Europe', *Annals of the American Academy of Political and Social Science*, May 1939, 37–44

Angell, Norman and Buxton, Dorothy F., *You and the Refugee* (London, 1939)

Bentwich, Norman, 'The League of Nations and Refugees', *British Year Book of International Law*, 1935, 114–129

    The Refugees from Germany: April 1933 to December 1935 (London, 1936)

    My Seventy-Seven Years (London, 1962)

    Wanderer Between Two Worlds (London, 1941)

Buxton, Dorothy F., *The Economics of the Refugee Problem* (London, n.d., 1939?)

Cecil, Robert Viscount, *All the Way* (London, 1949)

Channon, Sir Henry, *Chips, The Diaries of Sir Henry Channon* (London, 1967)

Cohen, Joseph L., *Salvaging German Jewry, A Guide to Those who Wish to Help* (London, 1939)

Cohn, Heinz and Gottfeld, E., *Auswanderungs-Vorschriften für Juden in Deutschland* (Berlin, 1938)

Comité des Délégations Juives, *La Question des Juifs allemands devant le Société des Nations* (Paris, 1933)

Estorick, Eric, 'The Evian Conference and the Intergovernmental Committee', *Annals of the American Academy of Political and Social Science*, May 1939, 136–142

Gedye, G. E. R., *Fallen Bastions* (London, 1939)

Gershone, Karen, *We Came as Children* (London, 1966)

Hansson, Michael, *Le Problème des réfugiés et la Société des Nations* (Geneva, 1938)

Holborn, Louise W., 'The League of Nations and the Refugee Problem', *Annals of the American Academy of Political and Social Science*, May, 1939, 124–135

Janowsky, Oscar I. and Fagen, M. M., *International Aspects of German Racial Policies* (New York, 1937)

Jennings, R. Yewdall, 'Some International Law Aspects of the Refugee Question', *British Year Book of International Law*, 1939, 98–114

League of Nations Union, *Refugees and the League* (London, 1935)

Lewis, Wyndham, *The Jews, Are They Human?* (London, 1939)

Macmillan, Harold, *Winds of Change, 1914–1939* (London, 1966)

Mosley, Sir Oswald, *My Life* (London, 1968)

Muggeridge, Malcolm, *The Thirties* (London, 1940, rev. ed. 1967)

Political and Economic Planning (PEP), *Are Refugees an Asset?* (London, 1944)

Hope Simpson, Sir John, *The Refugee Problem: Report of a Survey* (London, 1939)

    Refugees: A Review of the Situation Since September 1938 (London, August 1939)

    Refugees, Preliminary Report of a Survey (London, July 1938)

Templewood, Viscount, *Nine Troubled Years* (London, 1954)

Warburg, Max M., *Aus meinen Aufzeichnungen* (New York, 1952)

Wedgwood, Josiah C., *Memoirs of a Fighting Life* (London, 1941)

Weizmann, Chaim, *Trial and Error* (London, 1949)

Woolf, Virginia, *A Writer's Diary* (London, 1953)

II. SECONDARY SOURCES

Adams, Walter, 'The Refugee Scholars of the 1930s', *The Political Quarterly*, 39, No. 1 (January–March, 1968), 7–14

Adler-Rudel, S., 'The Evian Conference on the Refugee Question', *Leo Baeck Institute Year Book*, XII (1968), 251–265

Association of Jewish Refugees in Great Britain, *Britain's New Citizens* (London, 1951)

    Dispersion and Resettlement (London, 1955)

Bauer, Yehuda, *From Diplomacy to Resistance* (trans. ed., Philadelphia, 1970)

Ben Elissar, Eliahu, *La Diplomatie du IIIe. Reich et les Juifs, 1933–1939* (Paris, 1969)

Benewick, Robert, *Political Violence and Public Order* (London, 1969)

Benjamin, D. J., 'Australia and the Evian Conference', *Australian Jewish Historical Society Journal and Proceedings*, V (July, 1961), 215–233

Bennathan, Esra, 'Die demographische und wirtschaftliche Struktur der Juden', in W. E. Mosse, ed., *Entscheidungsjahr 1932* (Tübingen, 1965)

Bentwich, Norman, 'A Grim and Humiliating Story', *The Jewish Quarterly*, 16, No. 1 (57) (Spring, 1968)

    They Found Refuge (London, 1956)

Beveridge, Lord, *A Defence of Free Learning* (London, 1959)

Blau, Bruno, *Das Ausnahmerecht für die Juden in Deutschland 1933–1945* (Düsseldorf, 1954)

Brotman, A. G., 'Britain's Reaction to the Pogroms', *AJR Bulletin*, XIII, No. 11 (November, 1958), 5

Colvin, Ian, *The Chamberlain Cabinet* (London, 1971)

Cross, Colin, *The Fascists in Britain* (London, 1961)

De Jong, L., *Het Koninkrijk der Nederlanden in de tweede wereldoorlog*, vol. I (The Hague, 1969)

Edinger, Lewis J., *German Exile Politics* (Berkeley, 1956)

Feilchenfeld, Werner, *et al.*, *Haavara-Transfer nach Palästina und Einwanderung deutscher Juden 1933–1939* (Tübingen, 1940)

Feingold, Henry L., *The Politics of Rescue* (New Brunswick, N.J.), 1970

Fraser, Charles F., *Control of Aliens in the British Commonwealth of Nations* (London, 1940)

Frings, Paul, *Das internationale Flüchtlingsproblem, 1919–1950* (Frankfurt, 1951)

Garrard, John A., 'Parallels of Protest : English Reactions to Jewish and Commonwealth Immigration', *Race*, IX, No. 1 (July, 1967), 47–66

Genschel, Helmut, *Die Verdrängung der Juden aus der Wirtschaft im Dritten Reich* (Göttingen, 1966)

George, Margaret, *The Hollow Men* (London, 1967)

Gilbert, Martin, *The Roots of Appeasement* (London, 1966)

Grossmann, Kurt R., *Emigration* (Frankfurt, 1969)

Hearst, Ernest, 'The British and the Slaughter of the Jews', *Wiener Library Bulletin*, XXI, Nos. 1 and 2

Herlin, Hans, *Kein gelobtes Land, die Irrfahrt des 'St Louis'* (Hamburg, 1961)

Hilberg, Raoul, *The Destruction of the European Jews* (Chicago, 1961)

Hurewitz, J. C., *The Struggle for Palestine* (New York, 1950)

Hyamson, Albert W., *Palestine Under the Mandate, 1920–1948* (London, 1950)

Jasper, Ronald C. D., *George Bell, Bishop of Chichester* (London, 1967)

Jewish Central Information Office, *The Position of Jewish Refugees in England* (London, 1945)

Ball-Kaduri, Kurt, *Das Leben der Juden in Deutschland im Jahre 1933* (Frankfurt, 1963)

Karbach, Oscar, 'The Liquidation of the Jewish Community of Vienna', *Jewish Social Studies*, 1940, 255–278

Kent, Donald P., *The Refugee Intellectual* (New York, 1953)

Kimche, Jon and David, *The Secret Roads* (London, 1954)

Kimminich, Otto, *Der internationale Rechtsstatus des Flüchtlings* (Cologne, 1962)

Kochan, Lionel, *Pogrom 10 November 1938* (London, 1957)

Krausnick, Helmut, 'The Persecution of the Jews', in Krausnick *et al.*, eds., *Anatomy of the SS State* (London, 1968)

Krikler, Bernard, 'Boycotting Nazi Germany', *Wiener Library Bulletin*, XXIII, No. 4 (1969), 26–32

Kulischer, Eugene M., *The Displacement of Population in Europe* (Montreal, 1943)

   Europe on the Move: War and Population Changes 1917–1947 (New York, 1948)

Kulka, O. D., *Hatmurot b'maamadam uv'feilotam shel yehudei eiropa hamerkazit 1933–1939* (Changes in the Status and Activities of the Jews in Central Europe, 1933–1939) (Jerusalem, 1966)

Lamm, Hans, *Ueber die innere und äussere Entwicklung des deutschen Judentums im Dritten Reich* (Erlangen, 1951)

Ludwig, Carl, *Die Flüchtlingspolitik der Schweiz seit 1933 bis zur Gegenwart (1957)* (Bern, 1966)

Mandle, W. F., *Anti-Semitism and the British Union of Fascists* (London, 1968)

Marlowe, John, *The Seat of Pilate* (London, 1959)

Melka, R., 'Nazi Germany and the Palestine Question', *Middle Eastern Studies*, 5, No. 3 (October, 1969), 221–233

Monroe, Elizabeth, *Britain's Moment in the Middle East, 1914–1956* (London, 1965)

Morse, Arthur D., *While Six Million Died* (New York, 1967)

Mowat, Charles L., *Britain Between the Wars, 1918–1940* (London, 1955)

Murphy, H. B. M., *Flight and Resettlement* (Paris, 1955)

Naylor, John F., *Labour's International Policy; the Labour Party in the 1930s* (London, 1969)

Newsam, Sir Frank, *The Home Office* (London, 1954)

Parkes, James W., *The Emergence of the Jewish Problem, 1878–1939* (London, 1946)

Prinz, Artur, 'The Role of the Gestapo in Obstructing and Promoting Jewish Emigration', *Yad Washem Studies*, II (1958), 205–218

Proudfoot, Malcolm J., *European Refugees: 1939–1952* (London, 1957)

Roche, T. W. E., *The Key in the Lock; Immigration Control in England from 1066 to the Present Day* (London, 1969)

Röder, Werner, *Die deutschen sozialistischen Exilgruppen in Gross-Britannien, 1940–1945* (Hannover, 1969)

Rose, Norman, *Gentile Zionism and Anglo-Zionist Diplomacy, 1929–1939* (unpub. Ph.D thesis, London School of Economics, 1968)

Rosenstock, Werner, 'Exodus 1933–39; a Survey of Jewish Emigration from Germany', *Leo Baeck Institute Year Book*, I (1956), 373–390

Rosenthal, Erich, 'Trends of the Jewish Population in Germany, 1919–1939', *Jewish Social Studies*, VI (1944), 233–274

Royal Institute of International Affairs, *Great Britain and Palestine 1915–1945* (3rd ed., London, 1946)

    Surveys of International Affairs, 1933–1939

Schröder, Gustav, *Heimatlos auf hoher See* (Berlin, 1949)

Sharf, Andrew, *The British Press and Jews Under Nazi Rule* (London, 1964)

Stocks, Mary D., *Eleanor Rathbone* (London, 1949)

Stoessinger, John G., *The Refugee and the World Community* (Minneapolis, 1956)

Tartakower, Arieh and Grossmann, K. R., *The Jewish Refugee* (New York, 1944)

Thorne, Christopher, *The Approach of War, 1938–9* (London, 1967)

United Nations, Department of Social Affairs, *A Study of Statelessness* (New York, 1949)

Watt, D. C., *Britain Looks to Germany* (London, 1965)
    Personalities and Policies (London, 1965)

Wedgwood, C. V., *The Last of the Radicals, Josiah Wedgwood, MP* (London, 1951)

Wilson, Francesca M., *They Came as Strangers* (London, 1959)

Wischnitzer, Mark, 'Jewish Emigration from Germany 1933–1938', *Jewish Social Studies*, II (1940), 23–44
    To Dwell in Safety: the Story of Jewish Migration Since 1800 (Philadelphia, 1948)

Wyman, David S., *Paper Walls: America and the Refugee Crisis 1938–1941* (Amherst, Mass., 1968)

Wynot, Edward D., Jr., ' "A Necessary Cruelty", The Emergence of Official Anti-Semitism in Poland, 1936–39', *The American Historical Review*, Vol. 76, No. 4 (Oct. 1971), 1035–1058

Yisraeli, David, 'The Third Reich and the Transfer Agreement', *Journal of Contemporary History*, Vol. 6, No. 2 (1971), 129–148

Index